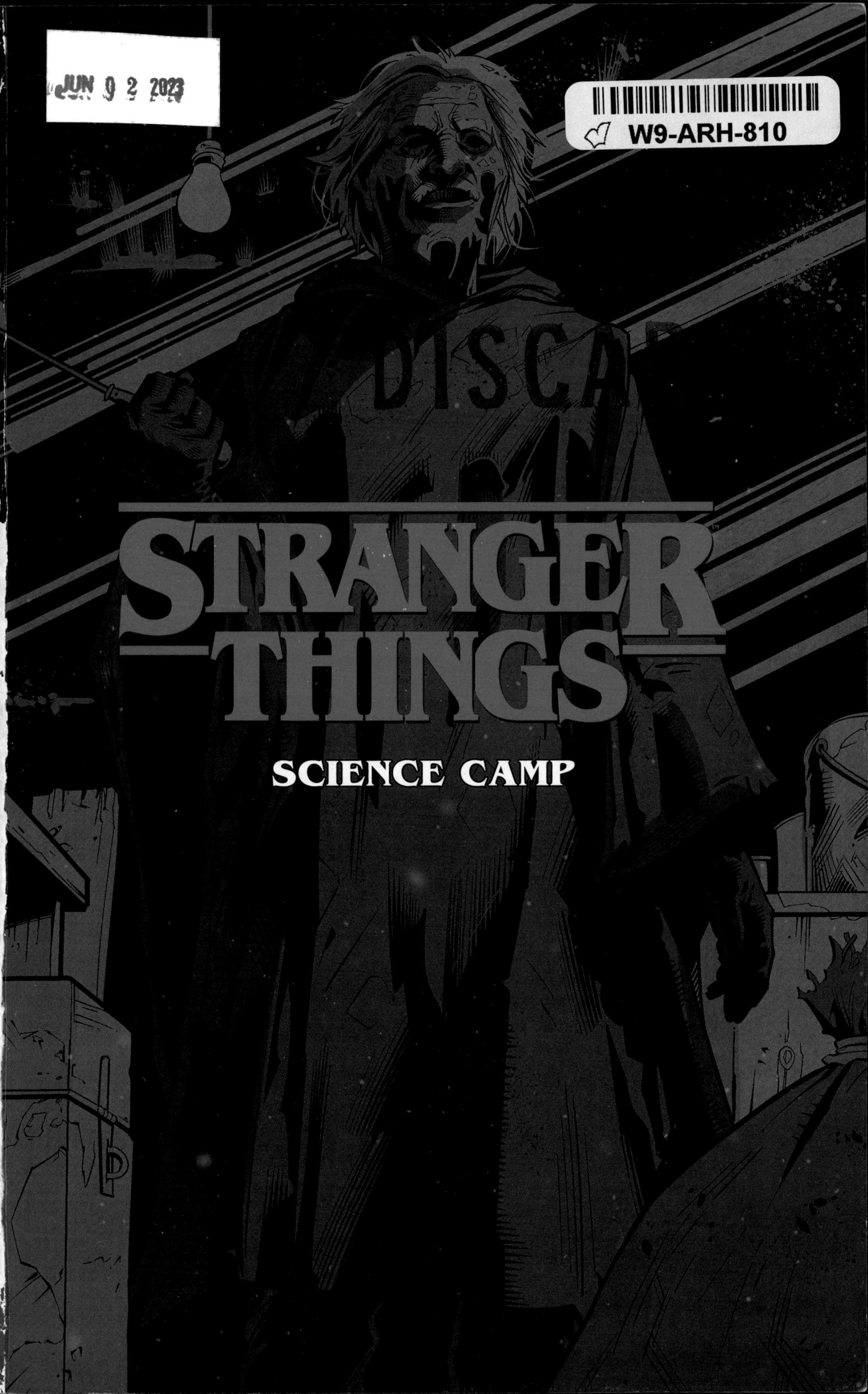

STRANGER THINGS

SCIENCE CAMP

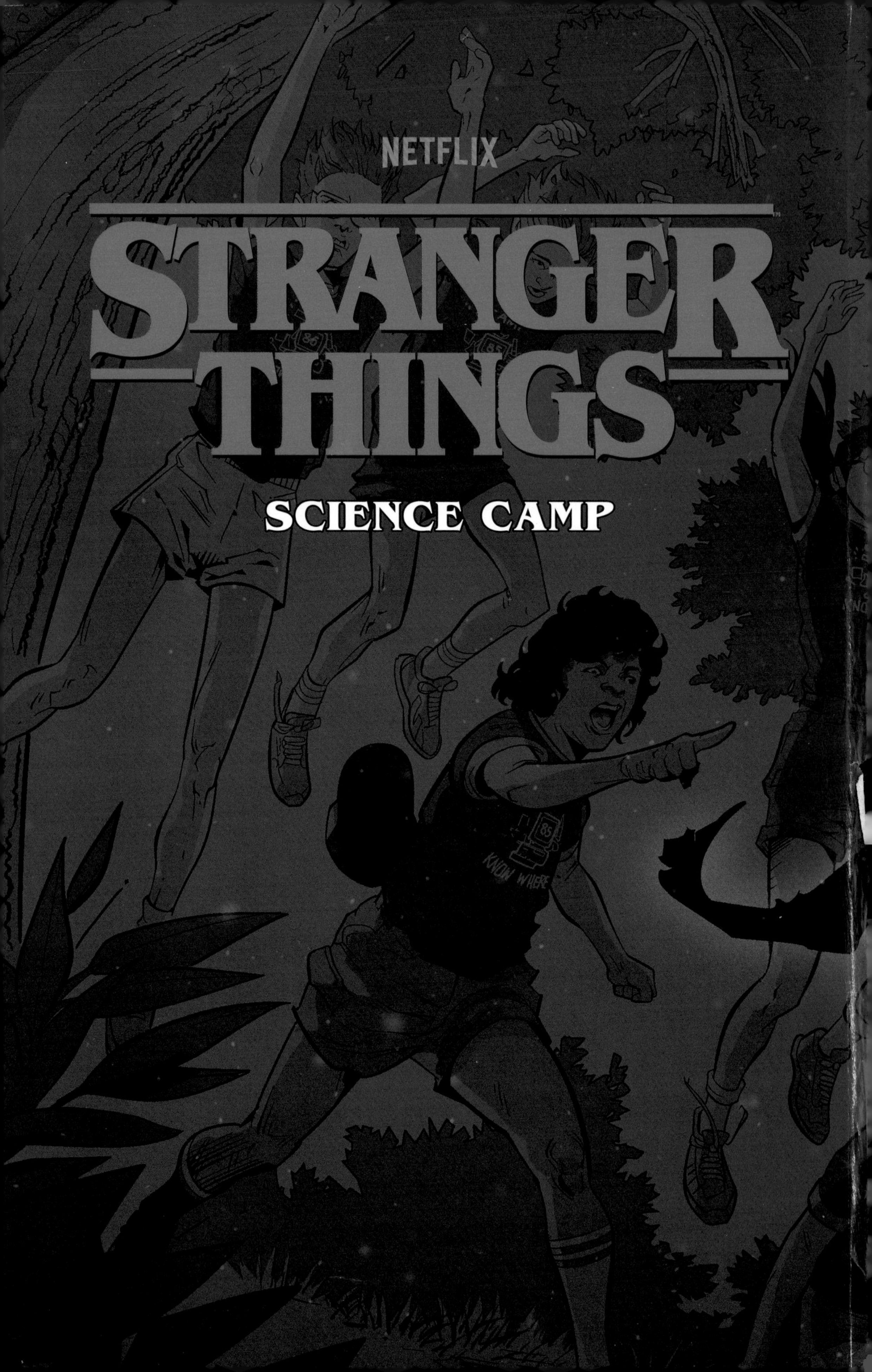
NETFLIX
STRANGER THINGS
SCIENCE CAMP
KNOW WHERE

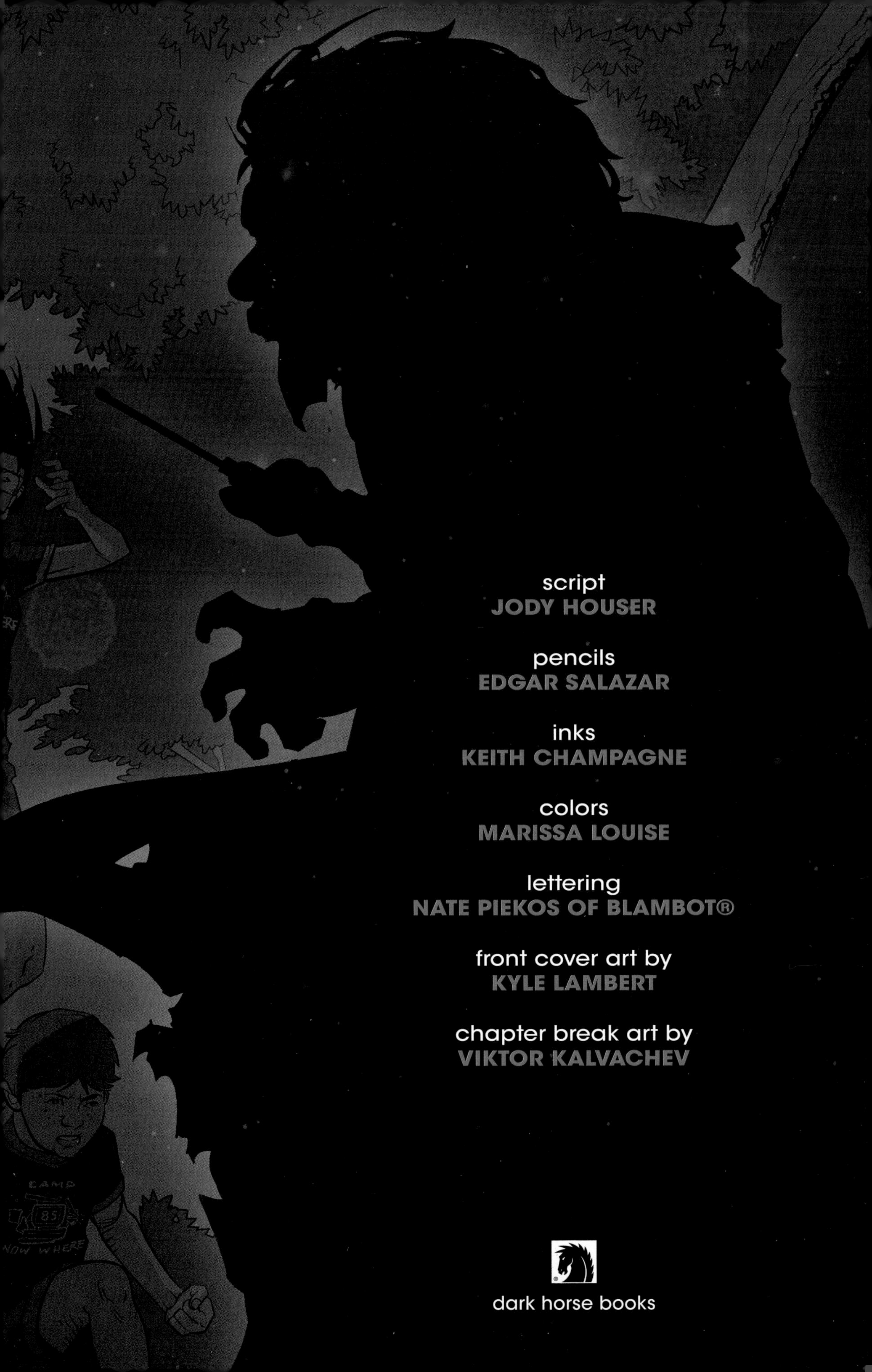
CAMP
85
NOW WHERE

script
JODY HOUSER

pencils
EDGAR SALAZAR

inks
KEITH CHAMPAGNE

colors
MARISSA LOUISE

lettering
NATE PIEKOS OF BLAMBOT®

front cover art by
KYLE LAMBERT

chapter break art by
VIKTOR KALVACHEV

dark horse books

president and publisher
MIKE RICHARDSON

editor
SPENCER CUSHING

assistant editor
KONNER KNUDSEN

collection designer
PATRICK SATTERFIELD

digital art technician
SAMANTHA HUMMER

Special thanks to NETFLIX, JOE LAWSON, SHANNON SCHRAM and KYLE LAMBERT.

Advertising Sales: ads@darkhorse.com | ComicShopLocator.com

This volume collects issue #1 through #4 of the Dark Horse comic book series
Stranger Things: Science Camp and the Free Comic Book Day 2020 story *Erica's Quest*.

Published by Dark Horse Books
A division of Dark Horse Comics LLC
10956 SE Main Street
Milwaukie, OR 97222

DarkHorse.com | Netflix.com

First edition: May 2021

Ebook ISBN: 978-1-50671-577-3
Trade Paperback ISBN: 978-1-50671-576-6

3 5 7 9 10 8 6 4
Printed in China

MIX
Paper from
responsible sources
FSC® C169962
www.fsc.org

NEIL HANKERSON executive vice president • TOM WEDDLE chief financial officer • DALE LAFOUNTAIN chief information officer • TIM WIESCH vice president of licensing • MATT PARKINSON vice president of marketing • VANESSA TODD-HOLMES vice president of production and scheduling • MARK BERNARDI vice president of book trade and digital Sales • RANDY LAHRMAN vice president of product development and sales • KEN LIZZI general counsel • DAVE MARSHALL editor in chief • DAVEY ESTRADA editorial director • CHRIS WARNER senior books editor • CARY GRAZZINI director of specialty projects • LIA RIBACCHI art director • MATT DRYER director of digital art and prepress • MICHAEL GOMBOS senior director of licensed publications • KARI YADRO director of custom programs • KARI TORSON director of international licensing

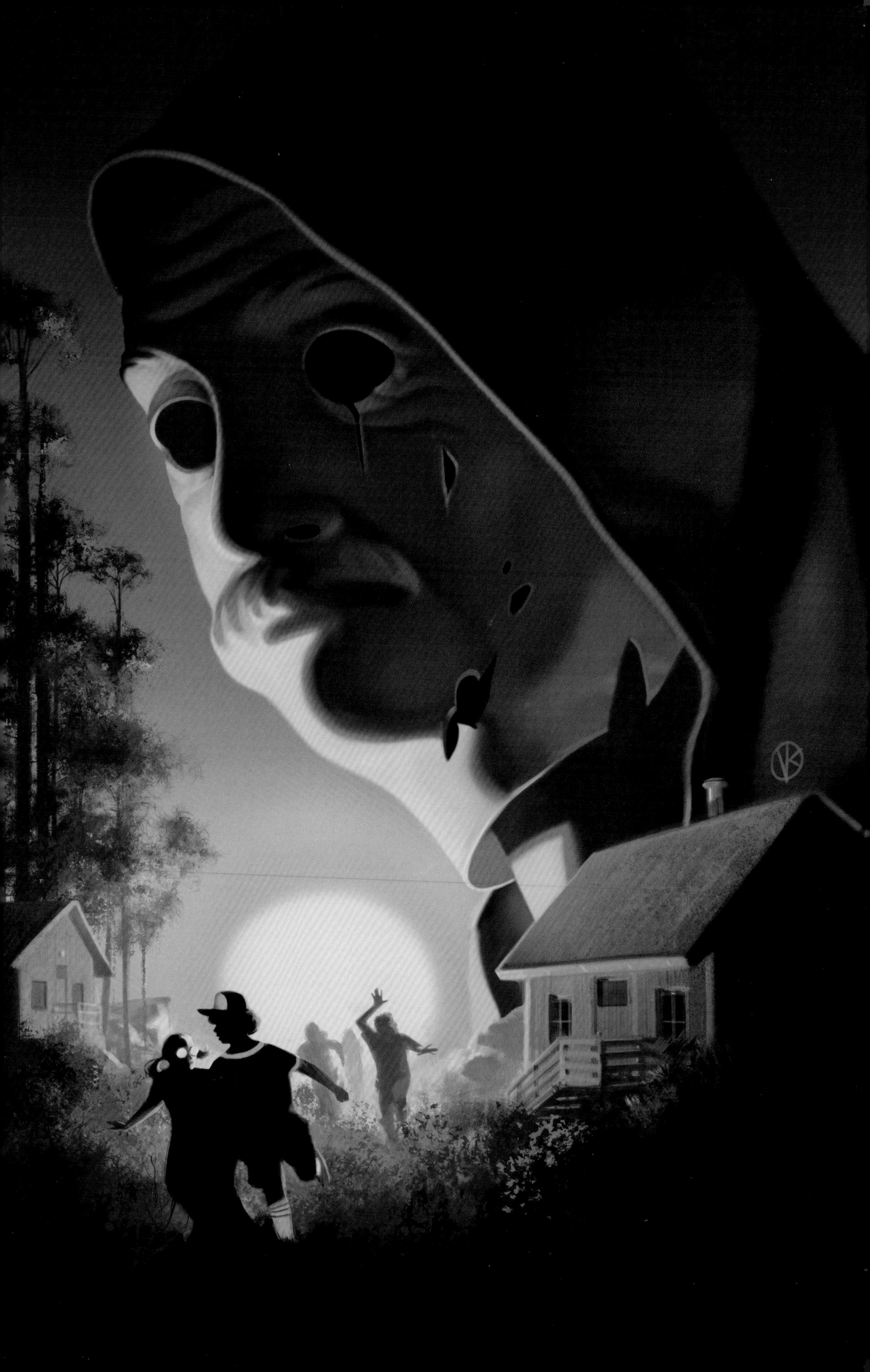

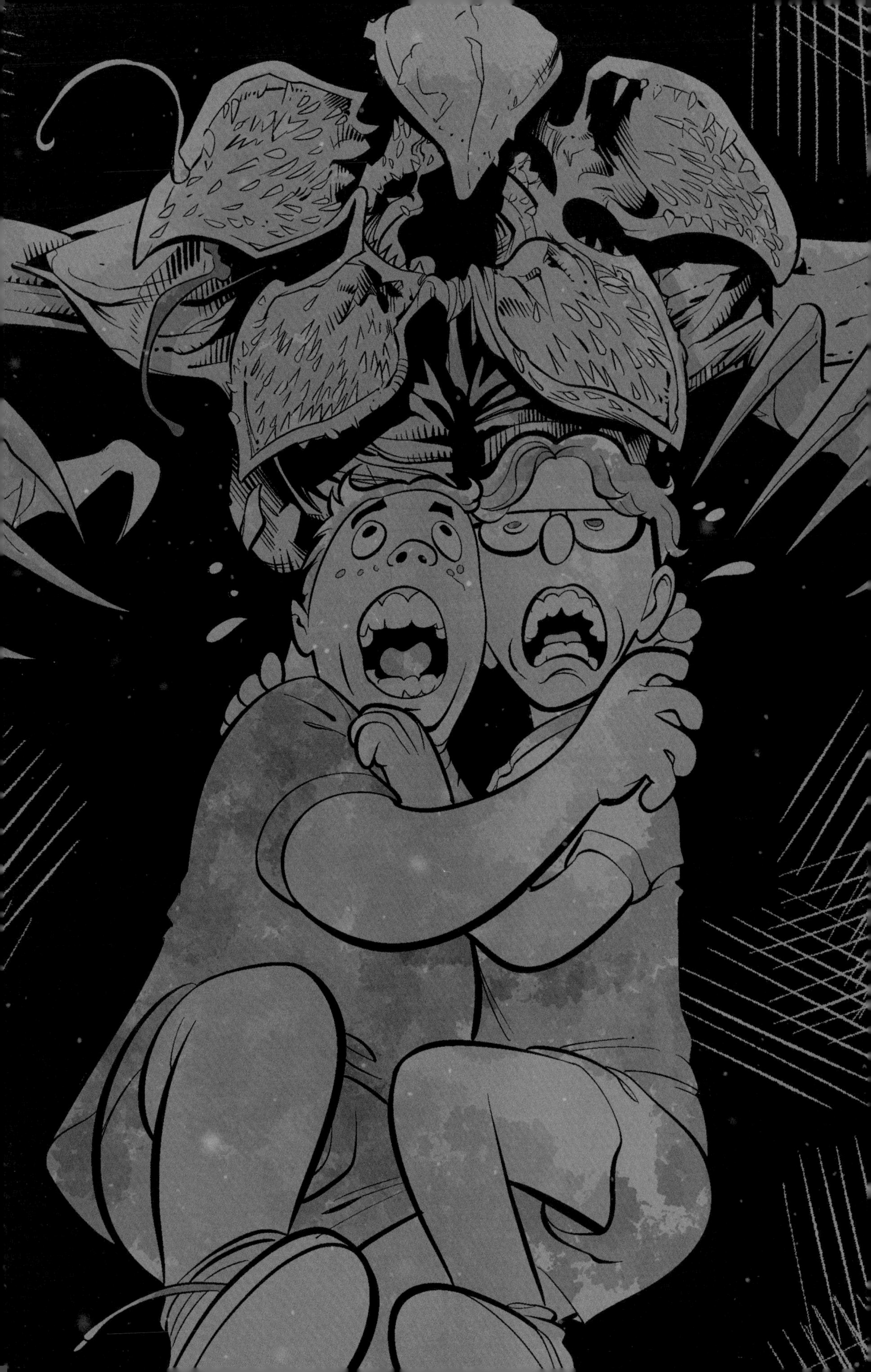

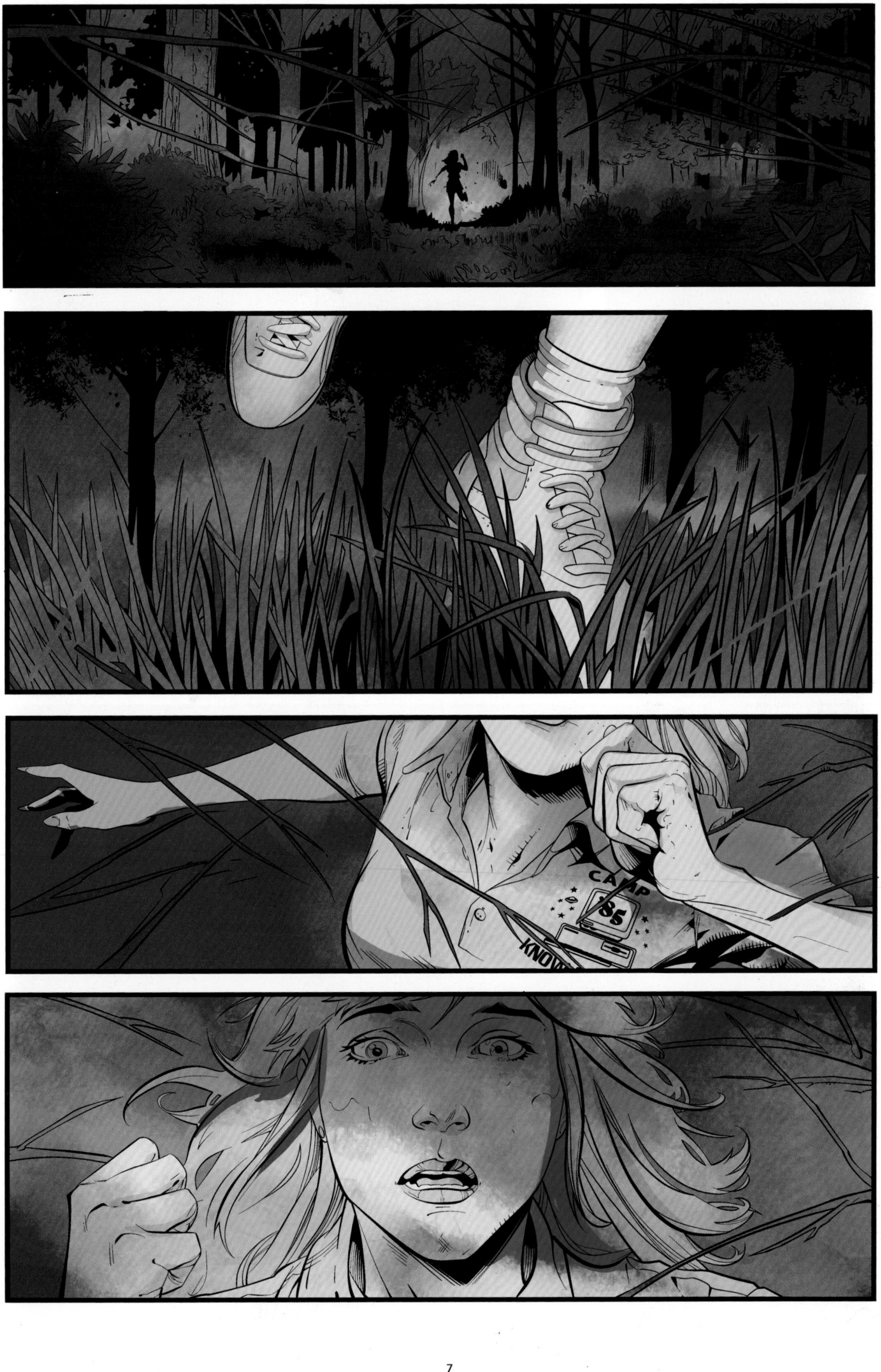
CAMP
'85

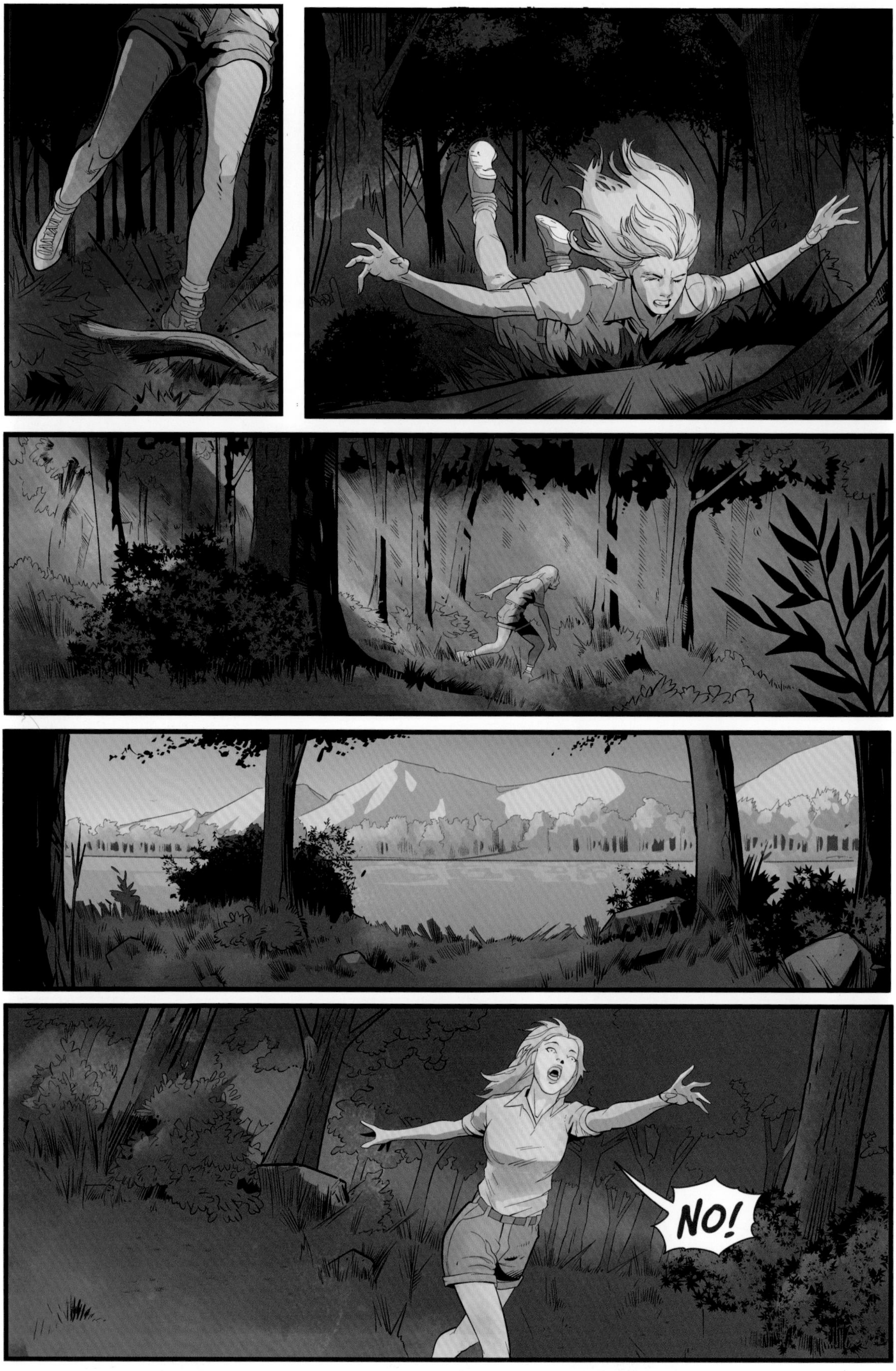
NO!

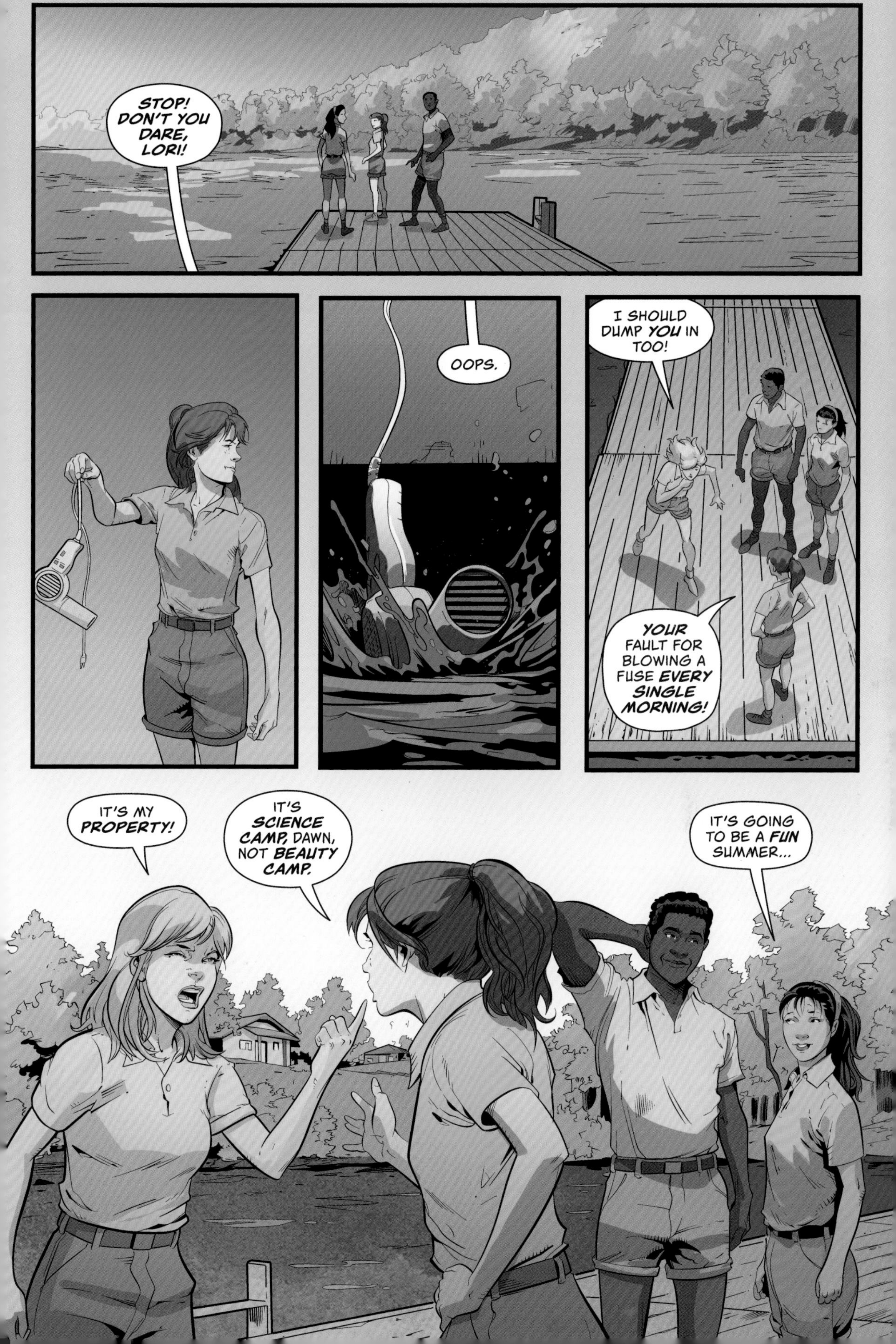
STOP! DON'T YOU DARE, LORI!
OOPS.
I SHOULD DUMP YOU IN TOO!
YOUR FAULT FOR BLOWING A FUSE EVERY SINGLE MORNING!
IT'S MY PROPERTY!
IT'S SCIENCE CAMP, DAWN, NOT BEAUTY CAMP.
IT'S GOING TO BE A FUN SUMMER...

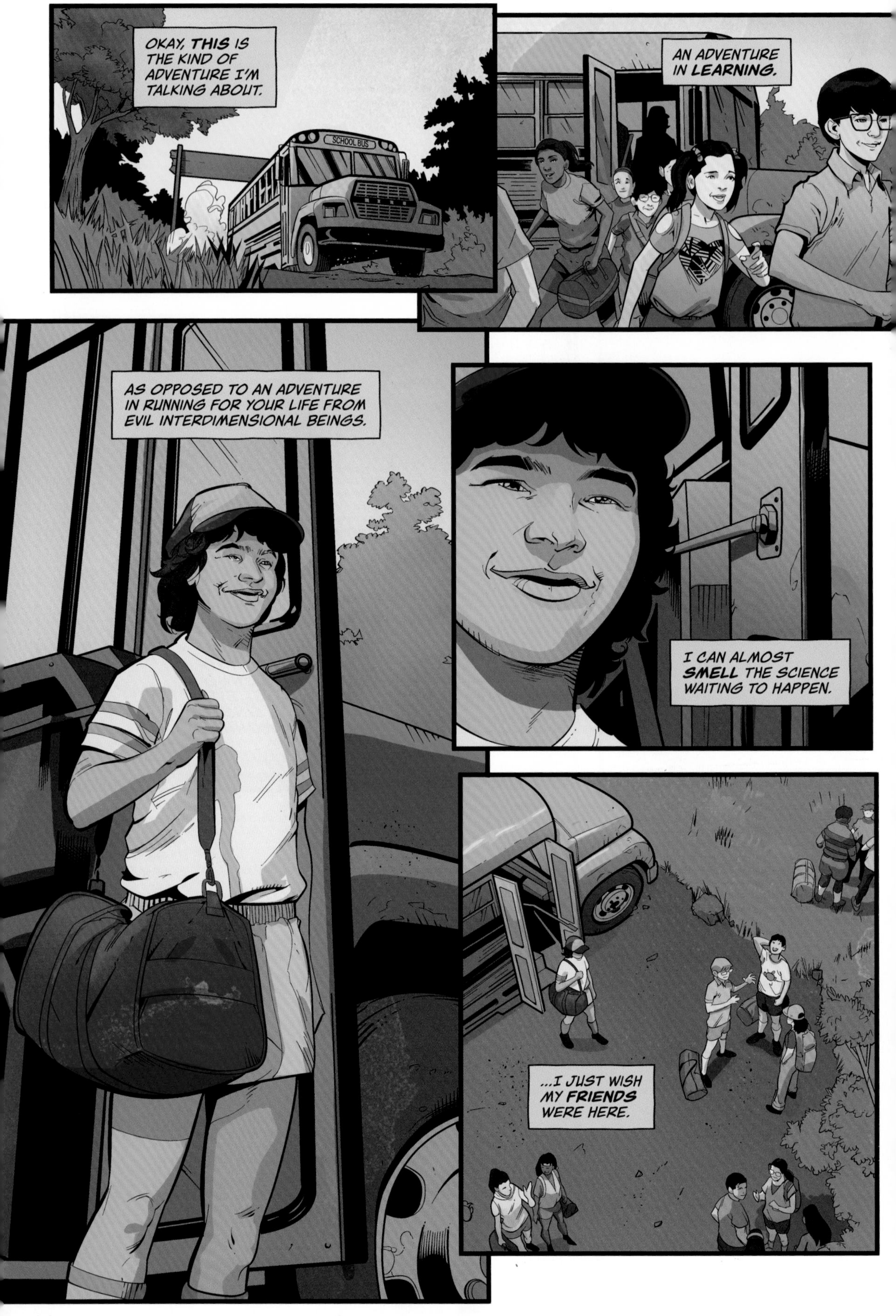
OKAY, **THIS** IS THE KIND OF ADVENTURE I'M TALKING ABOUT.
SCHOOL BUS
AN ADVENTURE IN **LEARNING**.
AS OPPOSED TO AN ADVENTURE IN RUNNING FOR YOUR LIFE FROM EVIL INTERDIMENSIONAL BEINGS.
I CAN ALMOST **SMELL** THE SCIENCE WAITING TO HAPPEN.
...I JUST WISH MY **FRIENDS** WERE HERE.

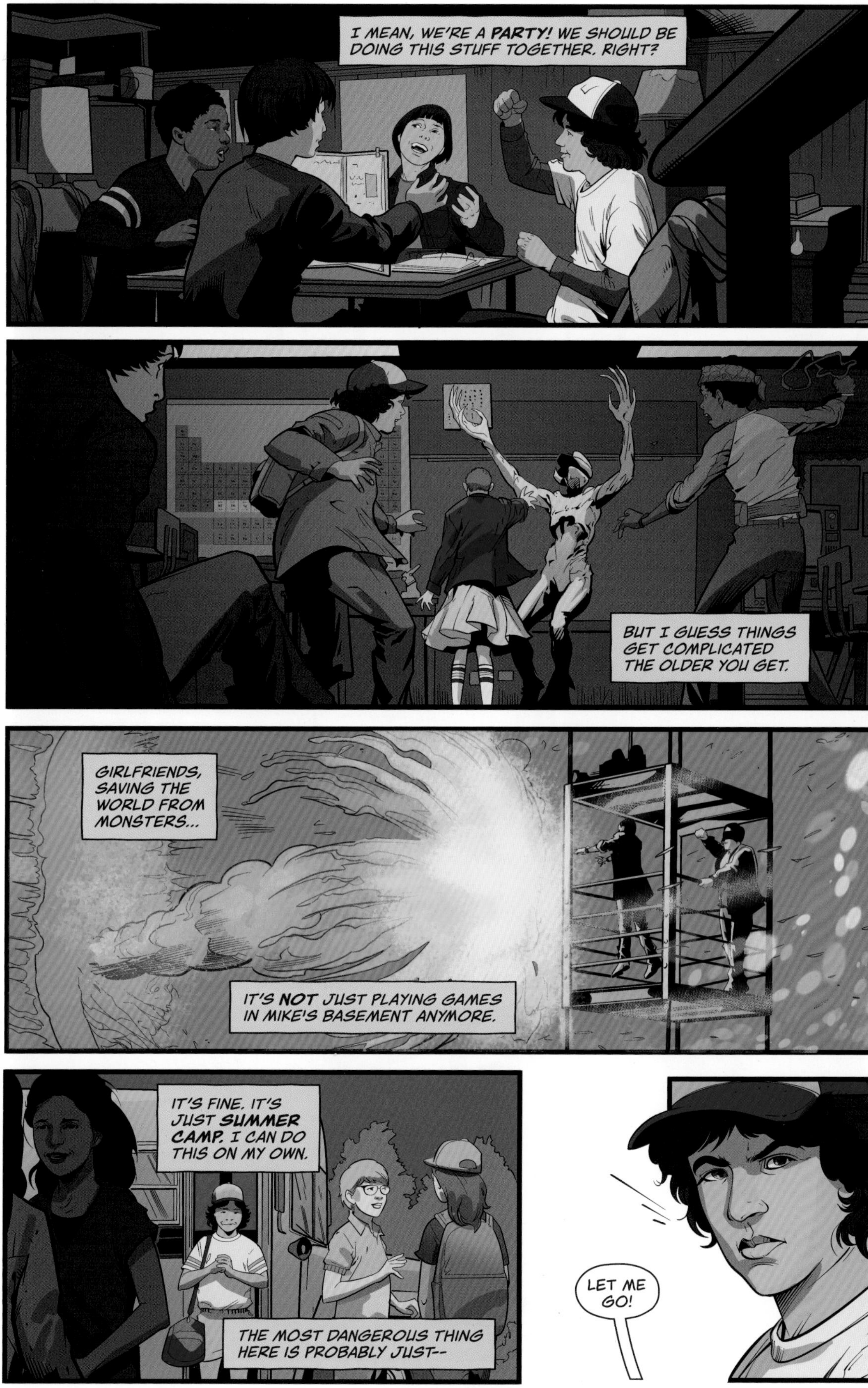
I MEAN, WE'RE A PARTY! WE SHOULD BE DOING THIS STUFF TOGETHER, RIGHT?
BUT I GUESS THINGS GET COMPLICATED THE OLDER YOU GET.
GIRLFRIENDS, SAVING THE WORLD FROM MONSTERS...
IT'S NOT JUST PLAYING GAMES IN MIKE'S BASEMENT ANYMORE.
IT'S FINE. IT'S JUST SUMMER CAMP. I CAN DO THIS ON MY OWN.
THE MOST DANGEROUS THING HERE IS PROBABLY JUST--
LET ME GO!

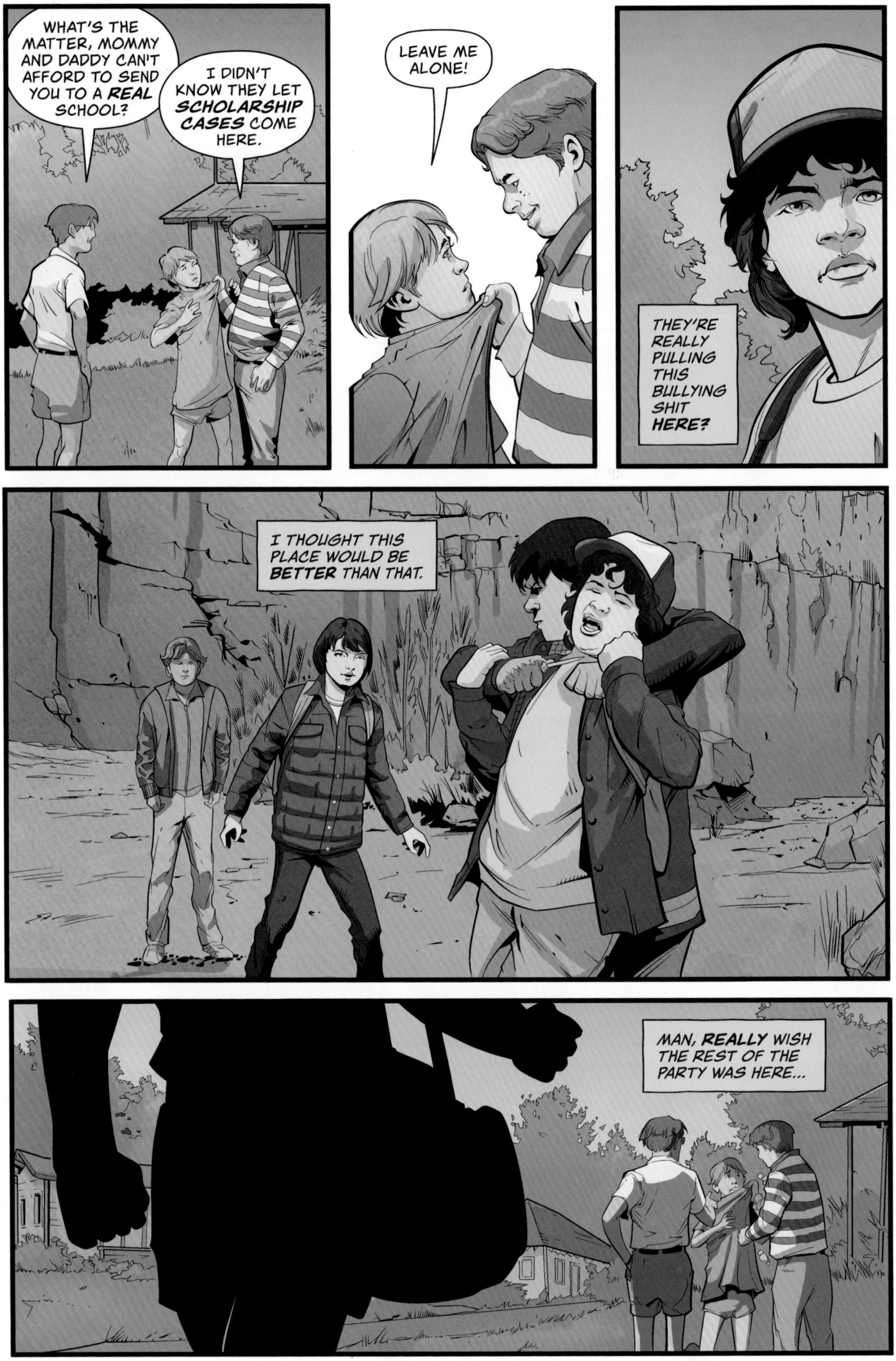

WHAT'S THE MATTER, MOMMY AND DADDY CAN'T AFFORD TO SEND YOU TO A REAL SCHOOL?
I DIDN'T KNOW THEY LET SCHOLARSHIP CASES COME HERE.
LEAVE ME ALONE!
THEY'RE REALLY PULLING THIS BULLYING SHIT HERE?
I THOUGHT THIS PLACE WOULD BE BETTER THAN THAT.
MAN, REALLY WISH THE REST OF THE PARTY WAS HERE...

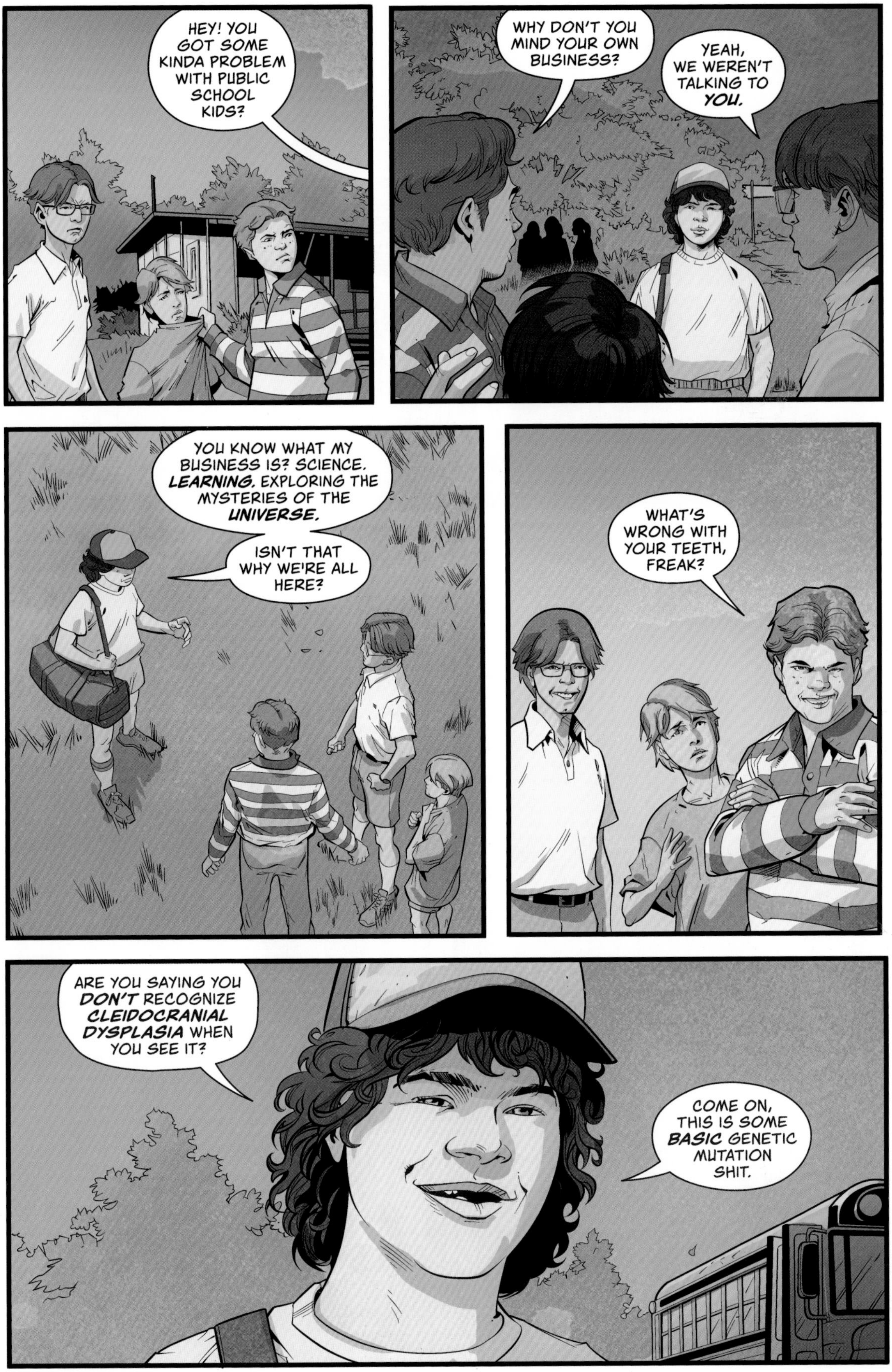
HEY! YOU GOT SOME KINDA PROBLEM WITH PUBLIC SCHOOL KIDS?
WHY DON'T YOU MIND YOUR OWN BUSINESS?
YEAH, WE WEREN'T TALKING TO *YOU.*
YOU KNOW WHAT MY BUSINESS IS? SCIENCE. *LEARNING.* EXPLORING THE MYSTERIES OF THE *UNIVERSE.*
ISN'T THAT WHY WE'RE ALL HERE?
WHAT'S WRONG WITH YOUR TEETH, FREAK?
ARE YOU SAYING YOU *DON'T* RECOGNIZE *CLEIDOCRANIAL DYSPLASIA* WHEN YOU SEE IT?
COME ON, THIS IS SOME *BASIC* GENETIC MUTATION SHIT.

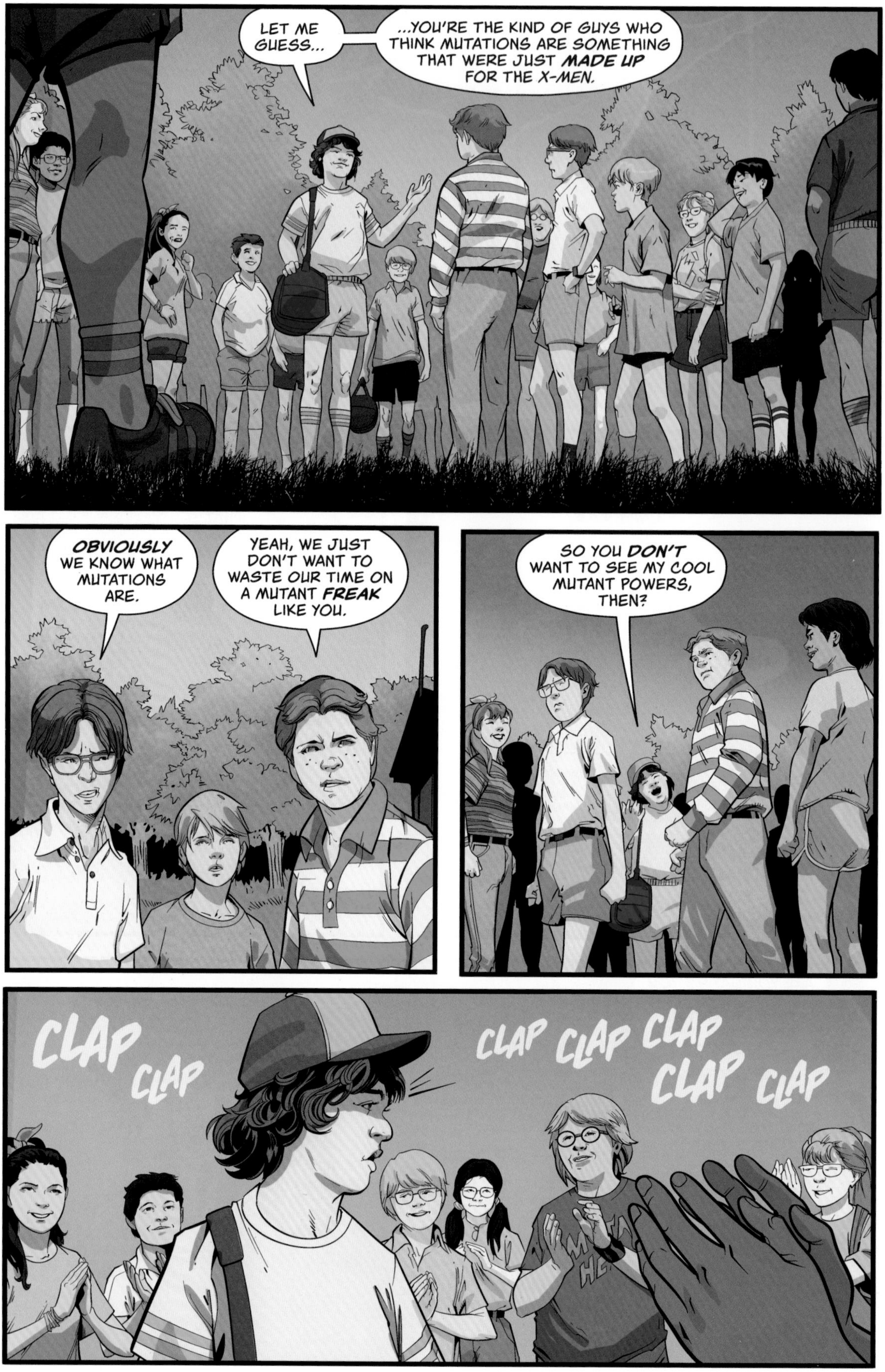
LET ME GUESS...
...YOU'RE THE KIND OF GUYS WHO THINK MUTATIONS ARE SOMETHING THAT WERE JUST MADE UP FOR THE X-MEN.
OBVIOUSLY WE KNOW WHAT MUTATIONS ARE.
YEAH, WE JUST DON'T WANT TO WASTE OUR TIME ON A MUTANT FREAK LIKE YOU.
SO YOU DON'T WANT TO SEE MY COOL MUTANT POWERS, THEN?
CLAP CLAP
CLAP CLAP CLAP
CLAP CLAP
CLAP

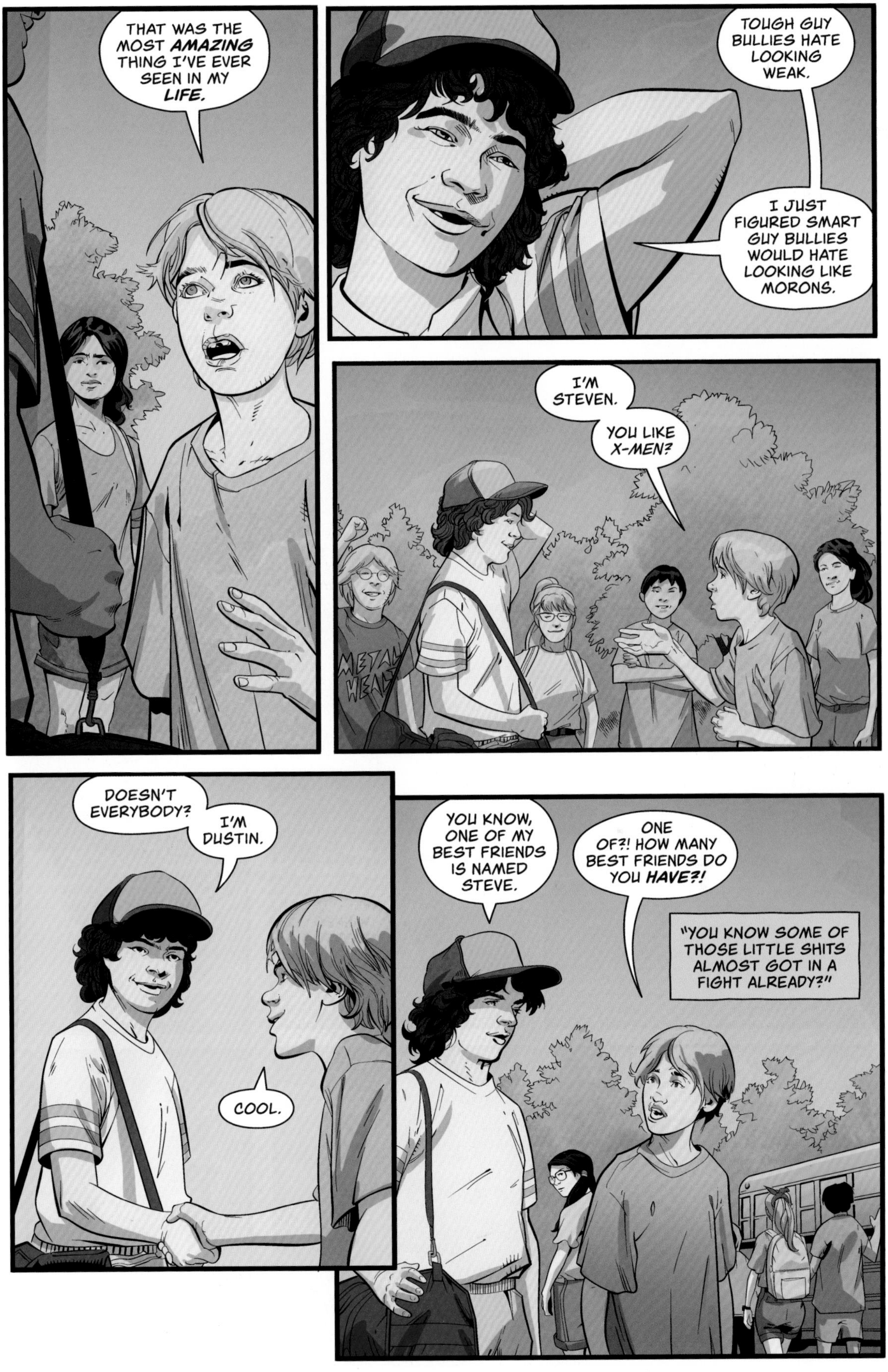
THAT WAS THE MOST **AMAZING** THING I'VE EVER SEEN IN MY **LIFE.**
TOUGH GUY BULLIES HATE LOOKING WEAK.
I JUST FIGURED SMART GUY BULLIES WOULD HATE LOOKING LIKE MORONS.
I'M STEVEN.
YOU LIKE X-MEN?
METAL HEAD
DOESN'T EVERYBODY?
I'M DUSTIN.
COOL.
YOU KNOW, ONE OF MY BEST FRIENDS IS NAMED STEVE.
ONE OF?! HOW MANY BEST FRIENDS DO YOU **HAVE?!**
"YOU KNOW SOME OF THOSE LITTLE SHITS ALMOST GOT IN A FIGHT ALREADY?"

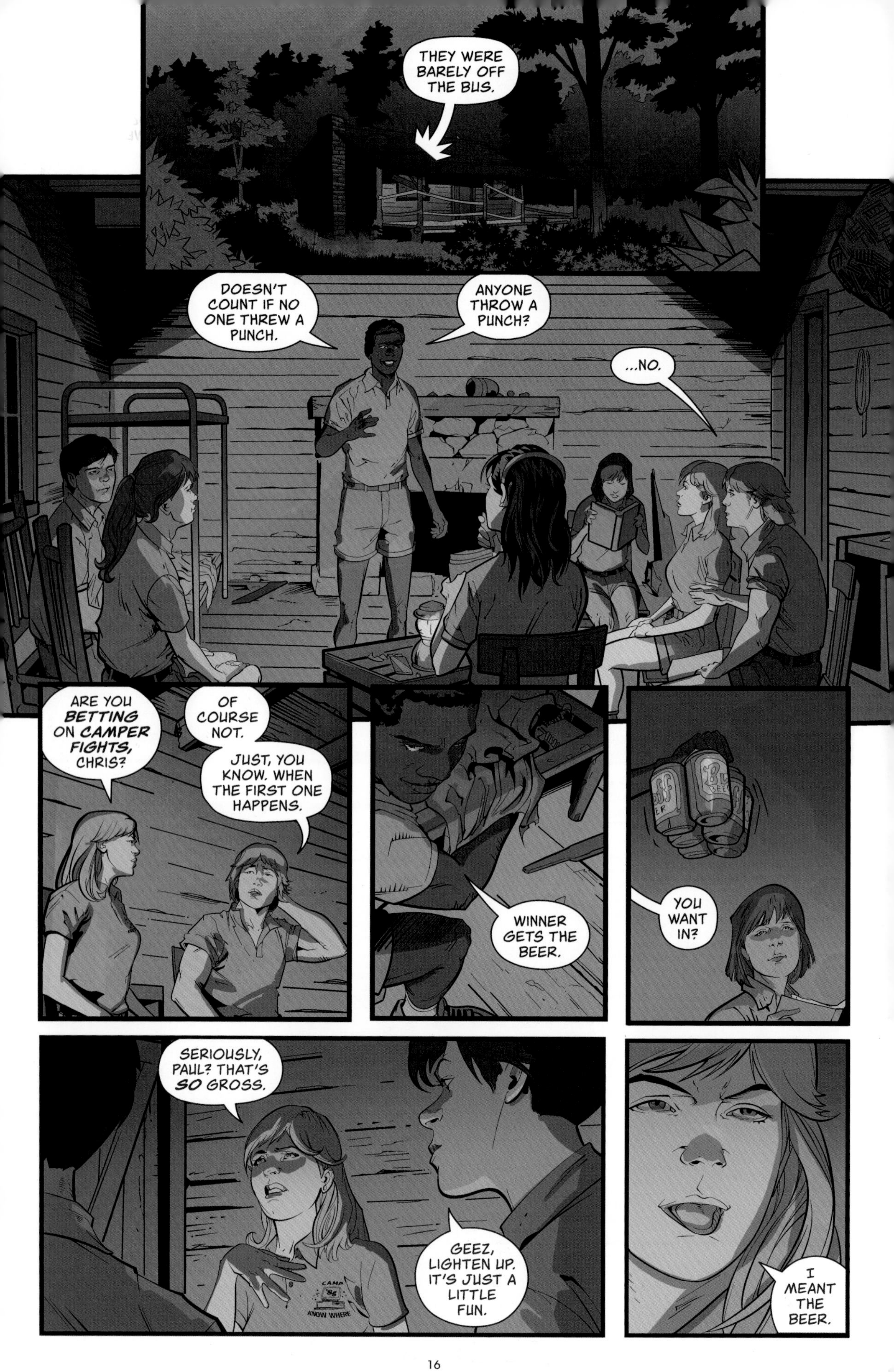
THEY WERE BARELY OFF THE BUS.
DOESN'T COUNT IF NO ONE THREW A PUNCH.
ANYONE THROW A PUNCH?
...NO.
ARE YOU BETTING ON CAMPER FIGHTS, CHRIS?
OF COURSE NOT.
JUST, YOU KNOW. WHEN THE FIRST ONE HAPPENS.
WINNER GETS THE BEER.
YOU WANT IN?
SERIOUSLY, PAUL? THAT'S SO GROSS.
GEEZ, LIGHTEN UP. IT'S JUST A LITTLE FUN.
I MEANT THE BEER.
CAMP '86 KNOW WHERE

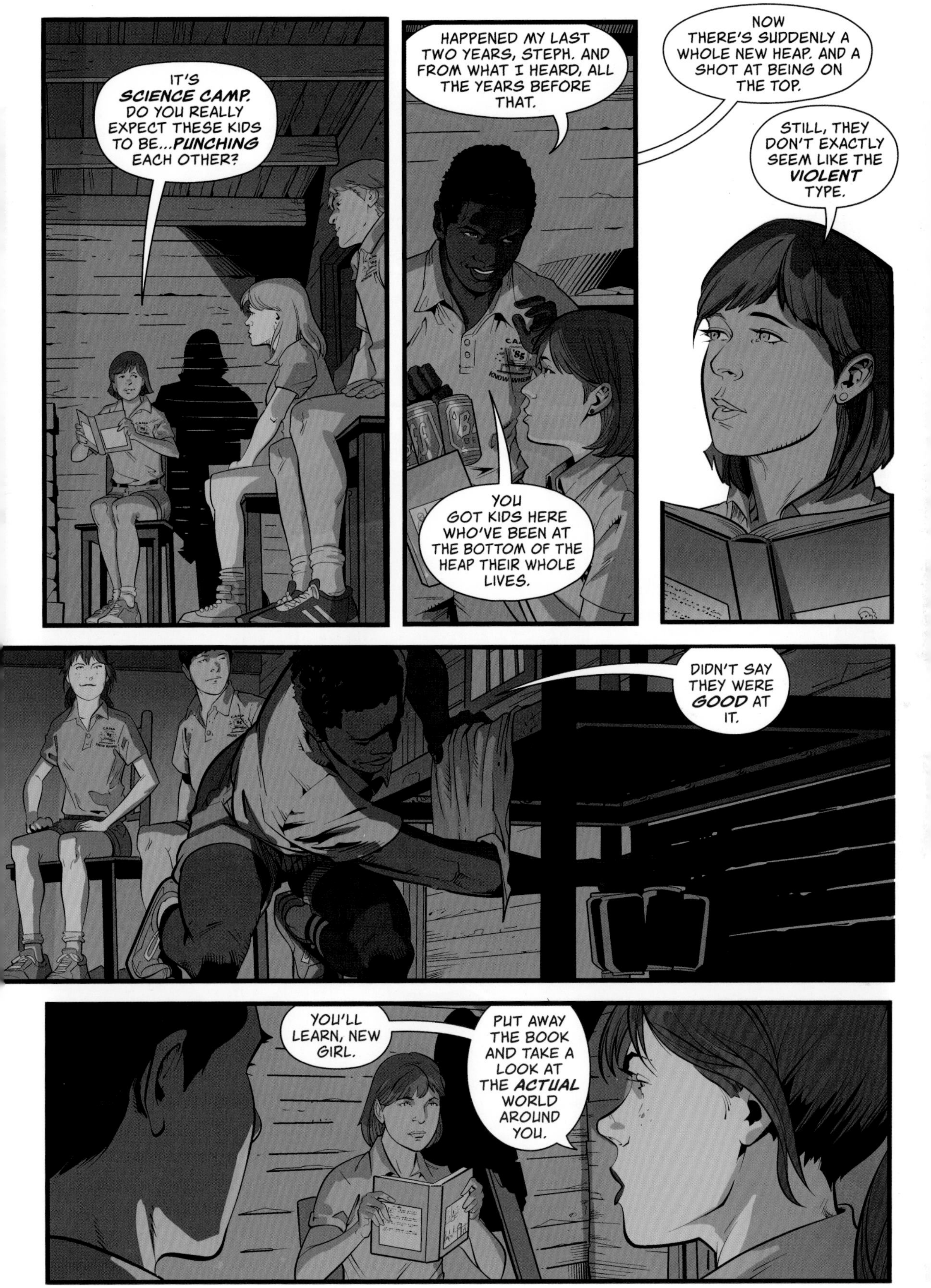
IT'S SCIENCE CAMP. DO YOU REALLY EXPECT THESE KIDS TO BE...PUNCHING EACH OTHER?
HAPPENED MY LAST TWO YEARS, STEPH. AND FROM WHAT I HEARD, ALL THE YEARS BEFORE THAT.
YOU GOT KIDS HERE WHO'VE BEEN AT THE BOTTOM OF THE HEAP THEIR WHOLE LIVES.
NOW THERE'S SUDDENLY A WHOLE NEW HEAP. AND A SHOT AT BEING ON THE TOP.
STILL, THEY DON'T EXACTLY SEEM LIKE THE VIOLENT TYPE.
DIDN'T SAY THEY WERE GOOD AT IT.
YOU'LL LEARN, NEW GIRL.
PUT AWAY THE BOOK AND TAKE A LOOK AT THE ACTUAL WORLD AROUND YOU.

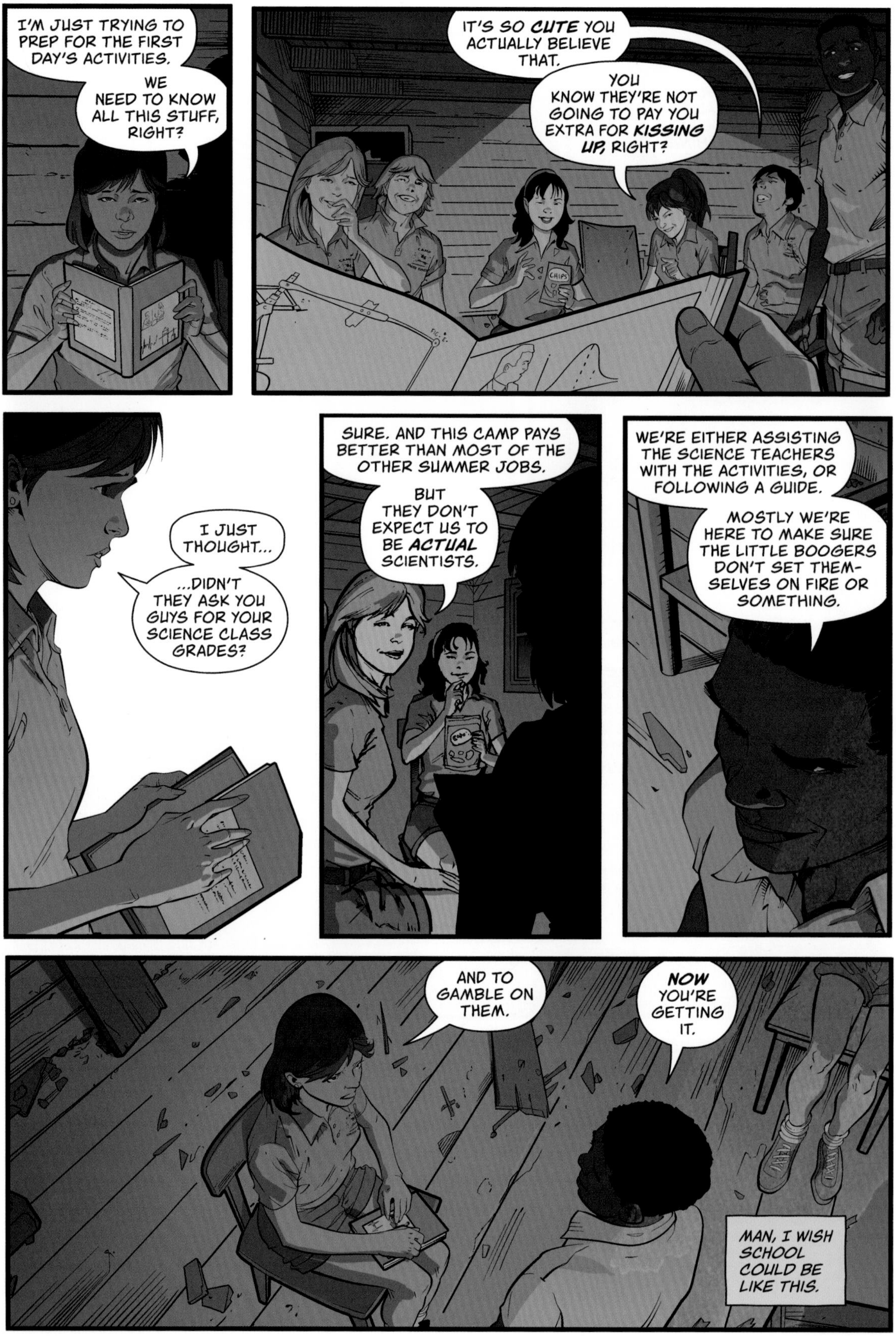

I'M JUST TRYING TO PREP FOR THE FIRST DAY'S ACTIVITIES.
WE NEED TO KNOW ALL THIS STUFF, RIGHT?
IT'S SO CUTE YOU ACTUALLY BELIEVE THAT.
YOU KNOW THEY'RE NOT GOING TO PAY YOU EXTRA FOR KISSING UP, RIGHT?
CHIPS
I JUST THOUGHT...
...DIDN'T THEY ASK YOU GUYS FOR YOUR SCIENCE CLASS GRADES?
SURE. AND THIS CAMP PAYS BETTER THAN MOST OF THE OTHER SUMMER JOBS.
BUT THEY DON'T EXPECT US TO BE ACTUAL SCIENTISTS.
WE'RE EITHER ASSISTING THE SCIENCE TEACHERS WITH THE ACTIVITIES, OR FOLLOWING A GUIDE.
MOSTLY WE'RE HERE TO MAKE SURE THE LITTLE BOOGERS DON'T SET THEM-SELVES ON FIRE OR SOMETHING.
AND TO GAMBLE ON THEM.
NOW YOU'RE GETTING IT.
MAN, I WISH SCHOOL COULD BE LIKE THIS.

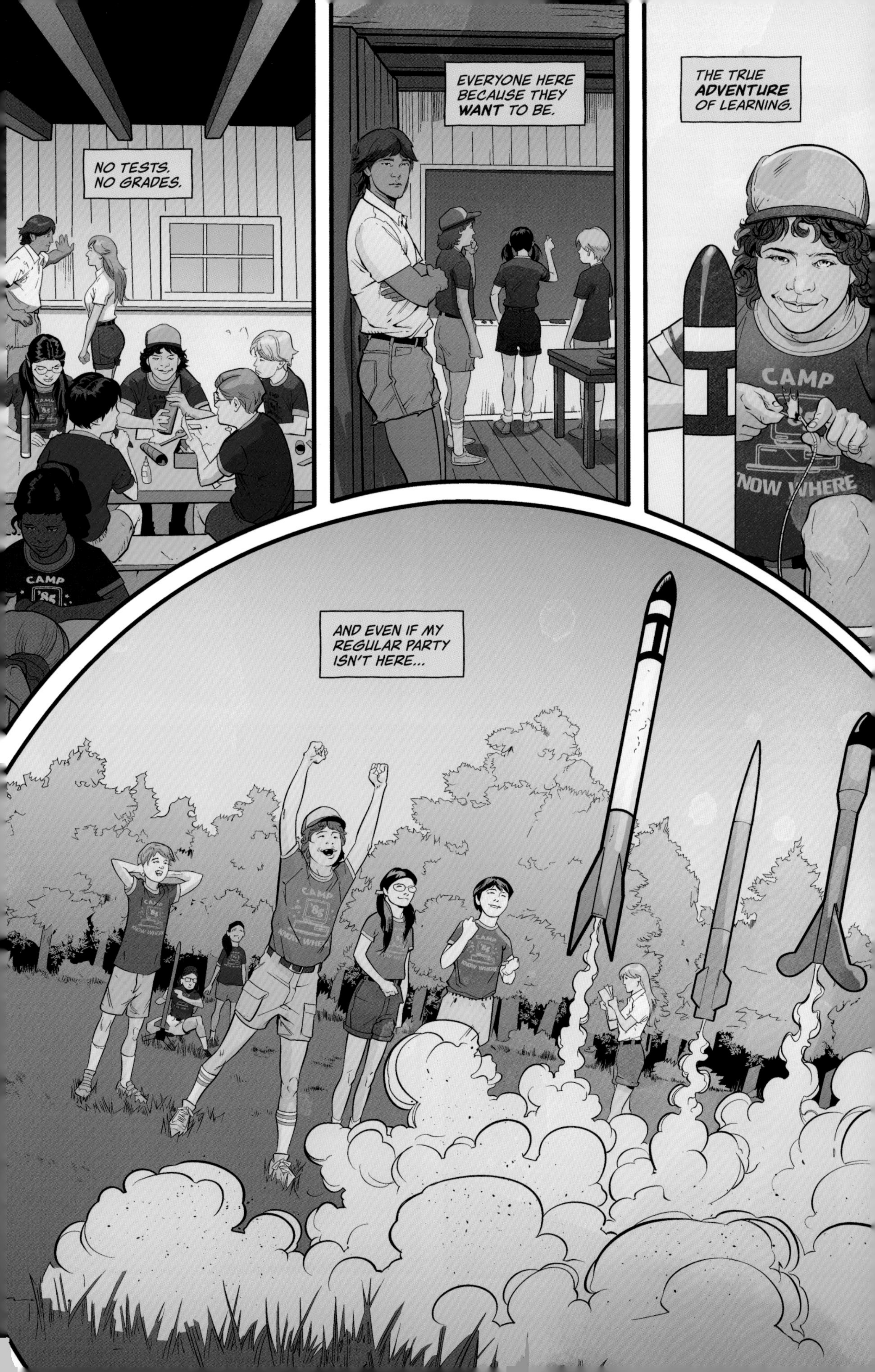
NO TESTS. NO GRADES.
CAMP
'85
EVERYONE HERE BECAUSE THEY WANT TO BE.
THE TRUE ADVENTURE OF LEARNING.
CAMP
NOW WHERE
AND EVEN IF MY REGULAR PARTY ISN'T HERE...
CAMP
'85
KNOW WHERE

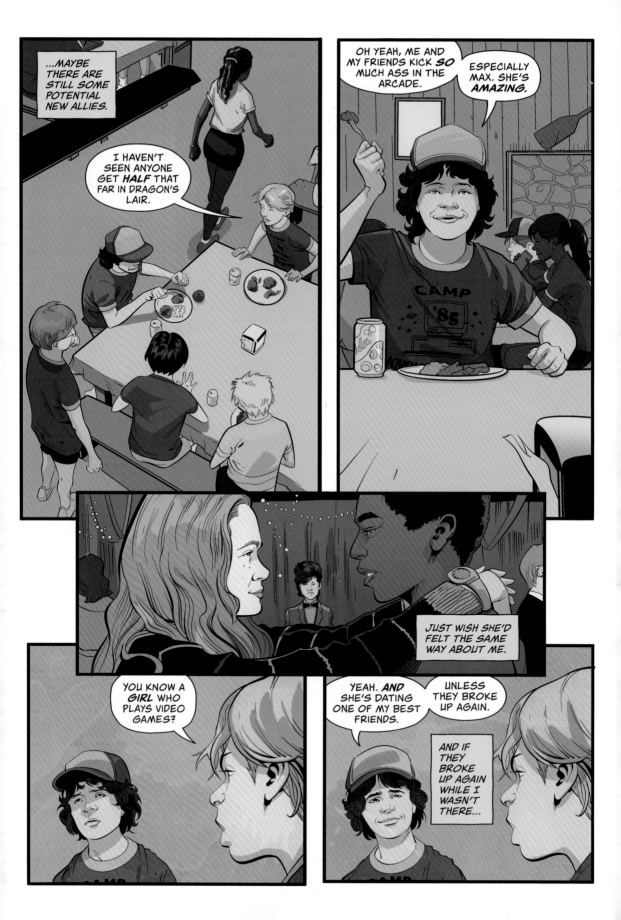

...MAYBE THERE ARE STILL SOME POTENTIAL NEW ALLIES.

I HAVEN'T SEEN ANYONE GET *HALF* THAT FAR IN DRAGON'S LAIR.

OH YEAH, ME AND MY FRIENDS KICK *SO* MUCH ASS IN THE ARCADE.

ESPECIALLY MAX. SHE'S *AMAZING.*

JUST WISH SHE'D FELT THE SAME WAY ABOUT ME.

YOU KNOW A *GIRL* WHO PLAYS VIDEO GAMES?

YEAH. *AND* SHE'S DATING ONE OF MY BEST FRIENDS.

UNLESS THEY BROKE UP AGAIN.

AND IF THEY BROKE UP AGAIN WHILE I WASN'T THERE...

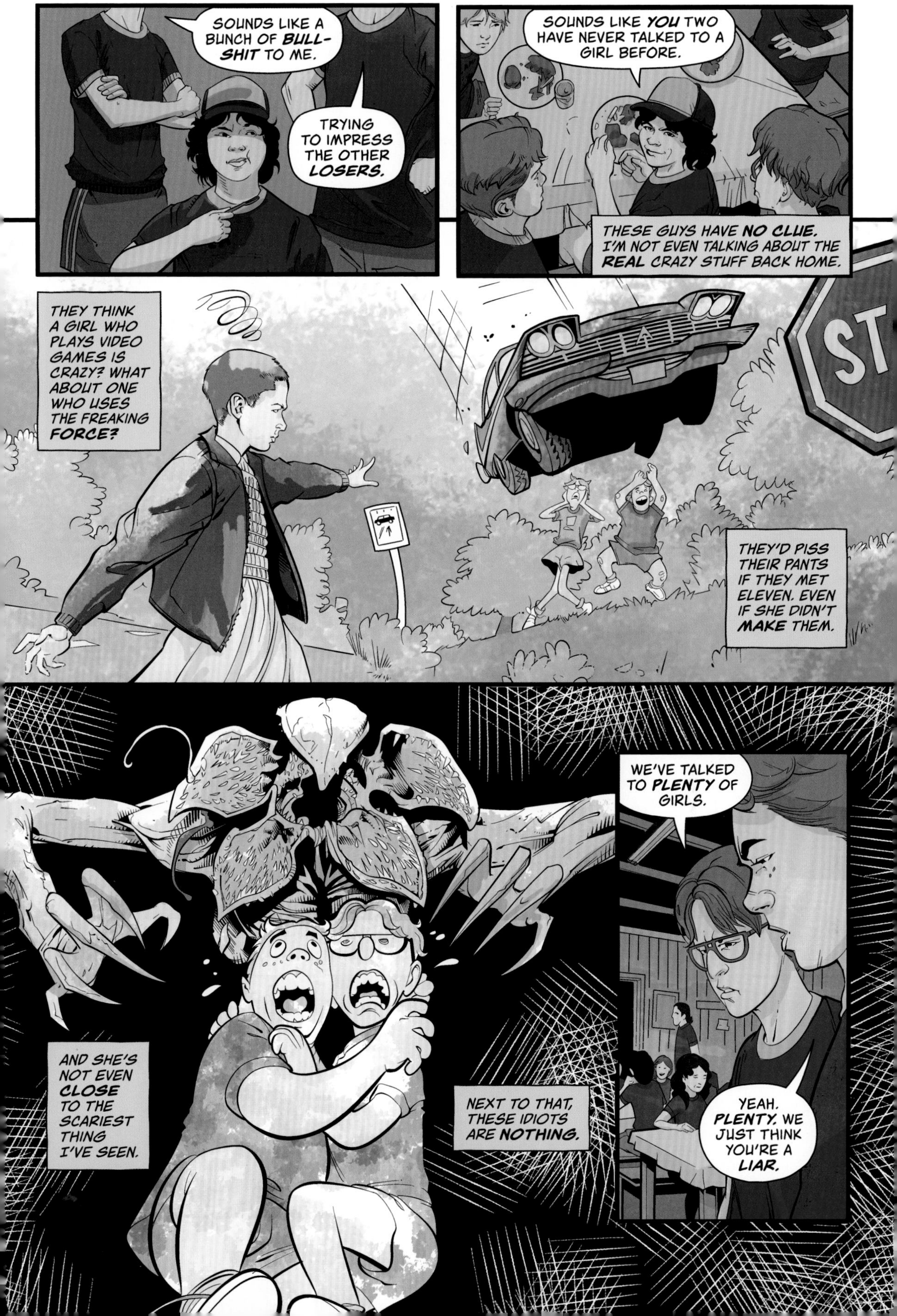

SOUNDS LIKE A BUNCH OF **BULL-SHIT** TO ME.
TRYING TO IMPRESS THE OTHER **LOSERS.**
SOUNDS LIKE ***YOU*** TWO HAVE NEVER TALKED TO A GIRL BEFORE.
*THESE GUYS HAVE **NO CLUE.** I'M NOT EVEN TALKING ABOUT THE **REAL** CRAZY STUFF BACK HOME.*
*THEY THINK A GIRL WHO PLAYS VIDEO GAMES IS CRAZY? WHAT ABOUT ONE WHO USES THE FREAKING **FORCE?***
ST
*THEY'D PISS THEIR PANTS IF THEY MET ELEVEN. EVEN IF SHE DIDN'T **MAKE** THEM.*
*AND SHE'S NOT EVEN **CLOSE** TO THE SCARIEST THING I'VE SEEN.*
*NEXT TO THAT, THESE IDIOTS ARE **NOTHING.***
WE'VE TALKED TO **PLENTY** OF GIRLS.
YEAH. **PLENTY.** WE JUST THINK YOU'RE A **LIAR.**

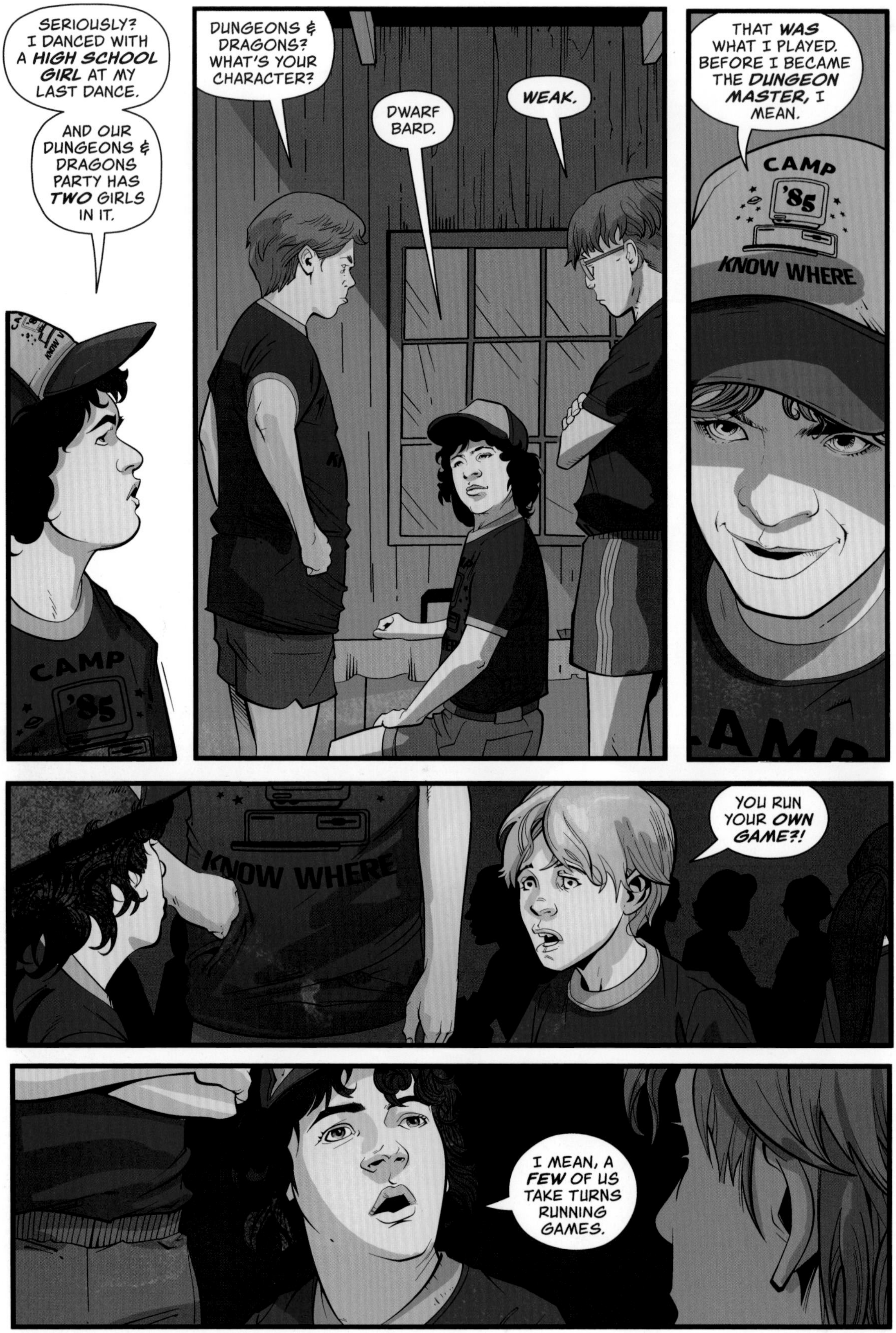
SERIOUSLY? I DANCED WITH A HIGH SCHOOL GIRL AT MY LAST DANCE.
AND OUR DUNGEONS & DRAGONS PARTY HAS TWO GIRLS IN IT.
CAMP '85
DUNGEONS & DRAGONS? WHAT'S YOUR CHARACTER?
DWARF BARD.
WEAK.
THAT WAS WHAT I PLAYED. BEFORE I BECAME THE DUNGEON MASTER, I MEAN.
CAMP '85 KNOW WHERE
KNOW WHERE
YOU RUN YOUR OWN GAME?!
I MEAN, A FEW OF US TAKE TURNS RUNNING GAMES.

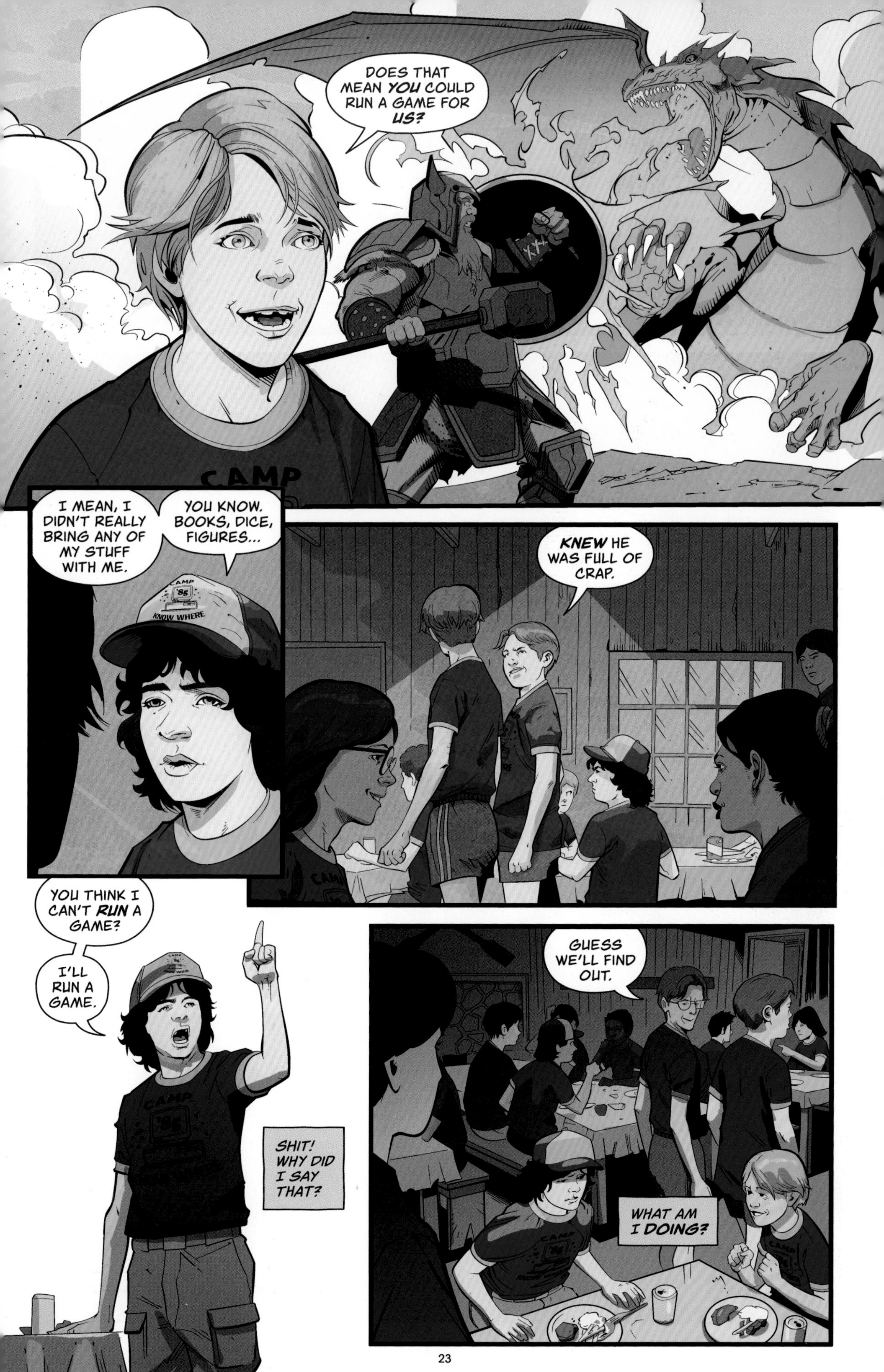
DOES THAT MEAN *YOU* COULD RUN A GAME FOR *US*?
I MEAN, I DIDN'T REALLY BRING ANY OF MY STUFF WITH ME.
YOU KNOW. BOOKS, DICE, FIGURES...
CAMP '85 KNOW WHERE
KNEW HE WAS FULL OF CRAP.
YOU THINK I CAN'T *RUN* A GAME?
I'LL RUN A GAME.
SHIT! WHY DID I SAY THAT?
GUESS WE'LL FIND OUT.
WHAT AM I DOING?

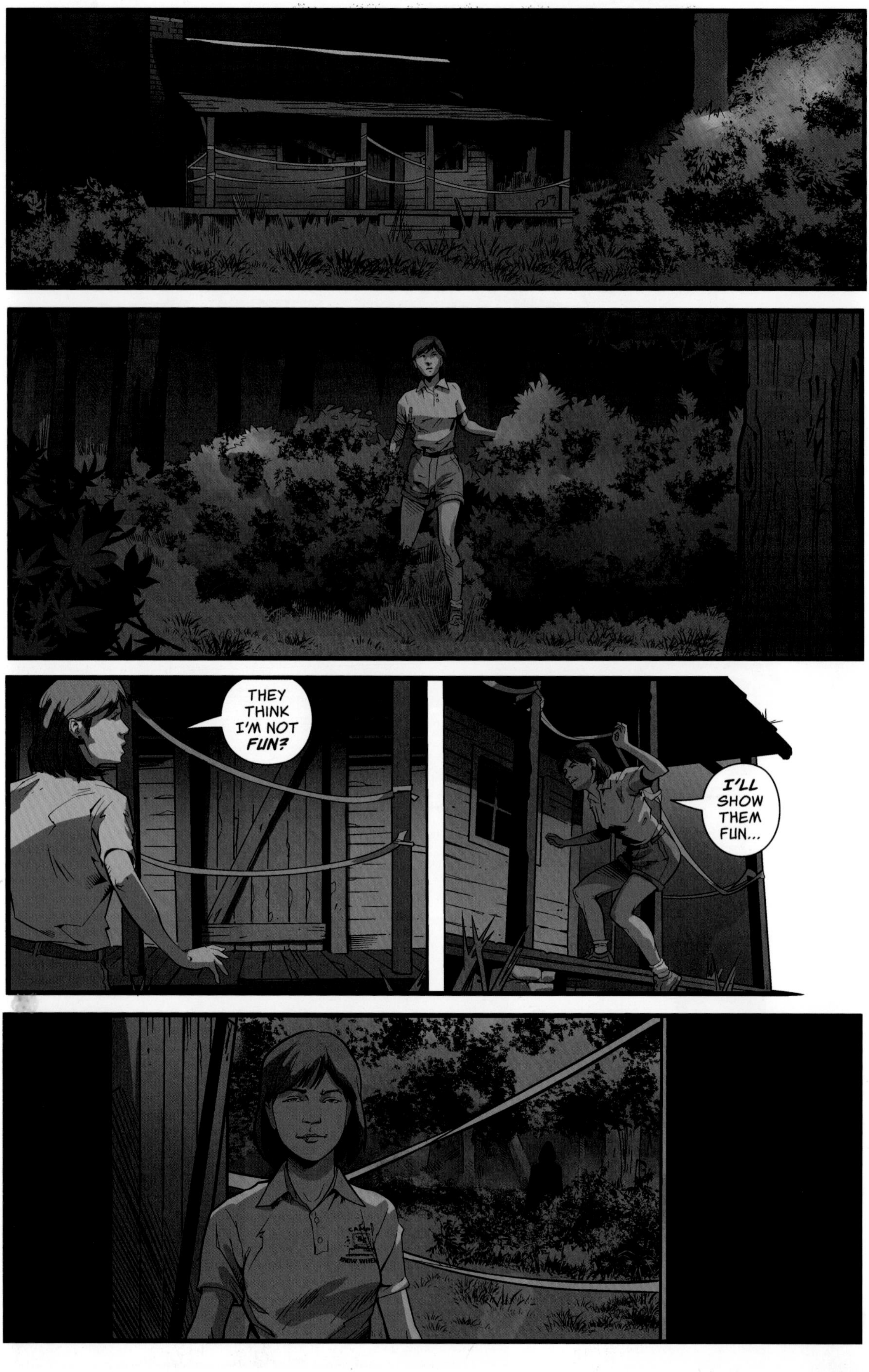
THEY THINK I'M NOT FUN?
I'LL SHOW THEM FUN...

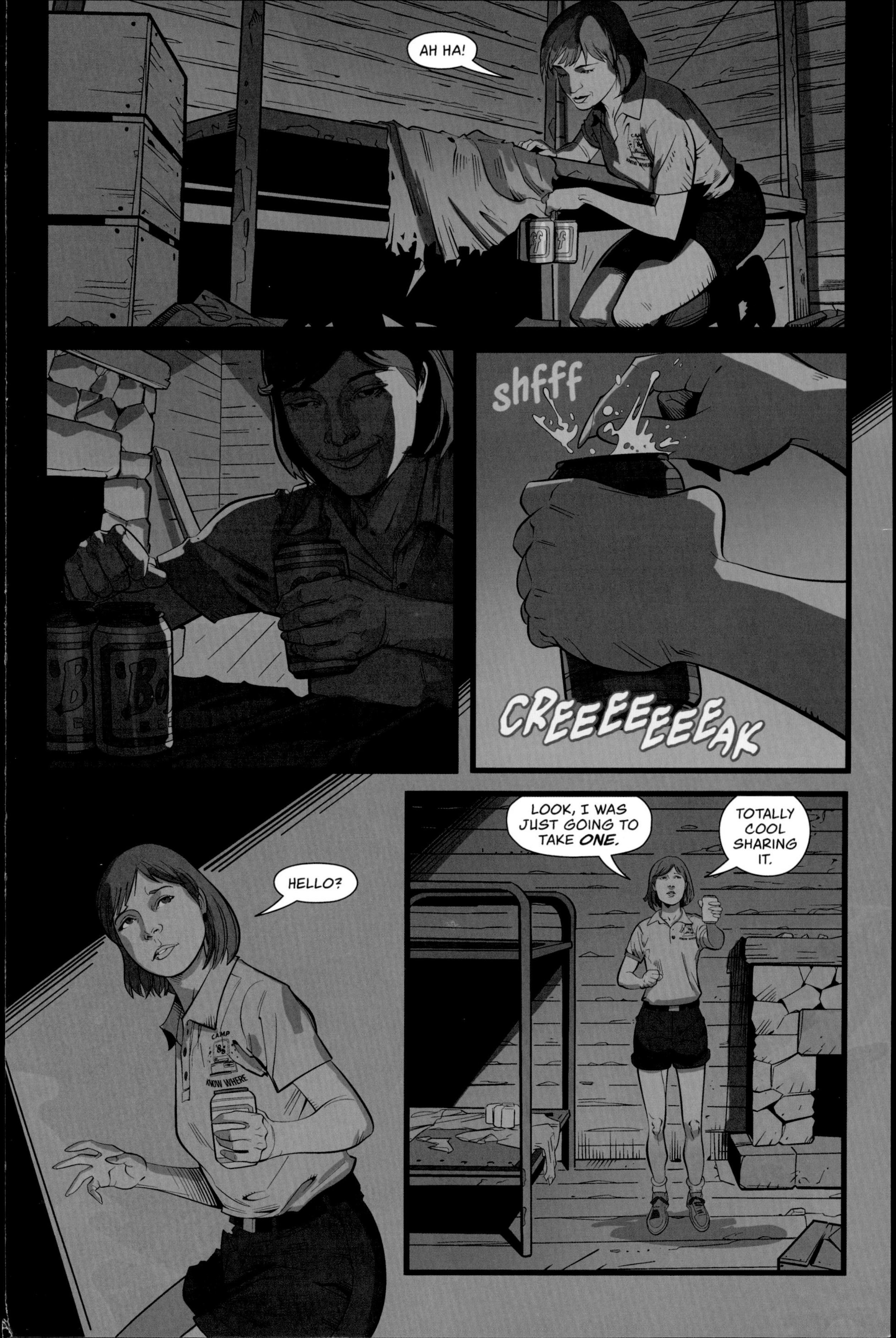
AH HA!
shfff
CREEEEEEEEAK
HELLO?
LOOK, I WAS JUST GOING TO TAKE *ONE*.
TOTALLY COOL SHARING IT.

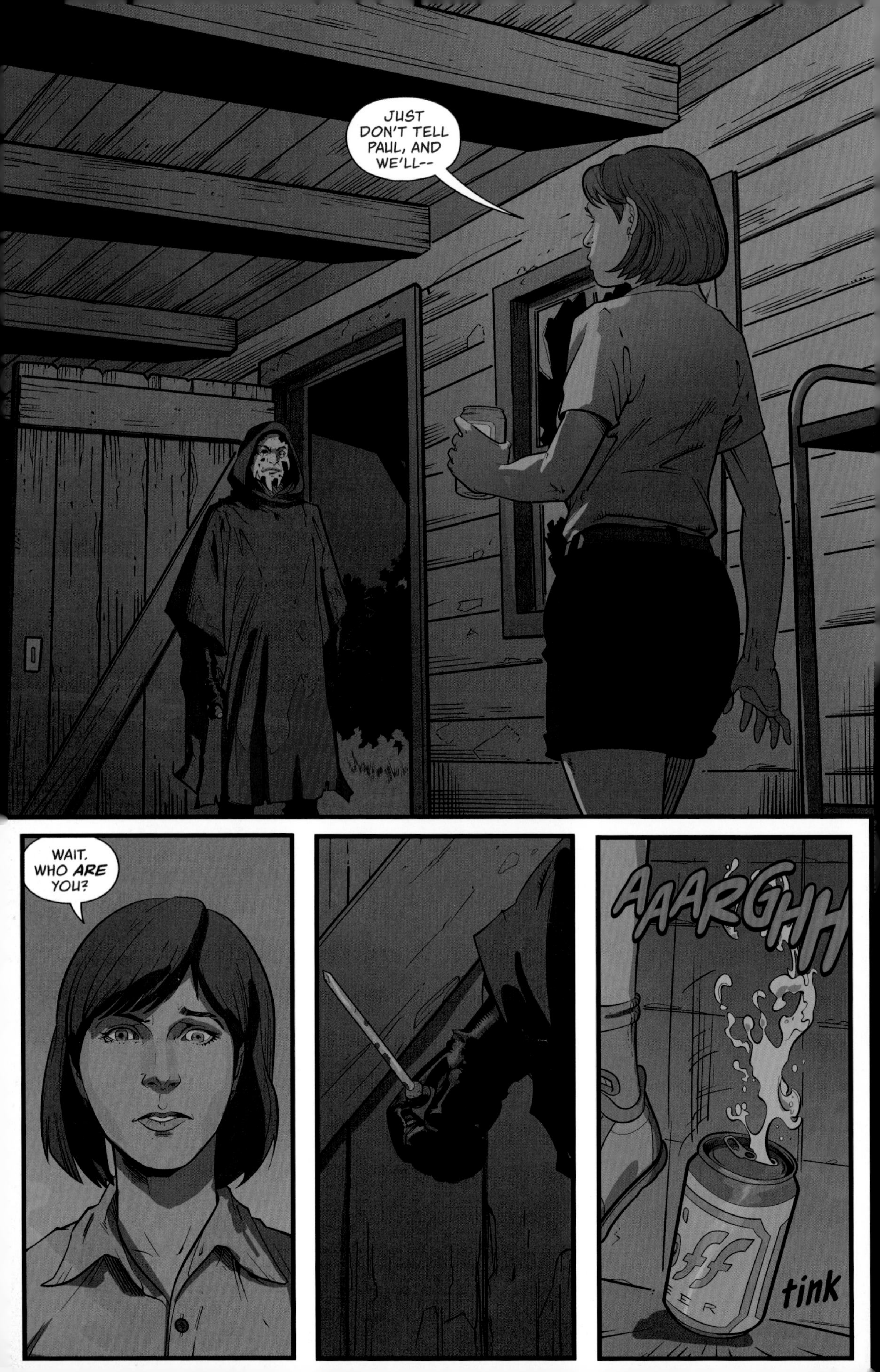
JUST DON'T TELL PAUL, AND WE'LL--
WAIT. WHO ARE YOU?
AAARGHH
tink

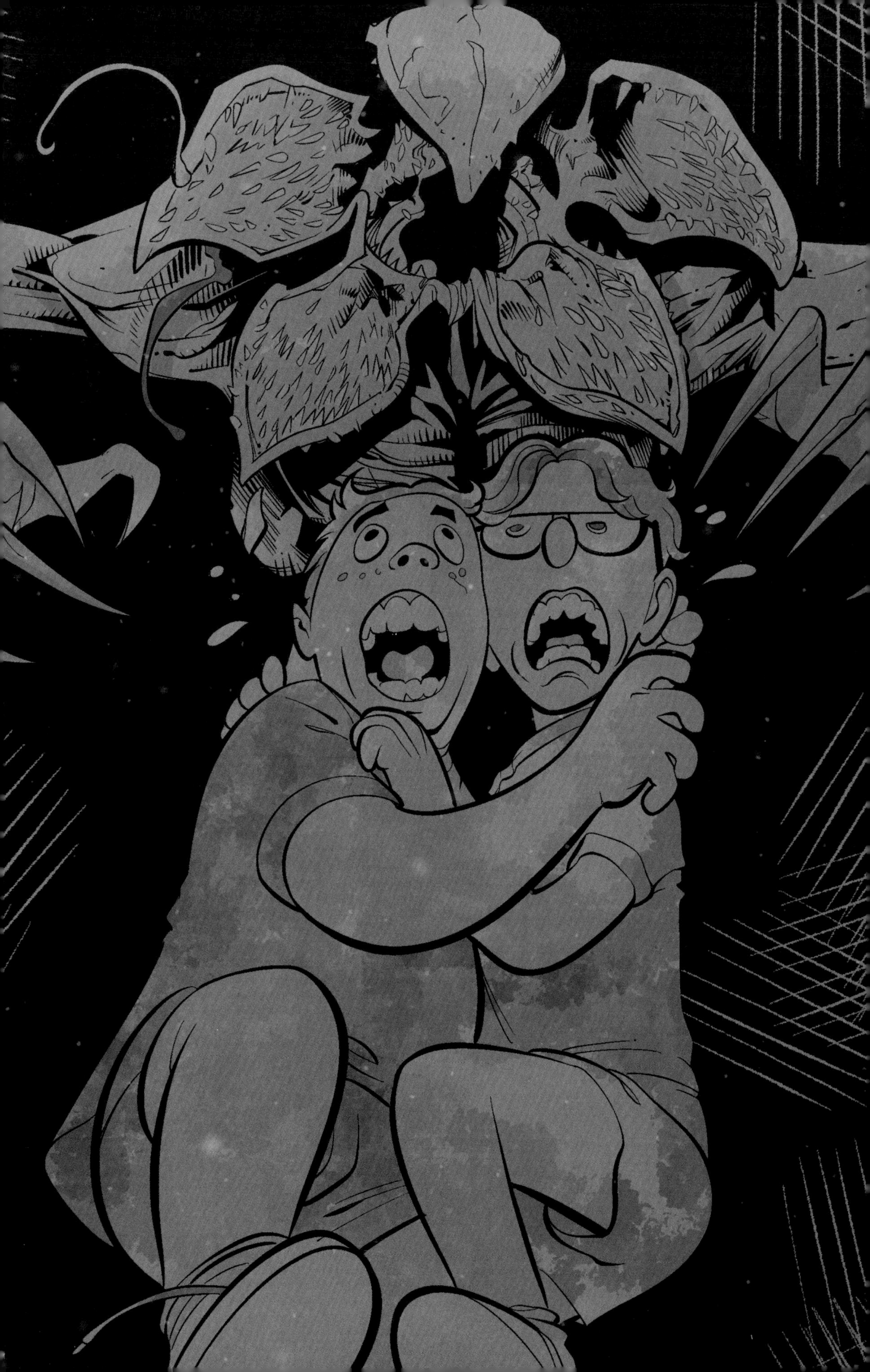

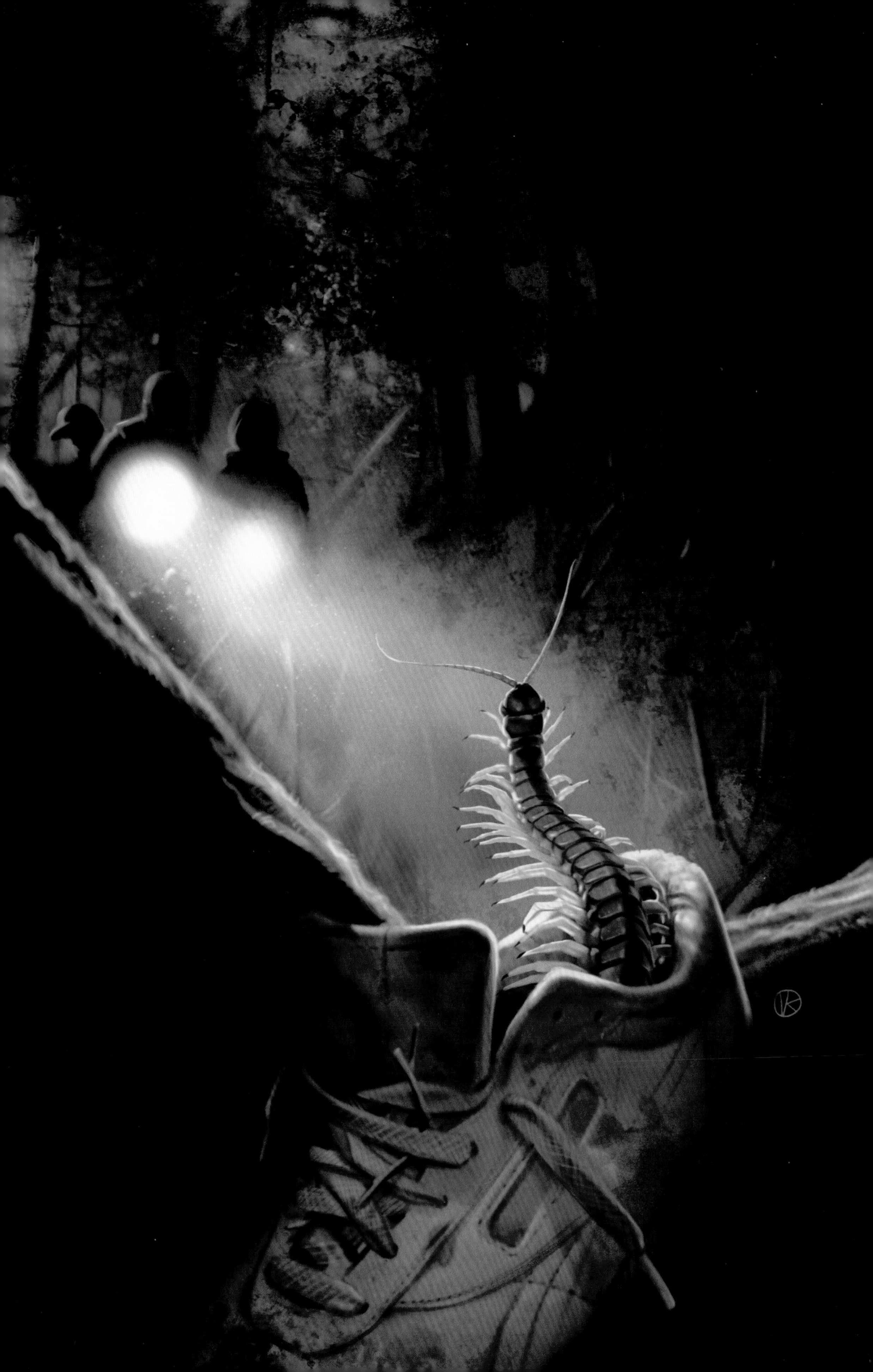

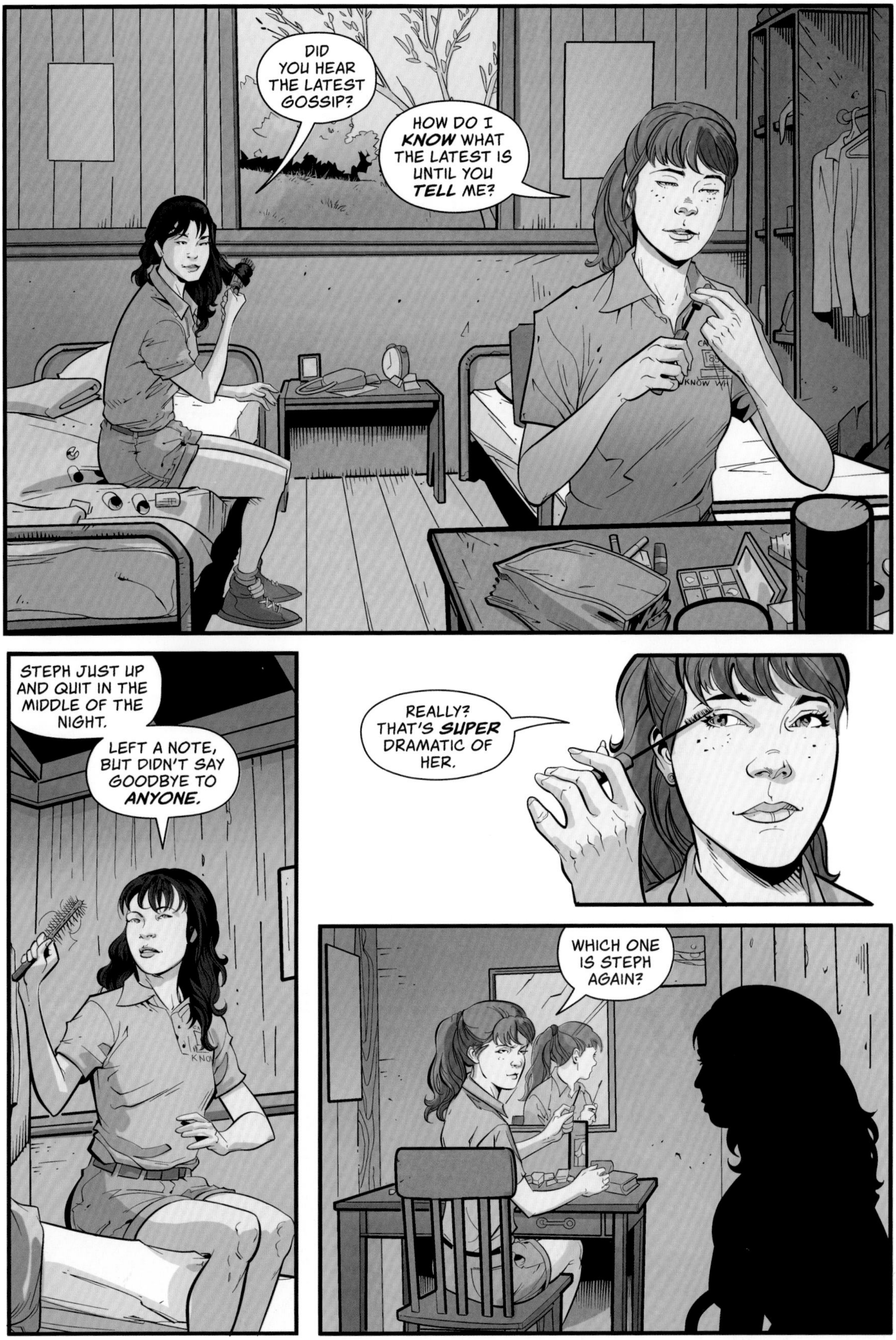

DID YOU HEAR THE LATEST GOSSIP?
HOW DO I *KNOW* WHAT THE LATEST IS UNTIL YOU *TELL* ME?
STEPH JUST UP AND QUIT IN THE MIDDLE OF THE NIGHT.
LEFT A NOTE, BUT DIDN'T SAY GOODBYE TO *ANYONE.*
REALLY? THAT'S *SUPER* DRAMATIC OF HER.
WHICH ONE IS STEPH AGAIN?

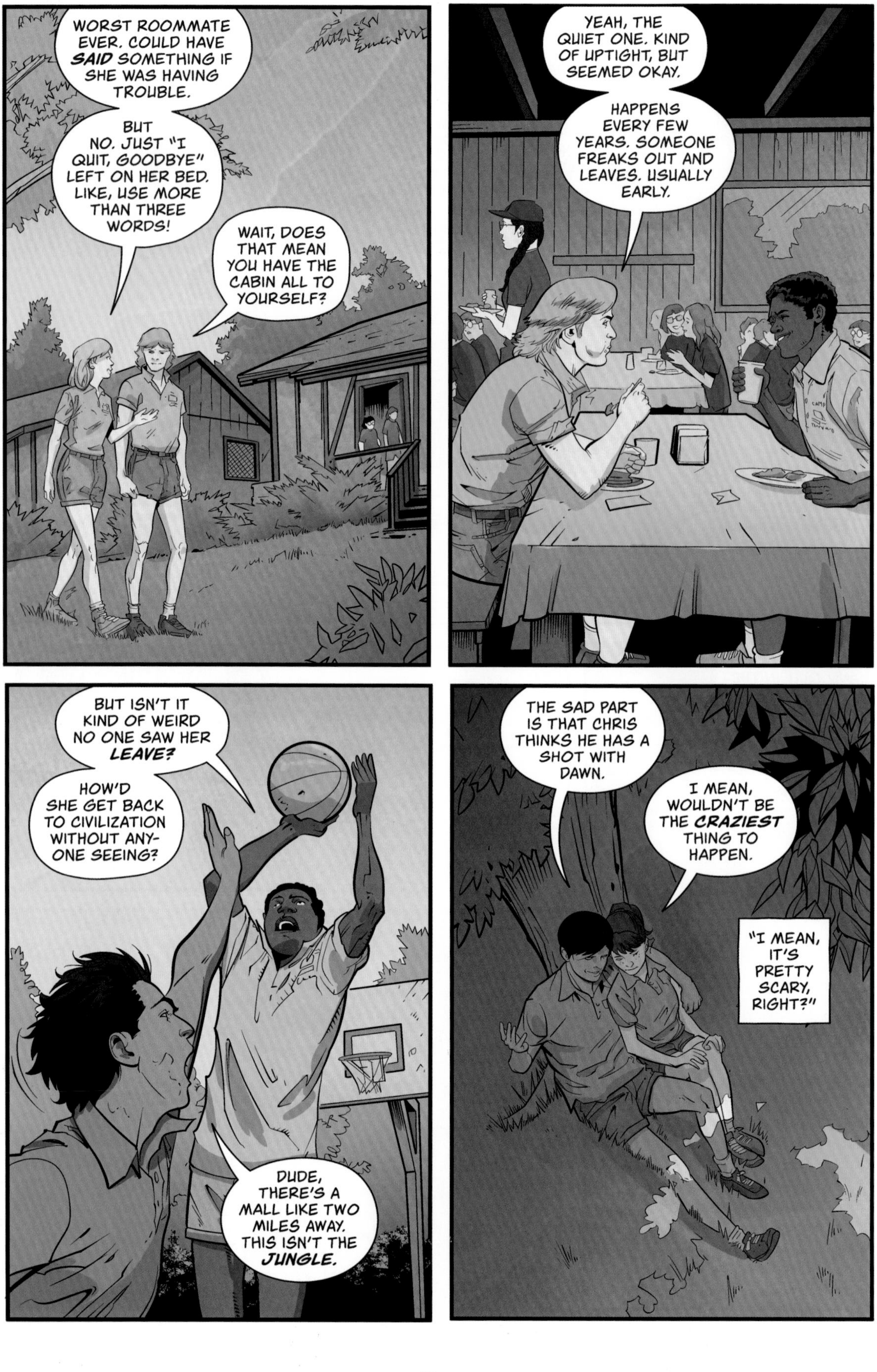
WORST ROOMMATE EVER. COULD HAVE SAID SOMETHING IF SHE WAS HAVING TROUBLE.
BUT NO. JUST "I QUIT, GOODBYE" LEFT ON HER BED. LIKE, USE MORE THAN THREE WORDS!
WAIT, DOES THAT MEAN YOU HAVE THE CABIN ALL TO YOURSELF?
YEAH, THE QUIET ONE. KIND OF UPTIGHT, BUT SEEMED OKAY.
HAPPENS EVERY FEW YEARS. SOMEONE FREAKS OUT AND LEAVES. USUALLY EARLY.
BUT ISN'T IT KIND OF WEIRD NO ONE SAW HER LEAVE?
HOW'D SHE GET BACK TO CIVILIZATION WITHOUT ANY-ONE SEEING?
DUDE, THERE'S A MALL LIKE TWO MILES AWAY. THIS ISN'T THE JUNGLE.
THE SAD PART IS THAT CHRIS THINKS HE HAS A SHOT WITH DAWN.
I MEAN, WOULDN'T BE THE CRAZIEST THING TO HAPPEN.
"I MEAN, IT'S PRETTY SCARY, RIGHT?"

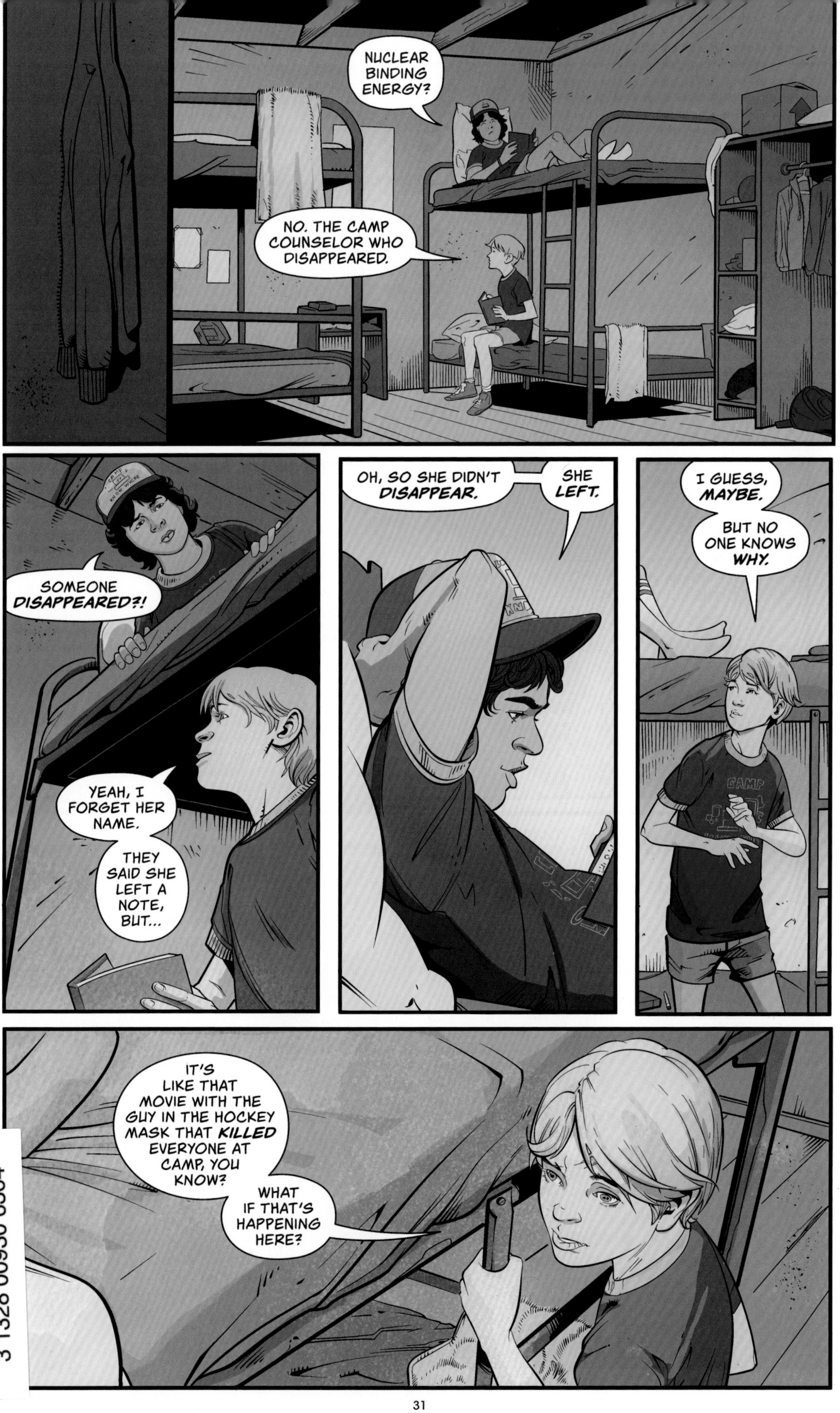
NUCLEAR BINDING ENERGY?
NO. THE CAMP COUNSELOR WHO DISAPPEARED.
SOMEONE DISAPPEARED?!
YEAH, I FORGET HER NAME.
THEY SAID SHE LEFT A NOTE, BUT...
OH, SO SHE DIDN'T DISAPPEAR.
SHE LEFT.
I GUESS, MAYBE.
BUT NO ONE KNOWS WHY.
IT'S LIKE THAT MOVIE WITH THE GUY IN THE HOCKEY MASK THAT KILLED EVERYONE AT CAMP, YOU KNOW?
WHAT IF THAT'S HAPPENING HERE?

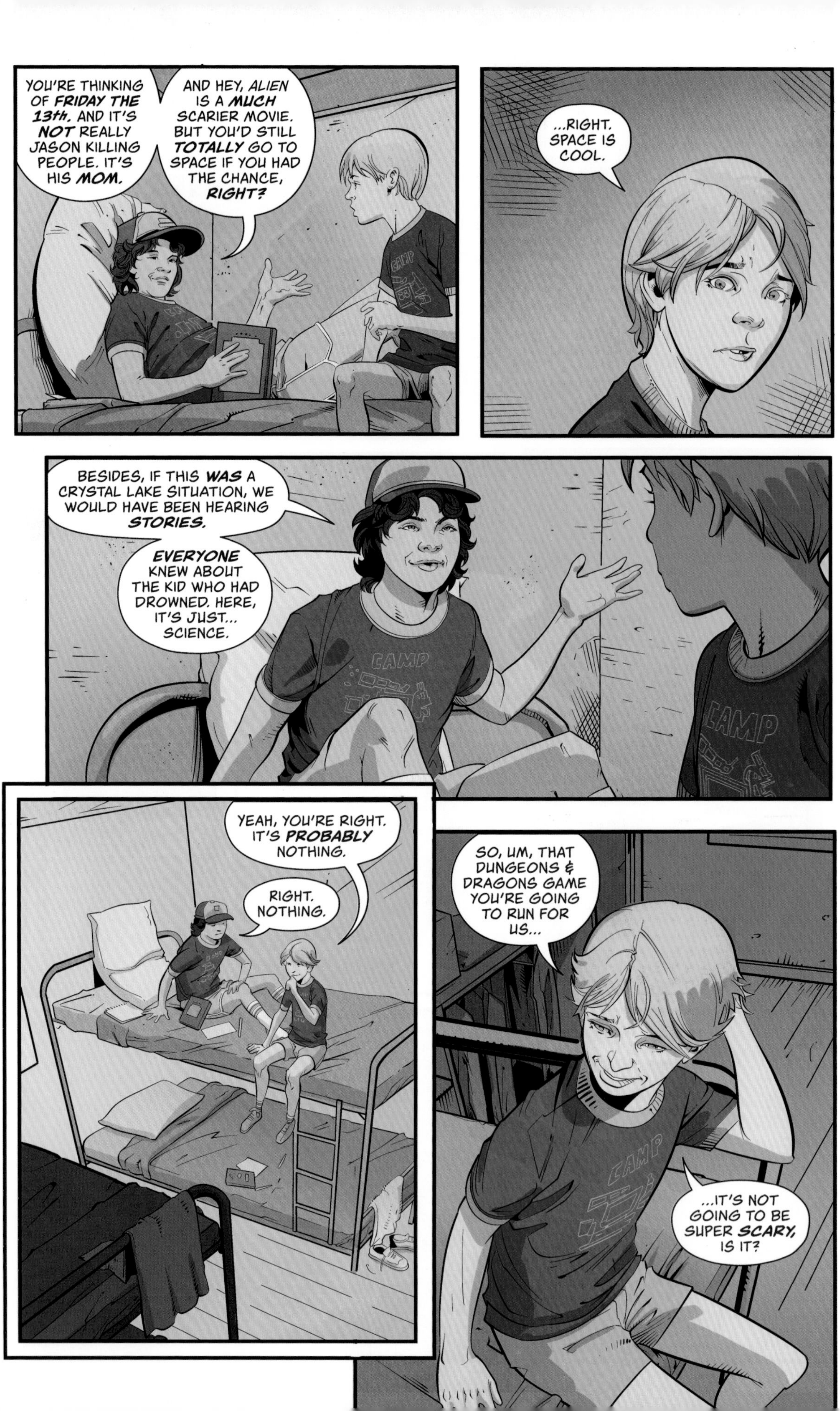
YOU'RE THINKING OF FRIDAY THE 13th. AND IT'S NOT REALLY JASON KILLING PEOPLE. IT'S HIS MOM.
AND HEY, ALIEN IS A MUCH SCARIER MOVIE. BUT YOU'D STILL TOTALLY GO TO SPACE IF YOU HAD THE CHANCE, RIGHT?
...RIGHT. SPACE IS COOL.
BESIDES, IF THIS WAS A CRYSTAL LAKE SITUATION, WE WOULD HAVE BEEN HEARING STORIES.
EVERYONE KNEW ABOUT THE KID WHO HAD DROWNED. HERE, IT'S JUST... SCIENCE.
CAMP
YEAH, YOU'RE RIGHT. IT'S PROBABLY NOTHING.
RIGHT. NOTHING.
SO, UM, THAT DUNGEONS & DRAGONS GAME YOU'RE GOING TO RUN FOR US...
...IT'S NOT GOING TO BE SUPER SCARY, IS IT?

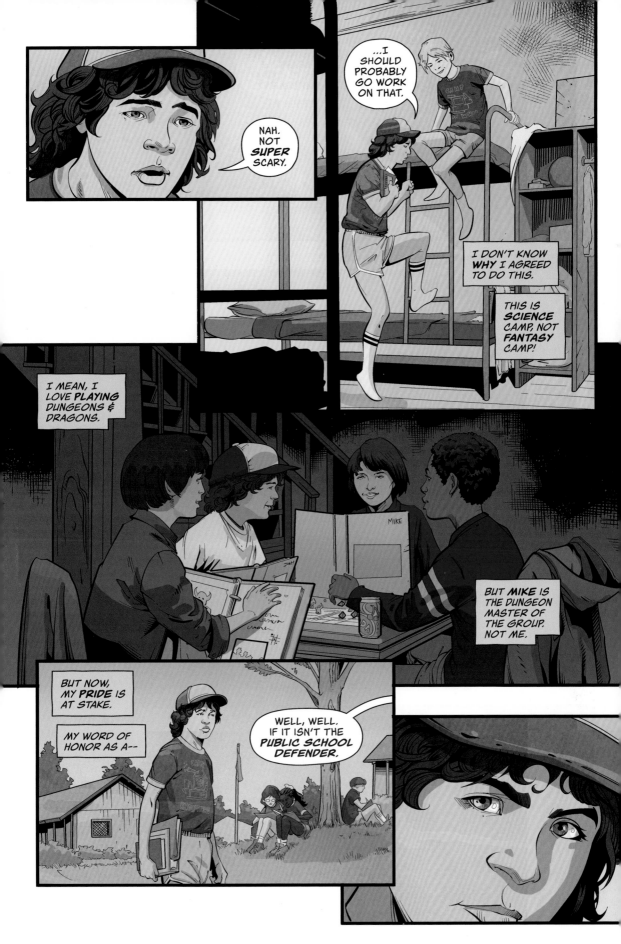

NAH. NOT **SUPER** SCARY.

...I SHOULD PROBABLY GO WORK ON THAT.

I DON'T KNOW **WHY** I AGREED TO DO THIS.

THIS IS **SCIENCE** CAMP, NOT **FANTASY** CAMP!

I MEAN, I LOVE **PLAYING DUNGEONS & DRAGONS.**

BUT **MIKE** IS THE DUNGEON MASTER OF THE GROUP. NOT ME.

BUT NOW, MY **PRIDE** IS AT STAKE.

MY WORD OF HONOR AS A--

WELL, WELL. IF IT ISN'T THE **PUBLIC SCHOOL** DEFENDER.

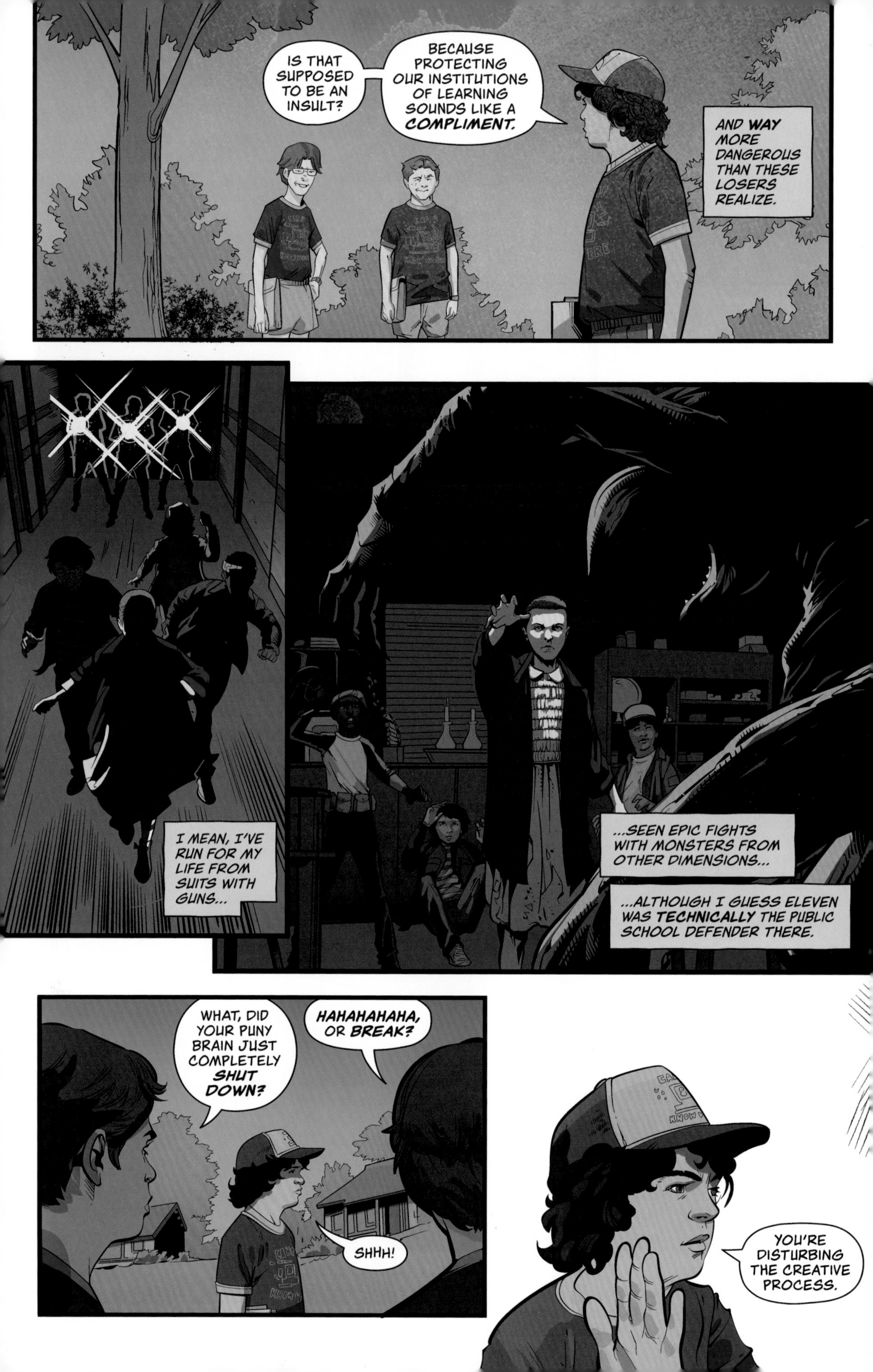
IS THAT SUPPOSED TO BE AN INSULT?
BECAUSE PROTECTING OUR INSTITUTIONS OF LEARNING SOUNDS LIKE A COMPLIMENT.
AND WAY MORE DANGEROUS THAN THESE LOSERS REALIZE.
I MEAN, I'VE RUN FOR MY LIFE FROM SUITS WITH GUNS...
...SEEN EPIC FIGHTS WITH MONSTERS FROM OTHER DIMENSIONS...
...ALTHOUGH I GUESS ELEVEN WAS TECHNICALLY THE PUBLIC SCHOOL DEFENDER THERE.
WHAT, DID YOUR PUNY BRAIN JUST COMPLETELY SHUT DOWN?
HAHAHAHAHA, OR BREAK?
SHHH!
YOU'RE DISTURBING THE CREATIVE PROCESS.

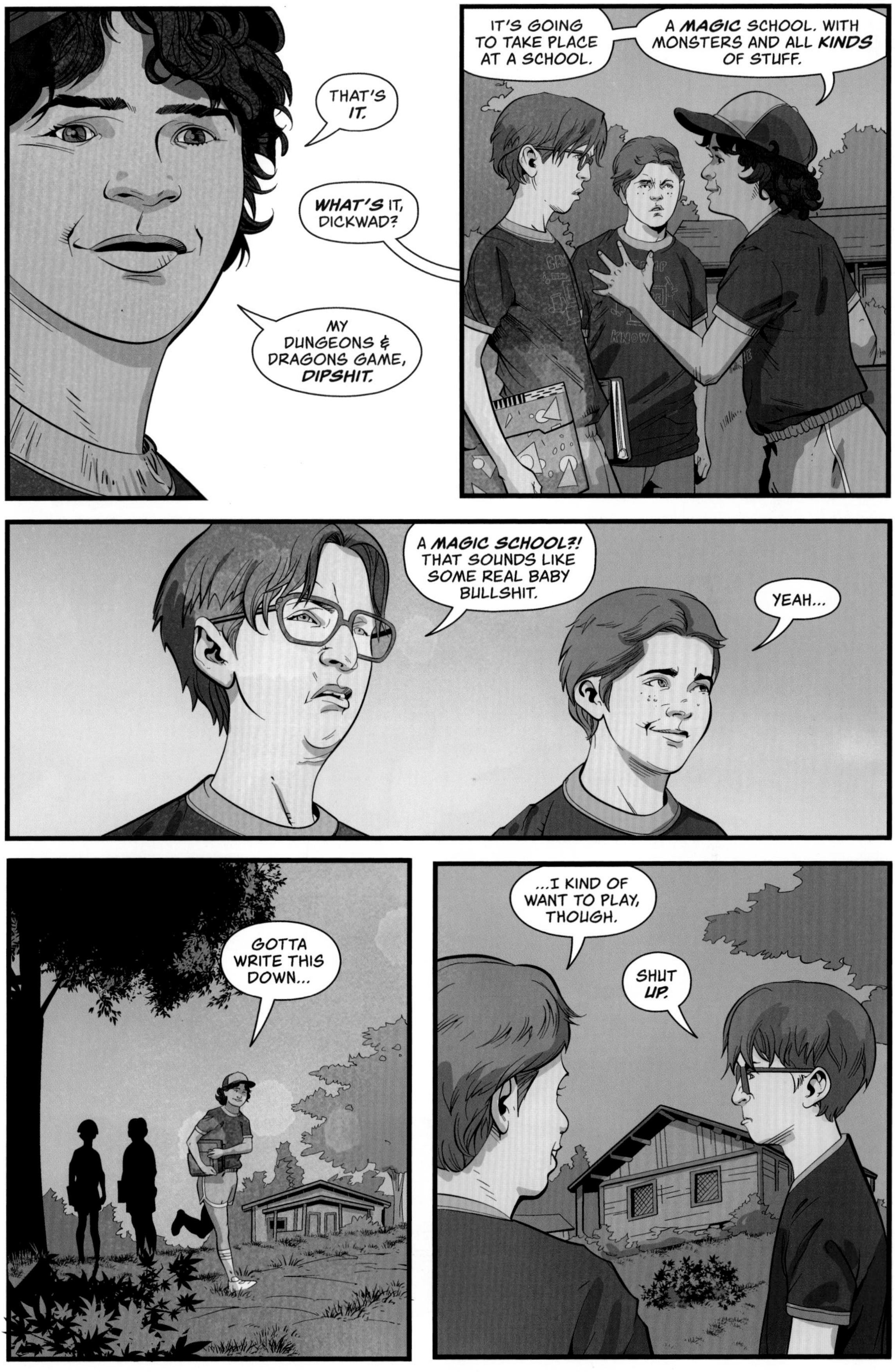
THAT'S IT.
WHAT'S IT, DICKWAD?
MY DUNGEONS & DRAGONS GAME, DIPSHIT.
IT'S GOING TO TAKE PLACE AT A SCHOOL.
A MAGIC SCHOOL. WITH MONSTERS AND ALL KINDS OF STUFF.
A MAGIC SCHOOL?! THAT SOUNDS LIKE SOME REAL BABY BULLSHIT.
YEAH...
GOTTA WRITE THIS DOWN...
...I KIND OF WANT TO PLAY, THOUGH.
SHUT UP.

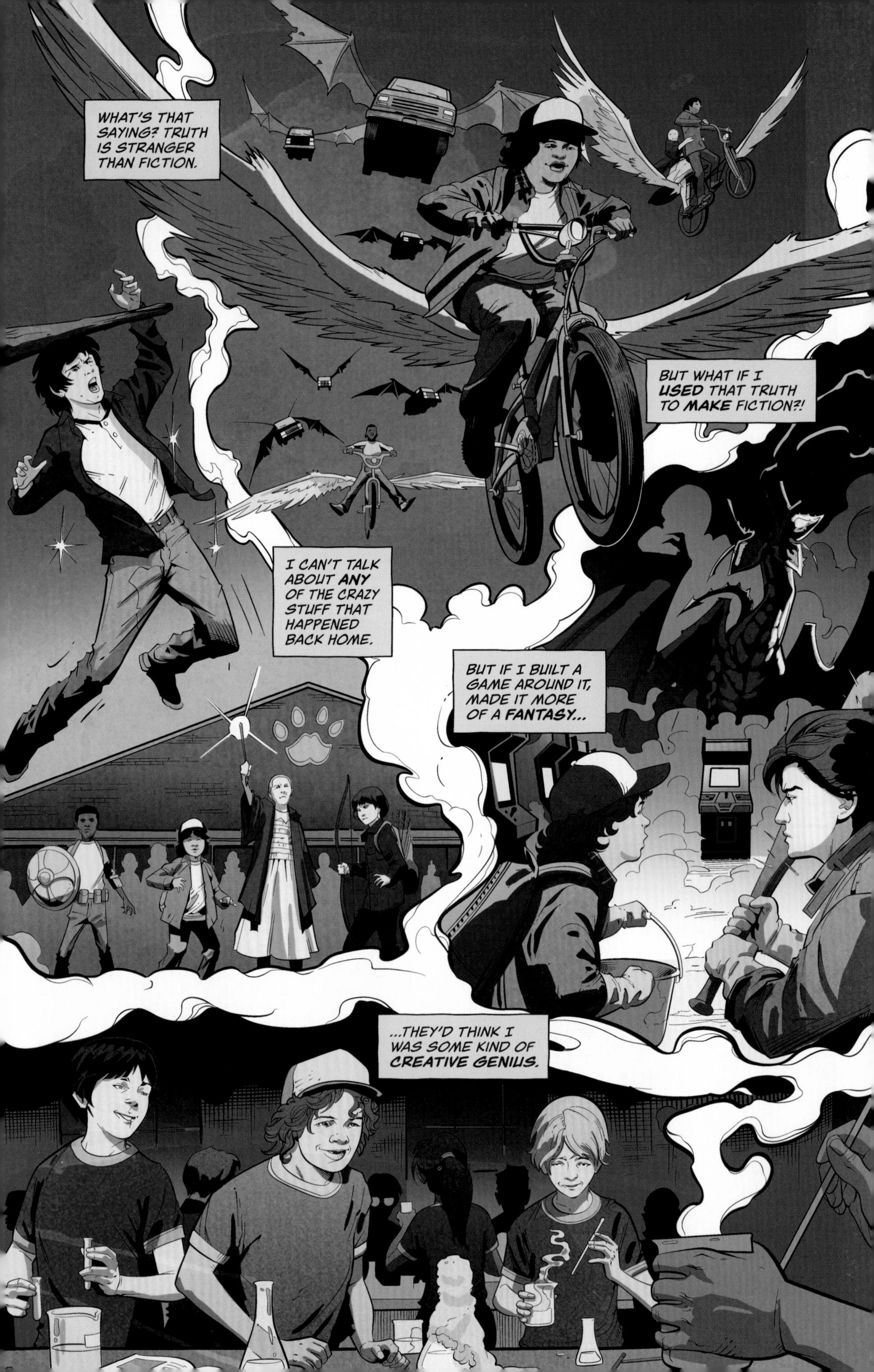
WHAT'S THAT SAYING? TRUTH IS STRANGER THAN FICTION.
BUT WHAT IF I USED THAT TRUTH TO MAKE FICTION?!
I CAN'T TALK ABOUT ANY OF THE CRAZY STUFF THAT HAPPENED BACK HOME.
BUT IF I BUILT A GAME AROUND IT, MADE IT MORE OF A FANTASY...
...THEY'D THINK I WAS SOME KIND OF CREATIVE GENIUS.

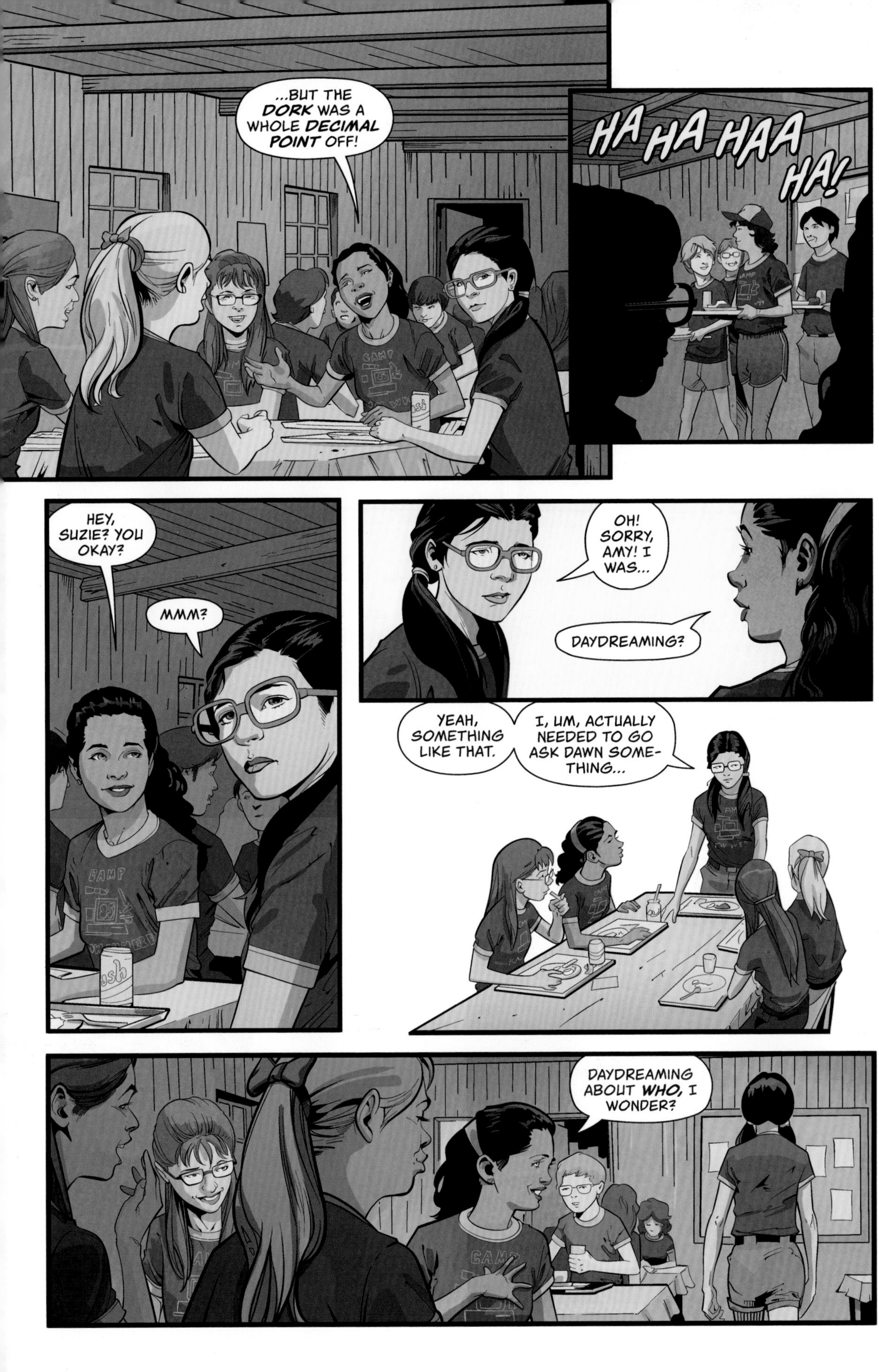
...BUT THE DORK WAS A WHOLE DECIMAL POINT OFF!
HA HA HAAA HA!
HEY, SUZIE? YOU OKAY?
MMM?
OH! SORRY, AMY! I WAS...
DAYDREAMING?
YEAH, SOMETHING LIKE THAT.
I, UM, ACTUALLY NEEDED TO GO ASK DAWN SOME-THING...
DAYDREAMING ABOUT WHO, I WONDER?

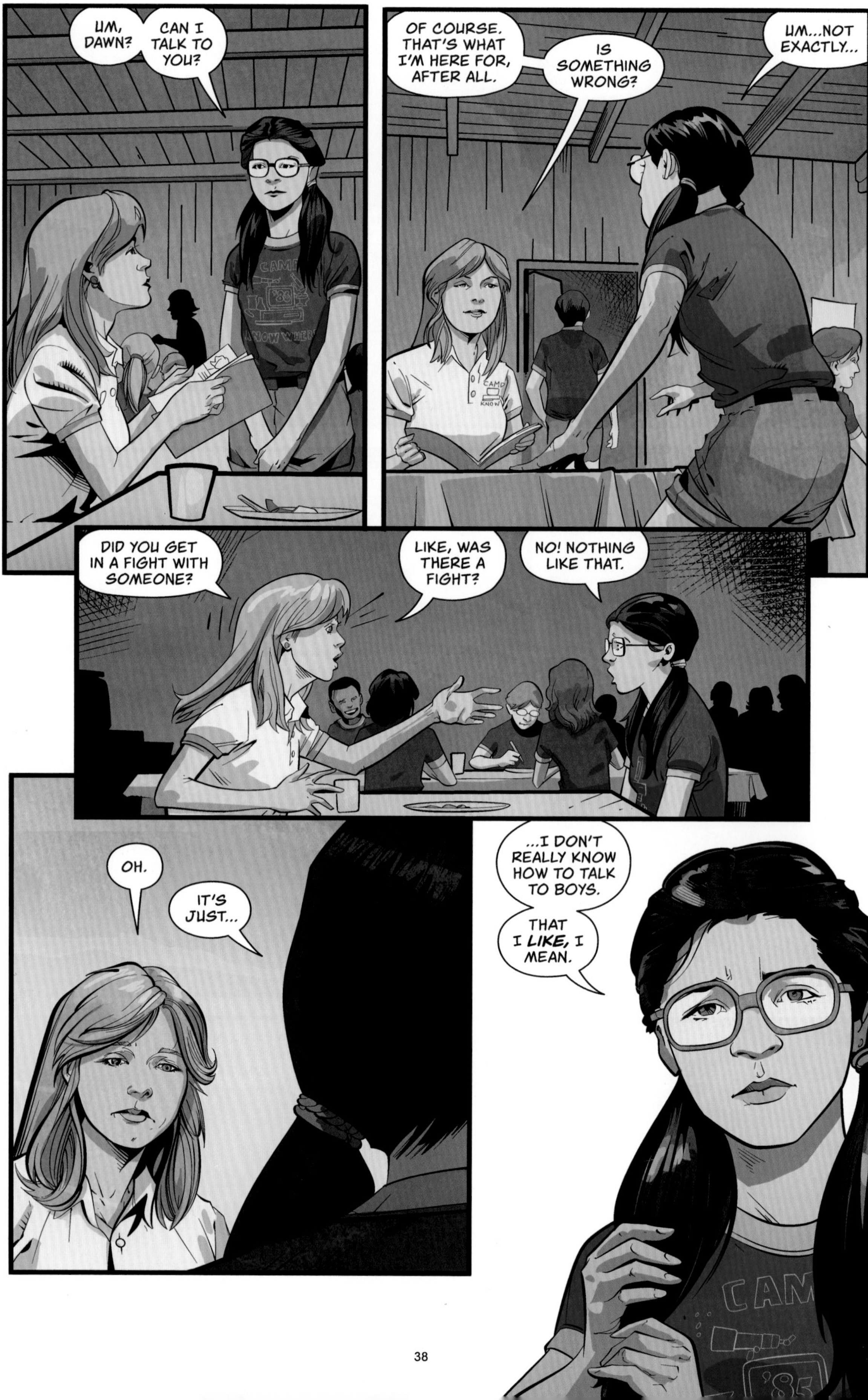
UM, DAWN?
CAN I TALK TO YOU?
OF COURSE. THAT'S WHAT I'M HERE FOR, AFTER ALL.
IS SOMETHING WRONG?
UM...NOT EXACTLY...
DID YOU GET IN A FIGHT WITH SOMEONE?
LIKE, WAS THERE A FIGHT?
NO! NOTHING LIKE THAT.
OH.
IT'S JUST...
...I DON'T REALLY KNOW HOW TO TALK TO BOYS.
THAT I *LIKE*, I MEAN.

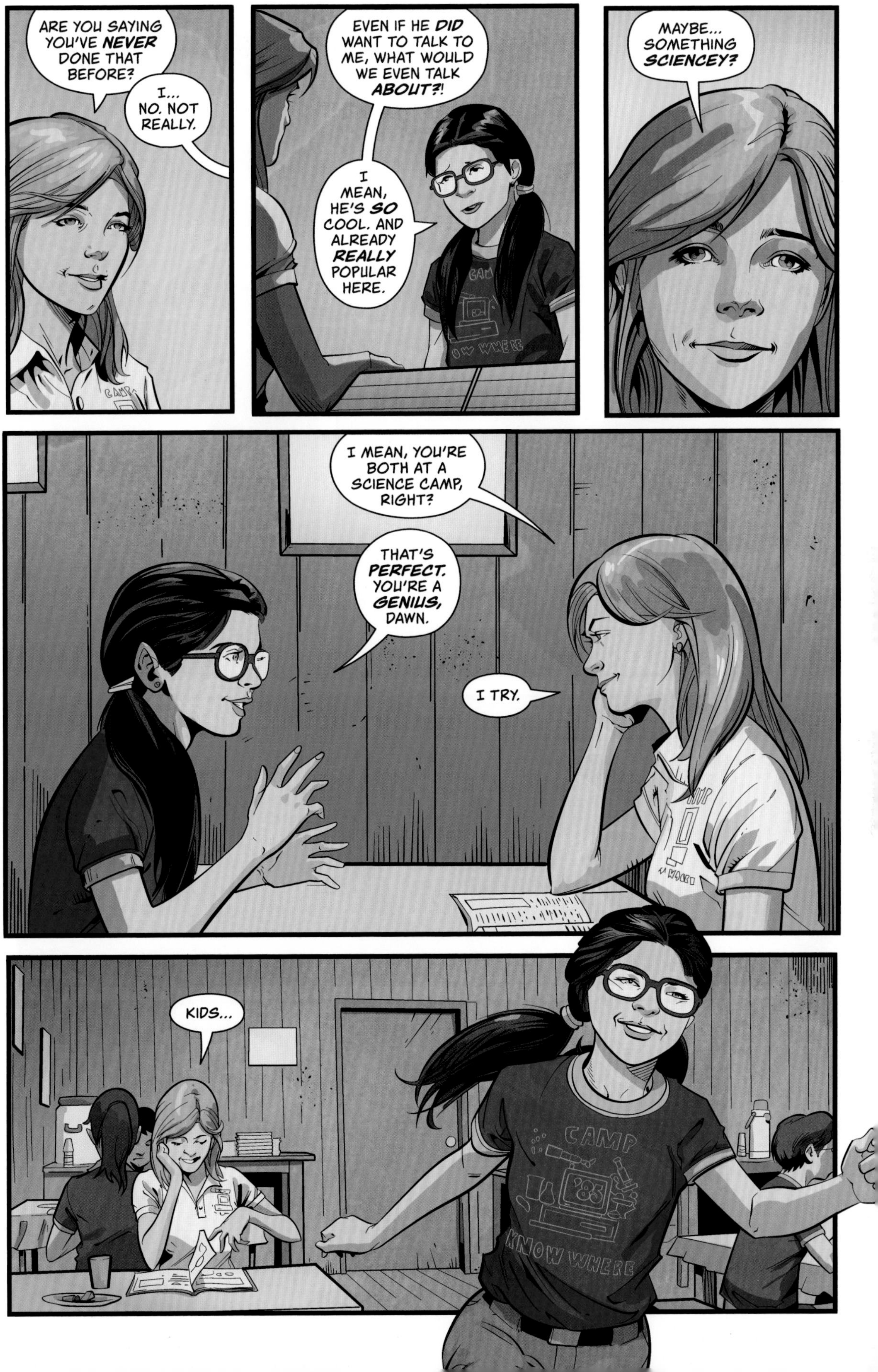
ARE YOU SAYING YOU'VE NEVER DONE THAT BEFORE?
I... NO. NOT REALLY.
EVEN IF HE DID WANT TO TALK TO ME, WHAT WOULD WE EVEN TALK ABOUT?!
I MEAN, HE'S SO COOL. AND ALREADY REALLY POPULAR HERE.
MAYBE... SOMETHING SCIENCEY?
I MEAN, YOU'RE BOTH AT A SCIENCE CAMP, RIGHT?
THAT'S PERFECT. YOU'RE A GENIUS, DAWN.
I TRY.
KIDS...
CAMP
'85
KNOW WHERE

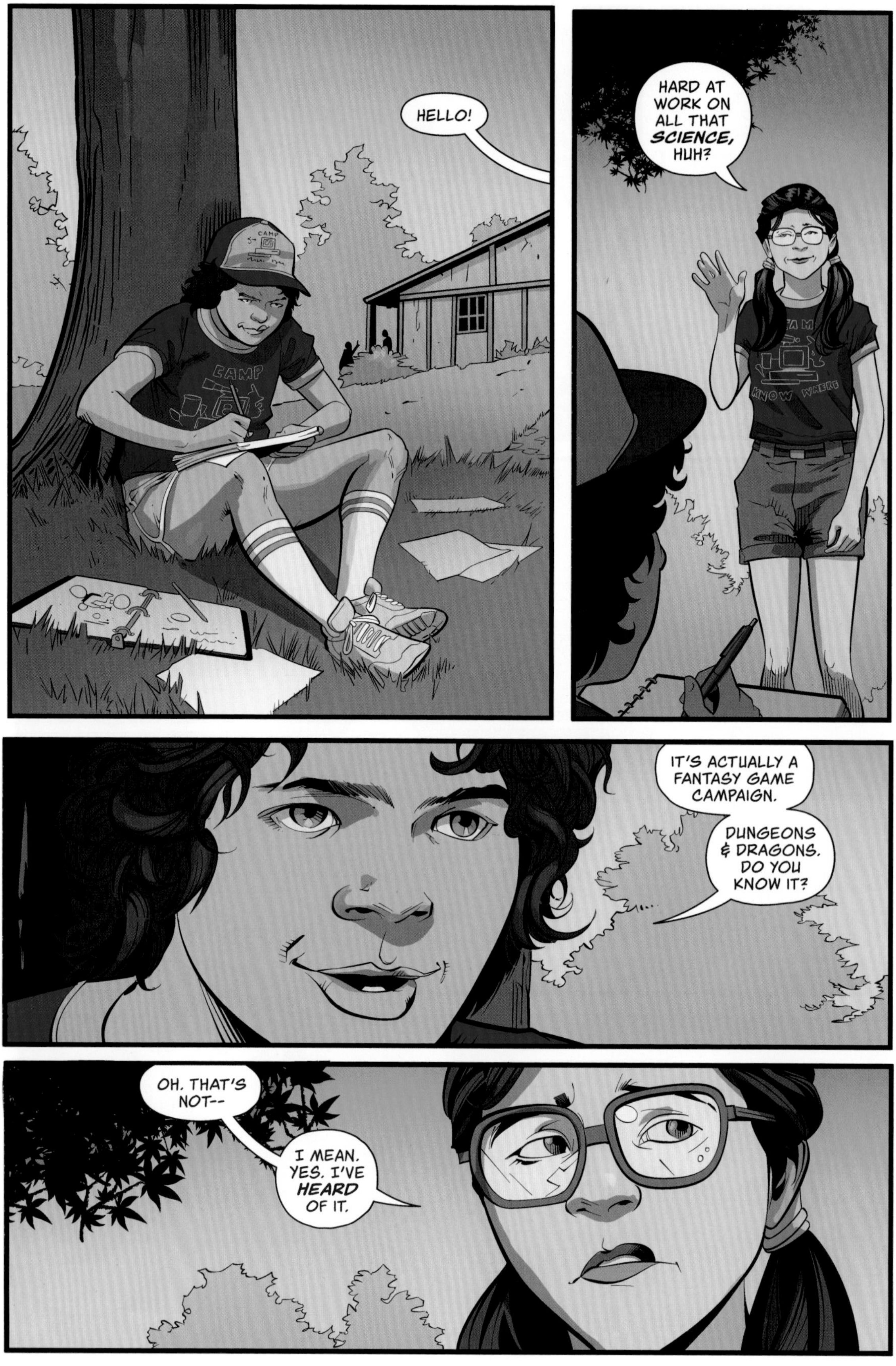
HELLO!
HARD AT WORK ON ALL THAT SCIENCE, HUH?
IT'S ACTUALLY A FANTASY GAME CAMPAIGN.
DUNGEONS & DRAGONS. DO YOU KNOW IT?
OH. THAT'S NOT--
I MEAN. YES. I'VE HEARD OF IT.

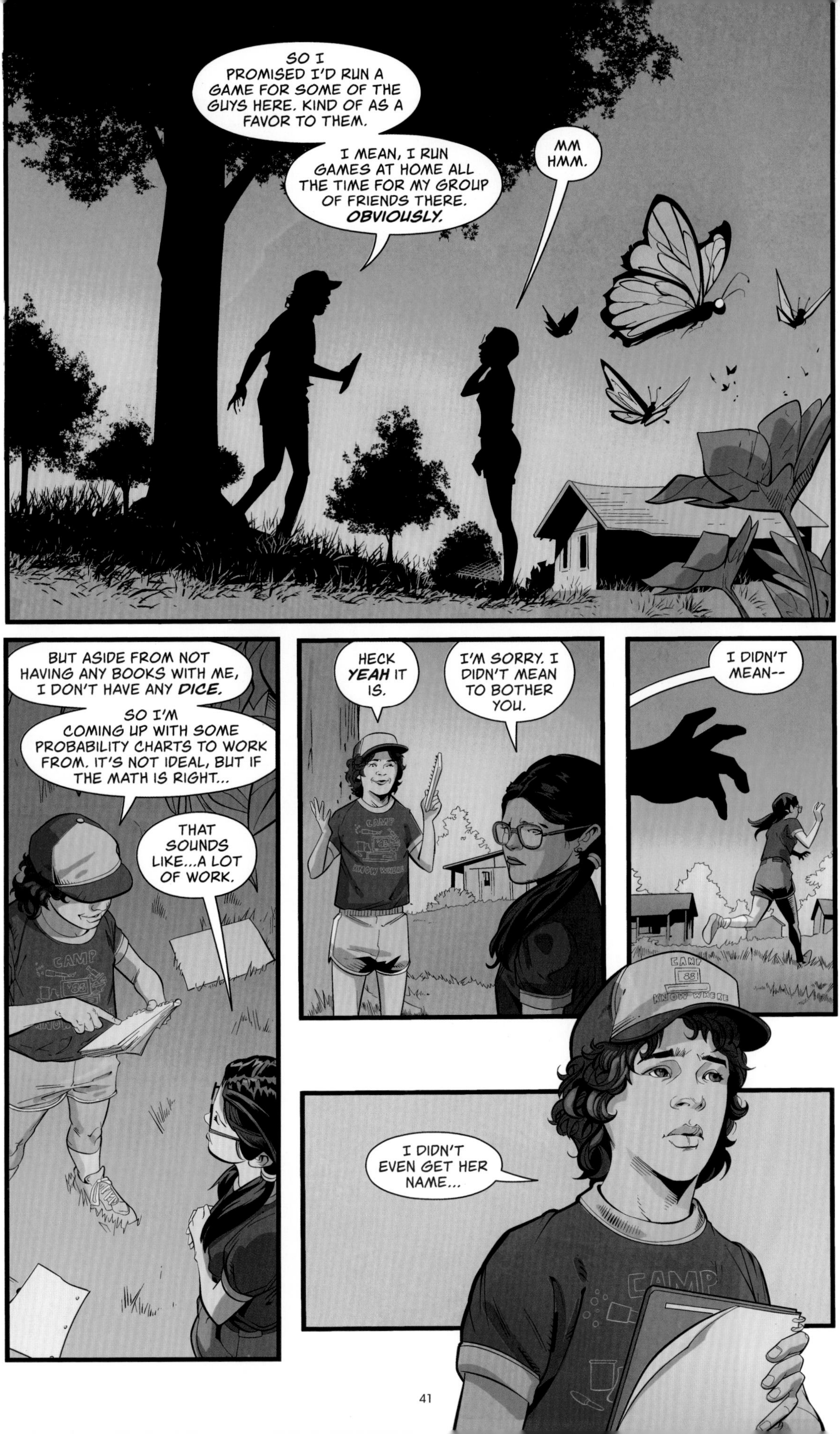
SO I PROMISED I'D RUN A GAME FOR SOME OF THE GUYS HERE. KIND OF AS A FAVOR TO THEM.
I MEAN, I RUN GAMES AT HOME ALL THE TIME FOR MY GROUP OF FRIENDS THERE. ***OBVIOUSLY.***
MM HMM.
BUT ASIDE FROM NOT HAVING ANY BOOKS WITH ME, I DON'T HAVE ANY ***DICE.***
SO I'M COMING UP WITH SOME PROBABILITY CHARTS TO WORK FROM. IT'S NOT IDEAL, BUT IF THE MATH IS RIGHT...
THAT SOUNDS LIKE...A LOT OF WORK.
HECK ***YEAH*** IT IS.
I'M SORRY. I DIDN'T MEAN TO BOTHER YOU.
I DIDN'T MEAN--
I DIDN'T EVEN GET HER NAME...

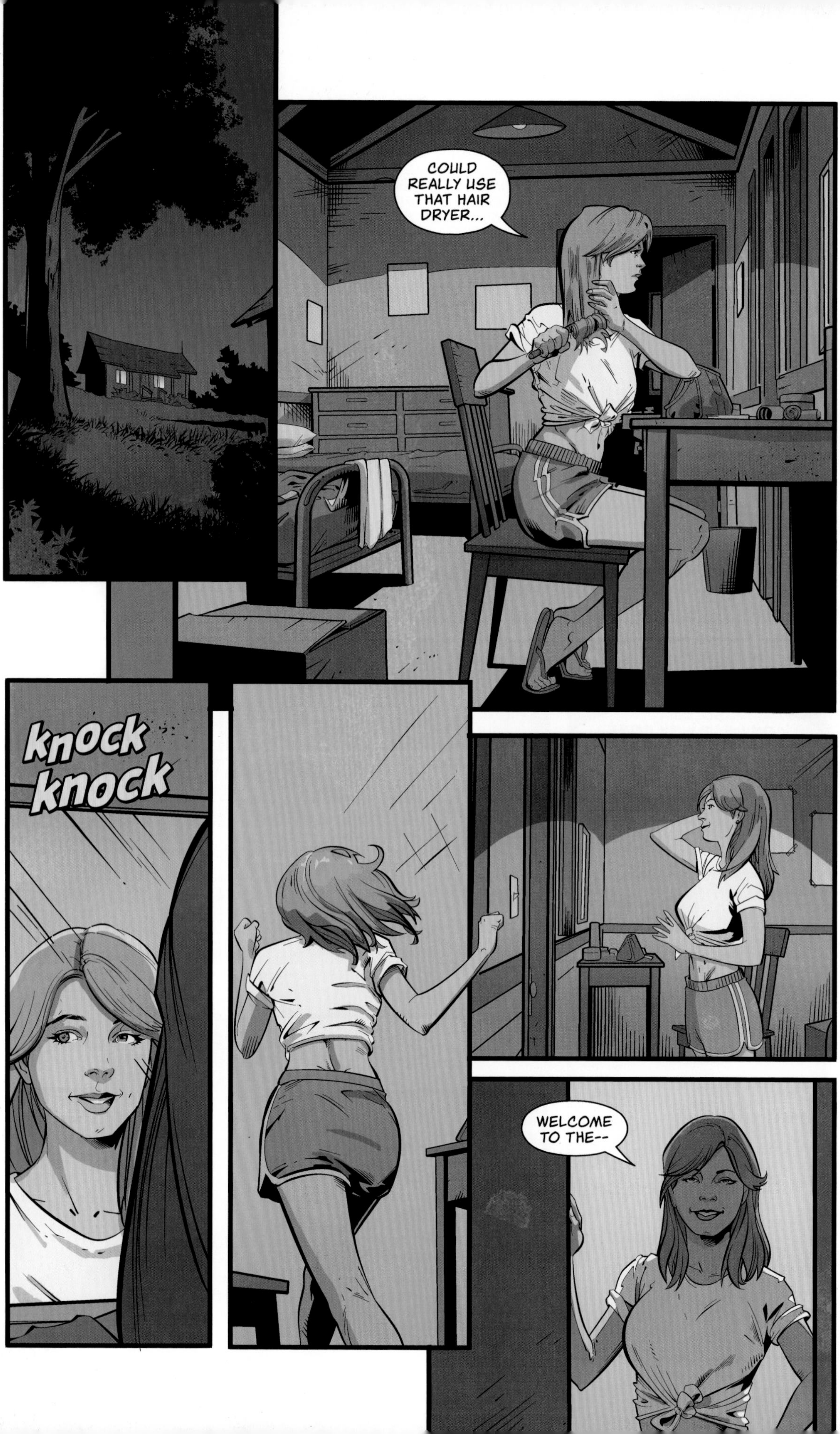
COULD REALLY USE THAT HAIR DRYER...
knock knock
WELCOME TO THE--

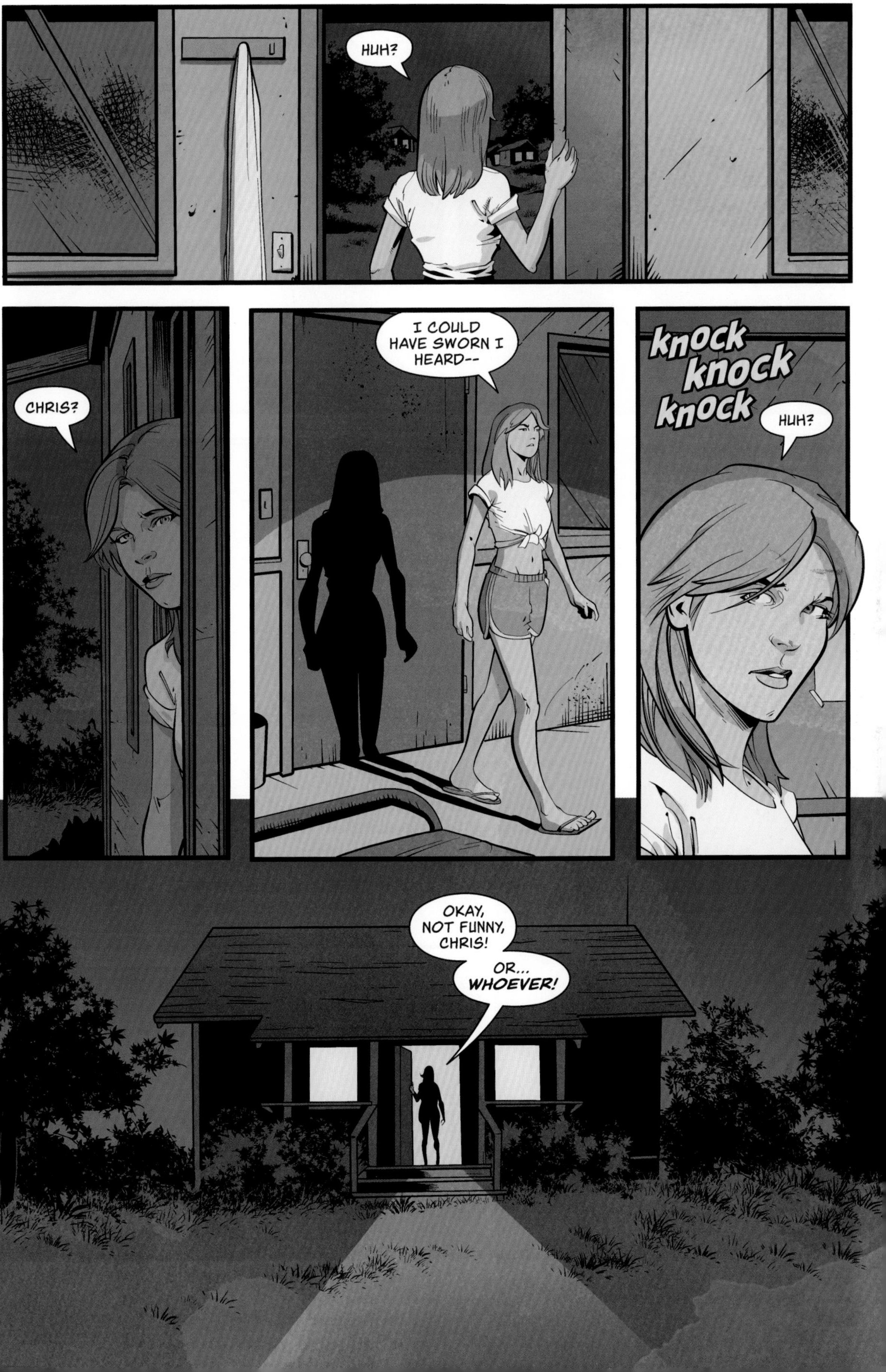
HUH?
CHRIS?
I COULD HAVE SWORN I HEARD--
knock knock knock
HUH?
OKAY, NOT FUNNY, CHRIS!
OR... WHOEVER!

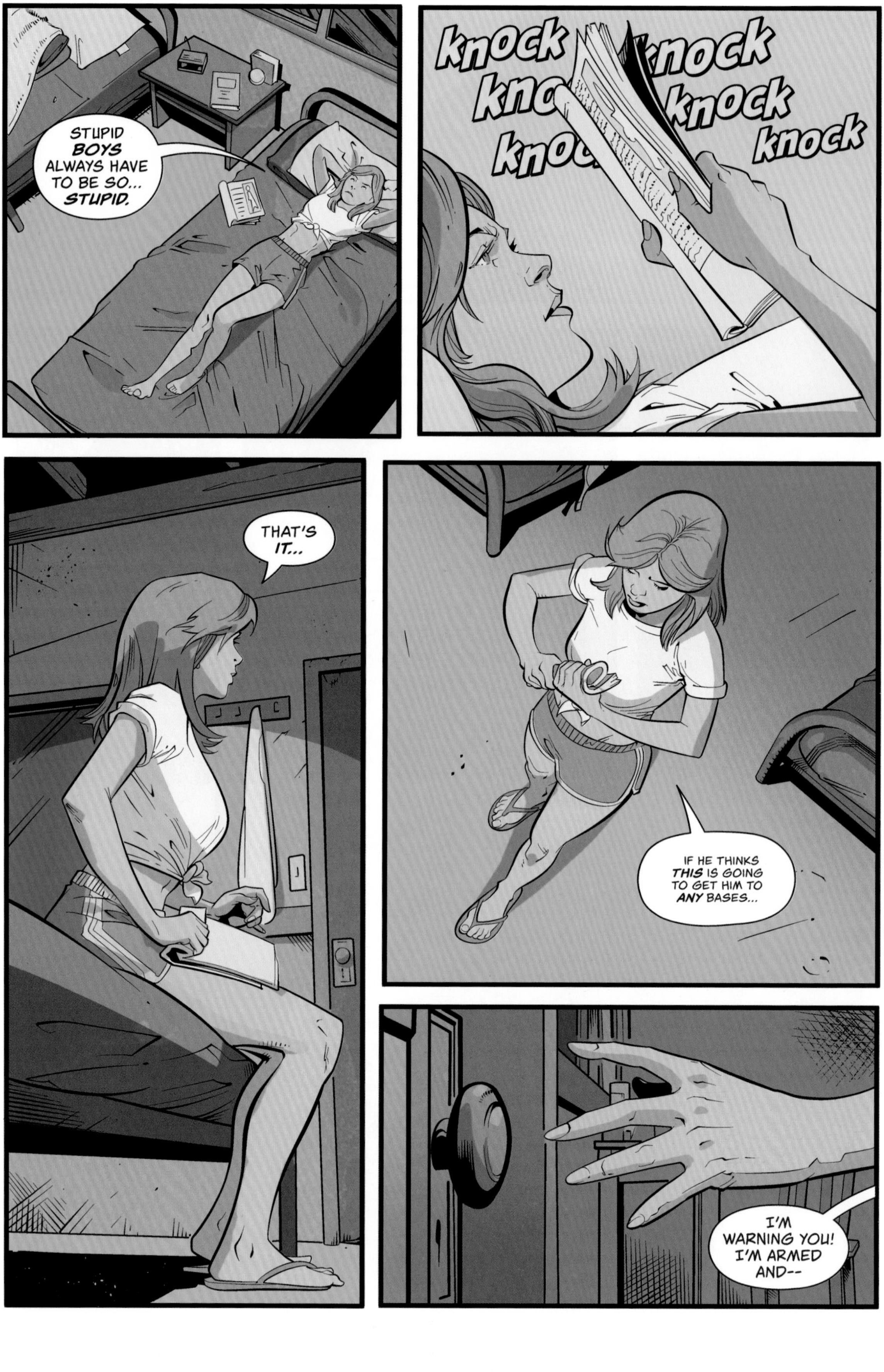
STUPID BOYS ALWAYS HAVE TO BE SO... STUPID.
knock knock knock knock knock knock
THAT'S IT...
IF HE THINKS THIS IS GOING TO GET HIM TO ANY BASES...
I'M WARNING YOU! I'M ARMED AND--

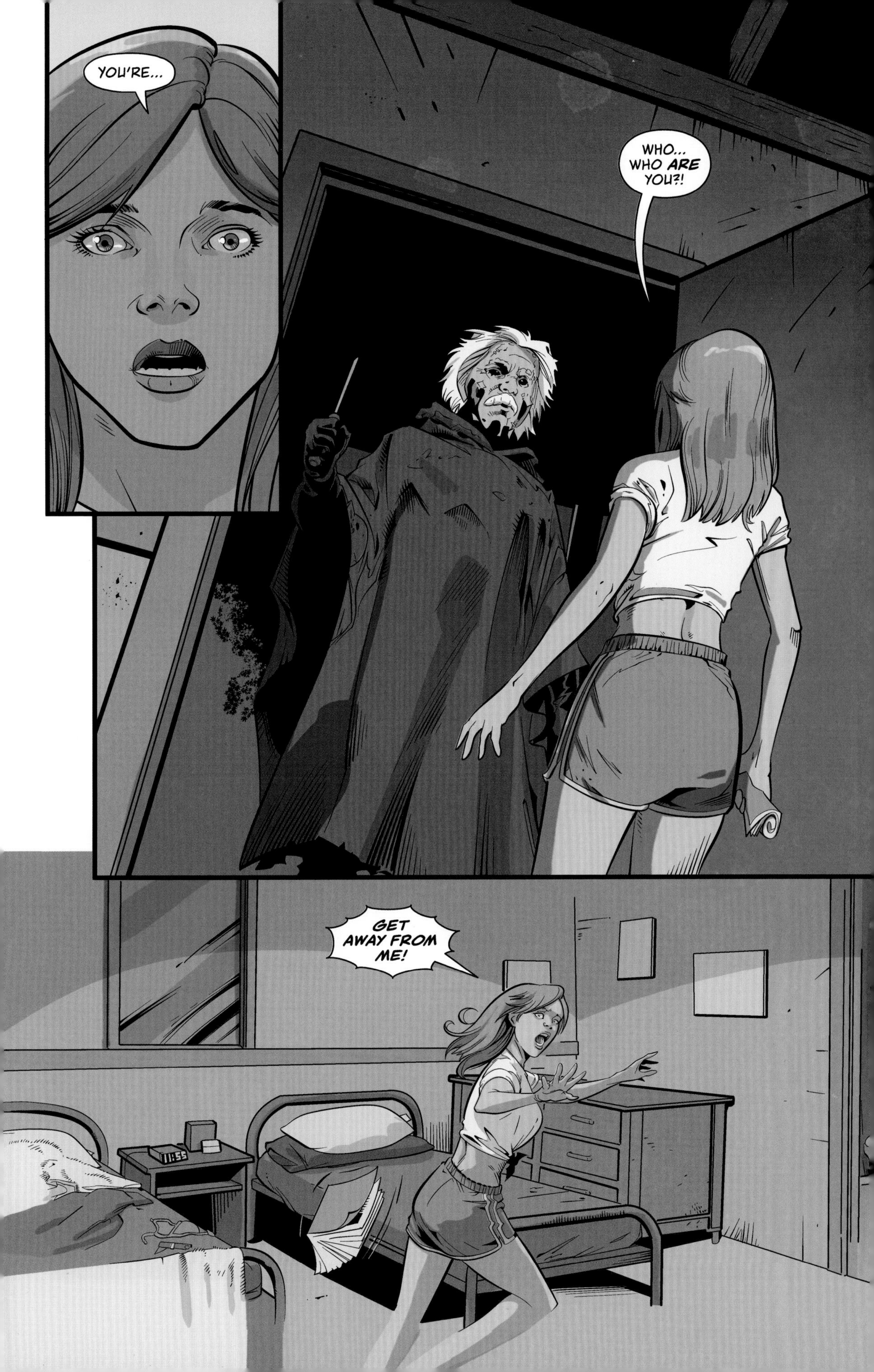
YOU'RE...
WHO... WHO ARE YOU?!
GET AWAY FROM ME!

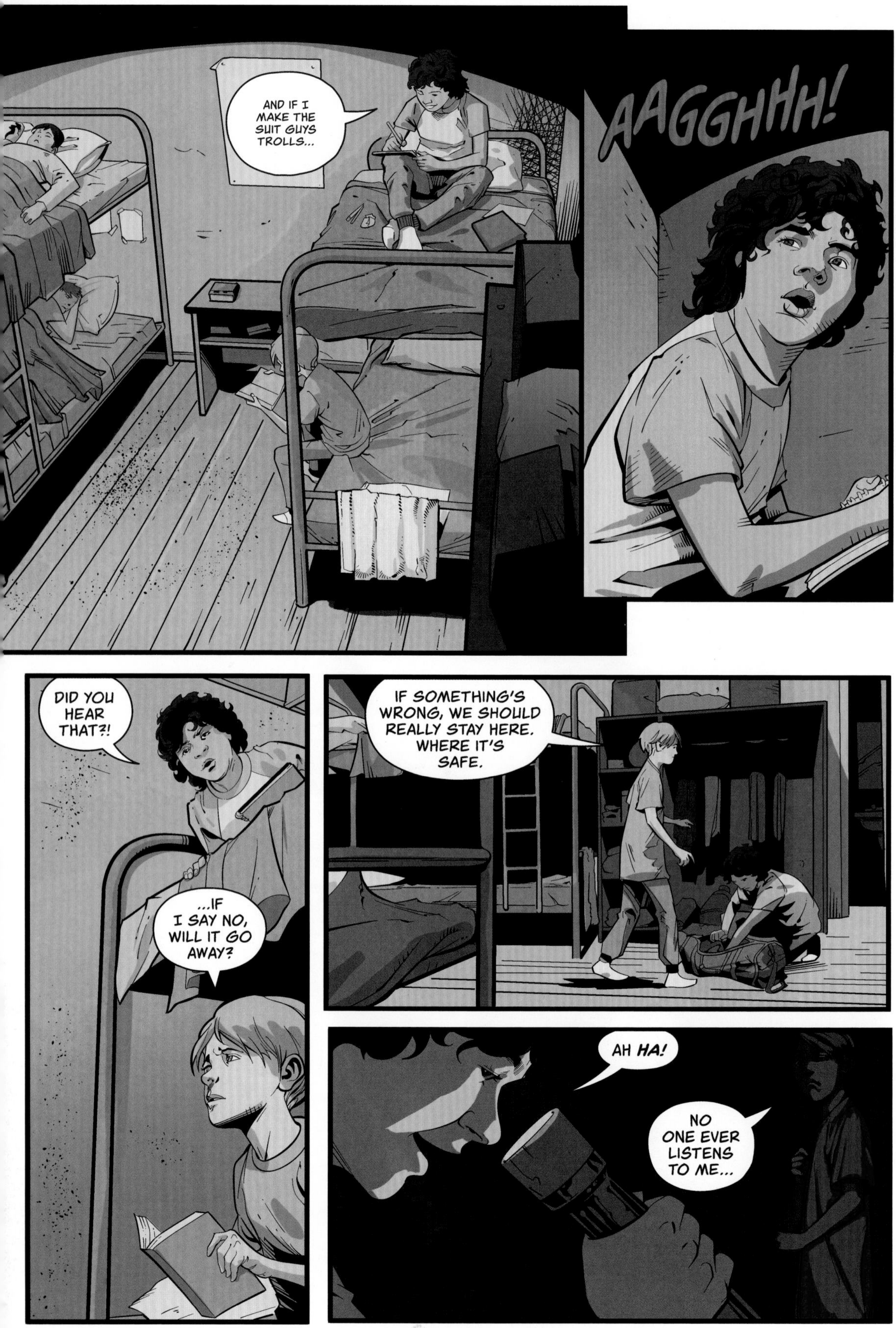
AND IF I MAKE THE SUIT GUYS TROLLS...
AAGGHHH!
DID YOU HEAR THAT?!
...IF I SAY NO, WILL IT GO AWAY?
IF SOMETHING'S WRONG, WE SHOULD REALLY STAY HERE. WHERE IT'S SAFE.
AH *HA!*
NO ONE EVER LISTENS TO ME...

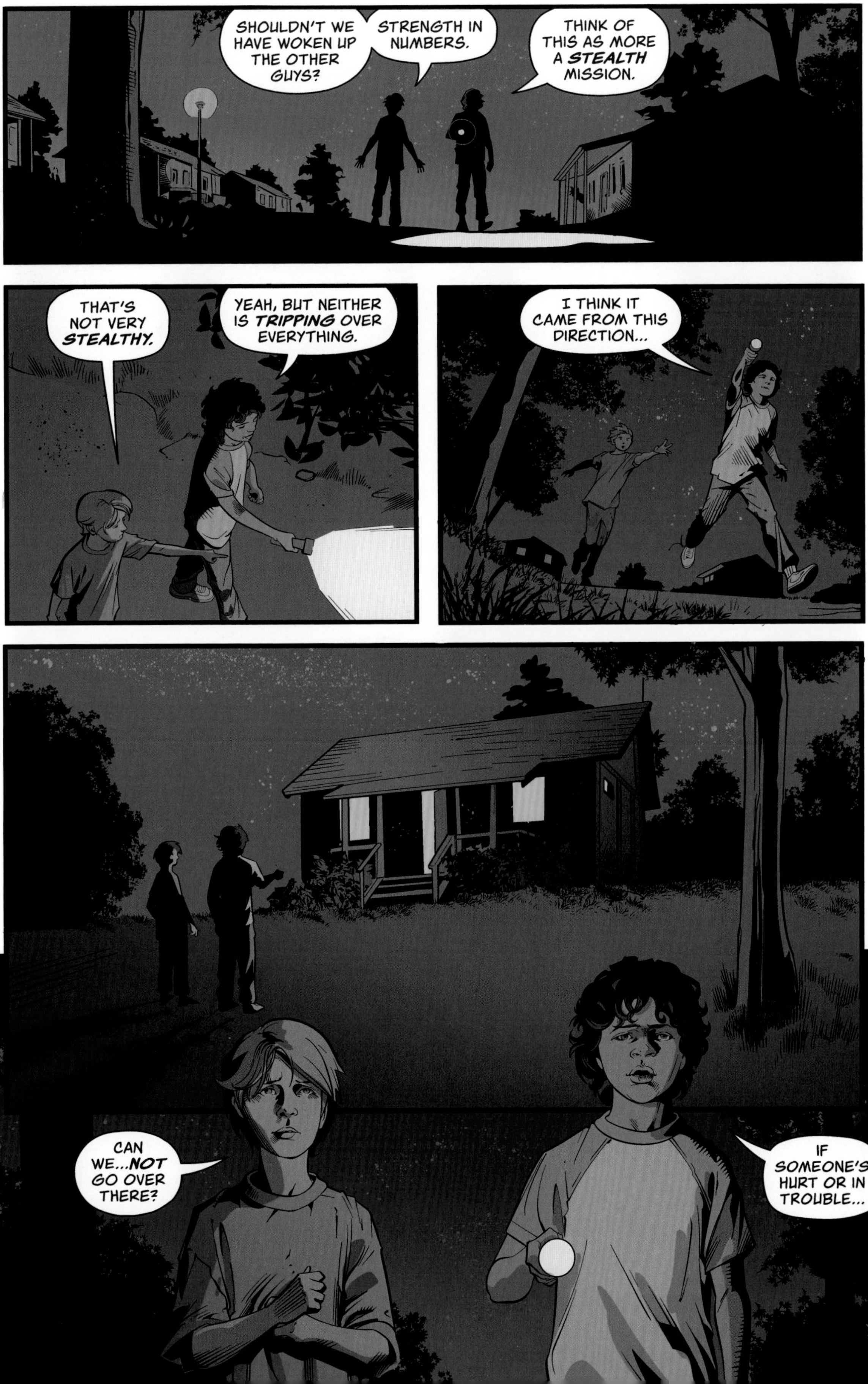
SHOULDN'T WE HAVE WOKEN UP THE OTHER GUYS?
STRENGTH IN NUMBERS.
THINK OF THIS AS MORE A STEALTH MISSION.
THAT'S NOT VERY STEALTHY.
YEAH, BUT NEITHER IS TRIPPING OVER EVERYTHING.
I THINK IT CAME FROM THIS DIRECTION...
CAN WE...NOT GO OVER THERE?
IF SOMEONE'S HURT OR IN TROUBLE...

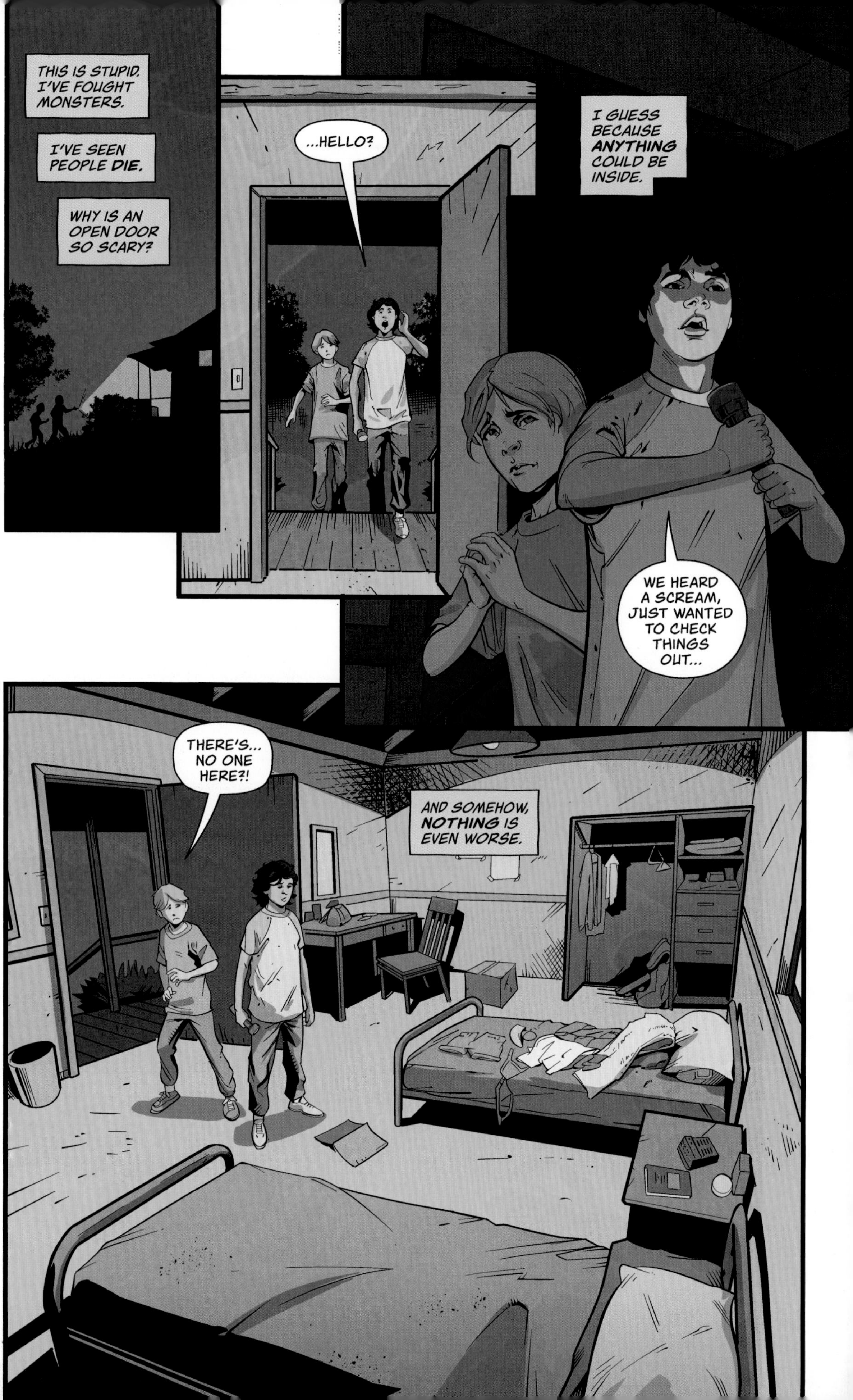
THIS IS STUPID. I'VE FOUGHT MONSTERS.
I'VE SEEN PEOPLE DIE.
WHY IS AN OPEN DOOR SO SCARY?
...HELLO?
I GUESS BECAUSE ANYTHING COULD BE INSIDE.
WE HEARD A SCREAM, JUST WANTED TO CHECK THINGS OUT...
THERE'S... NO ONE HERE?!
AND SOMEHOW, NOTHING IS EVEN WORSE.

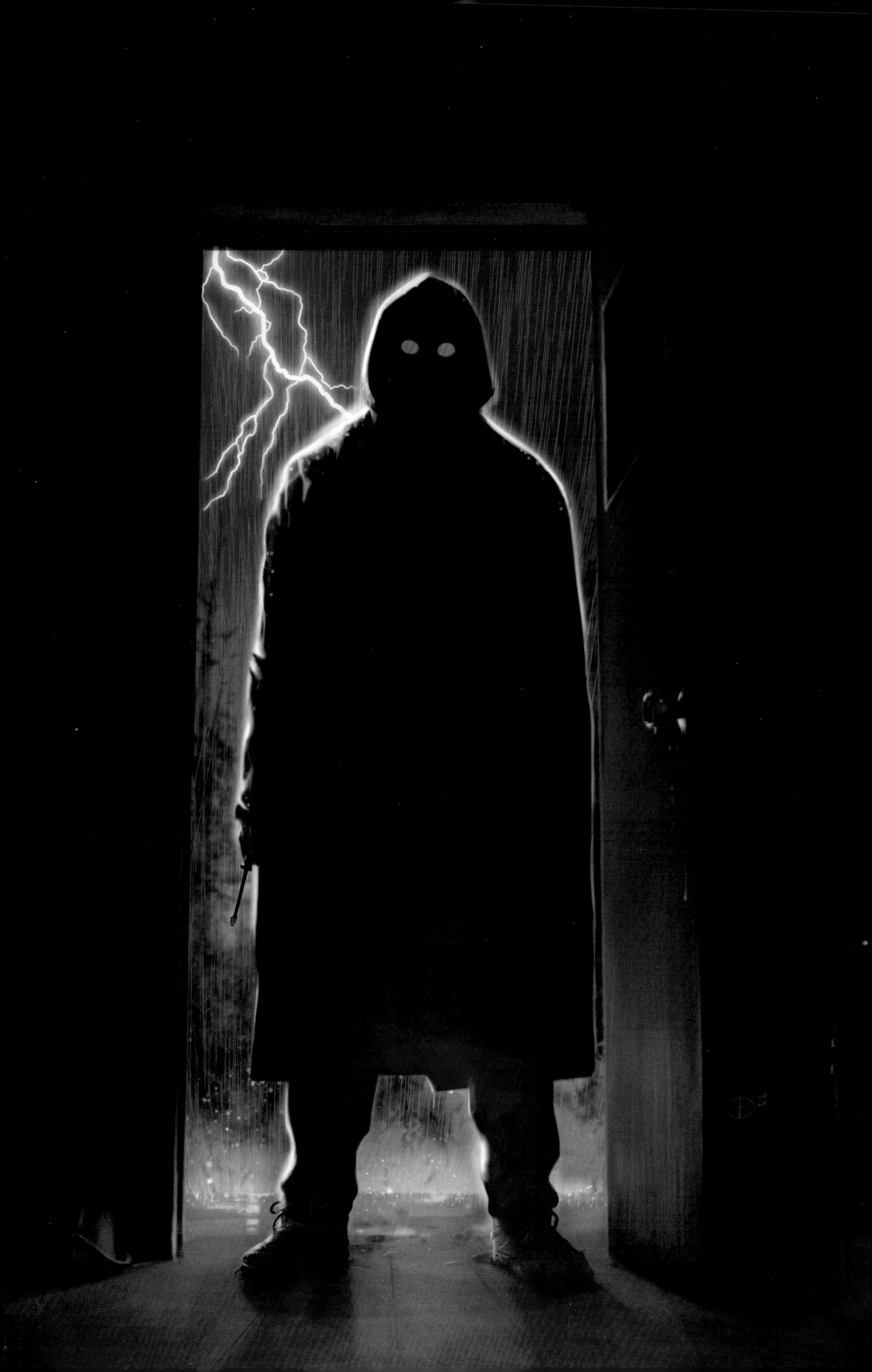

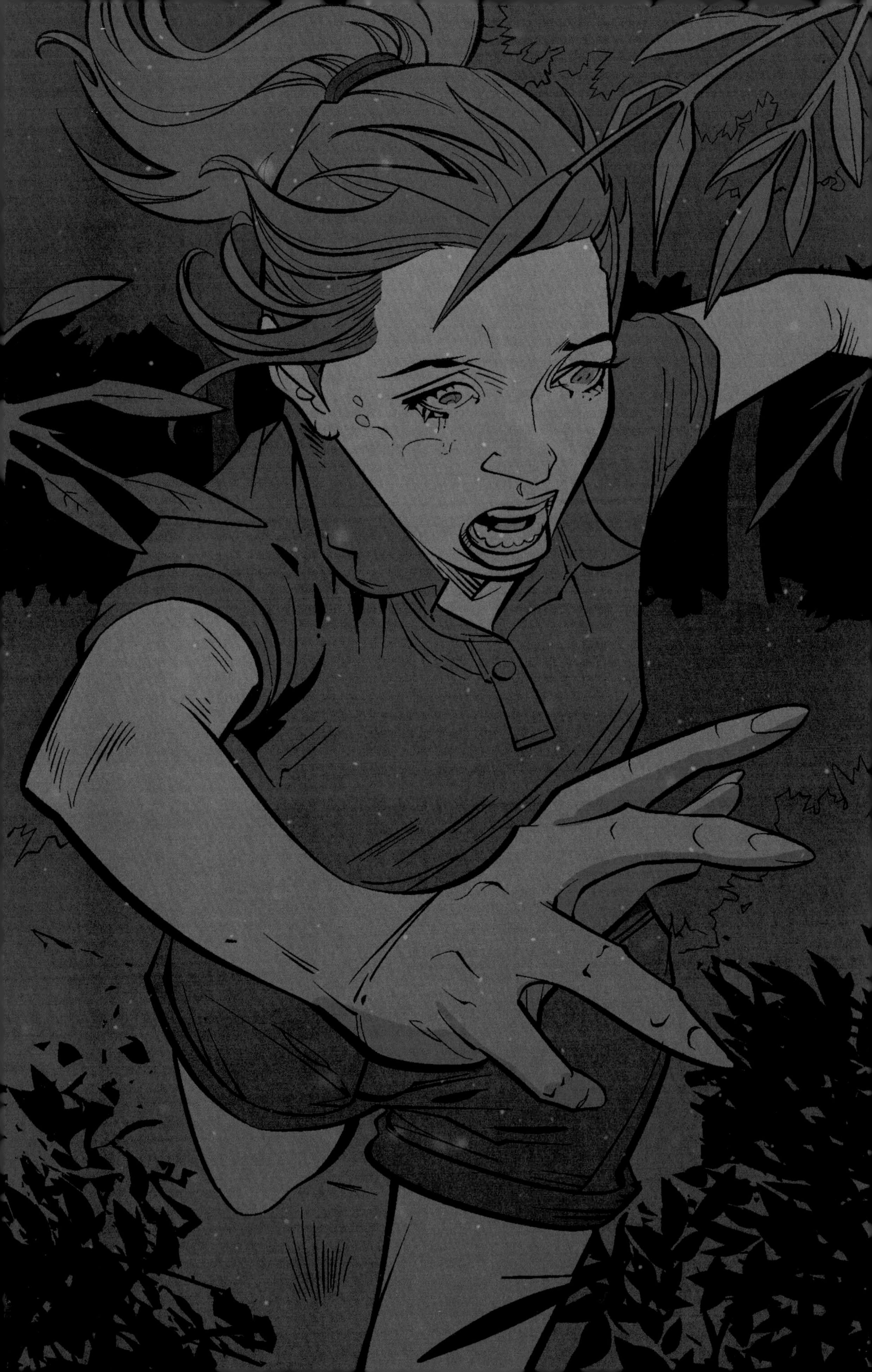

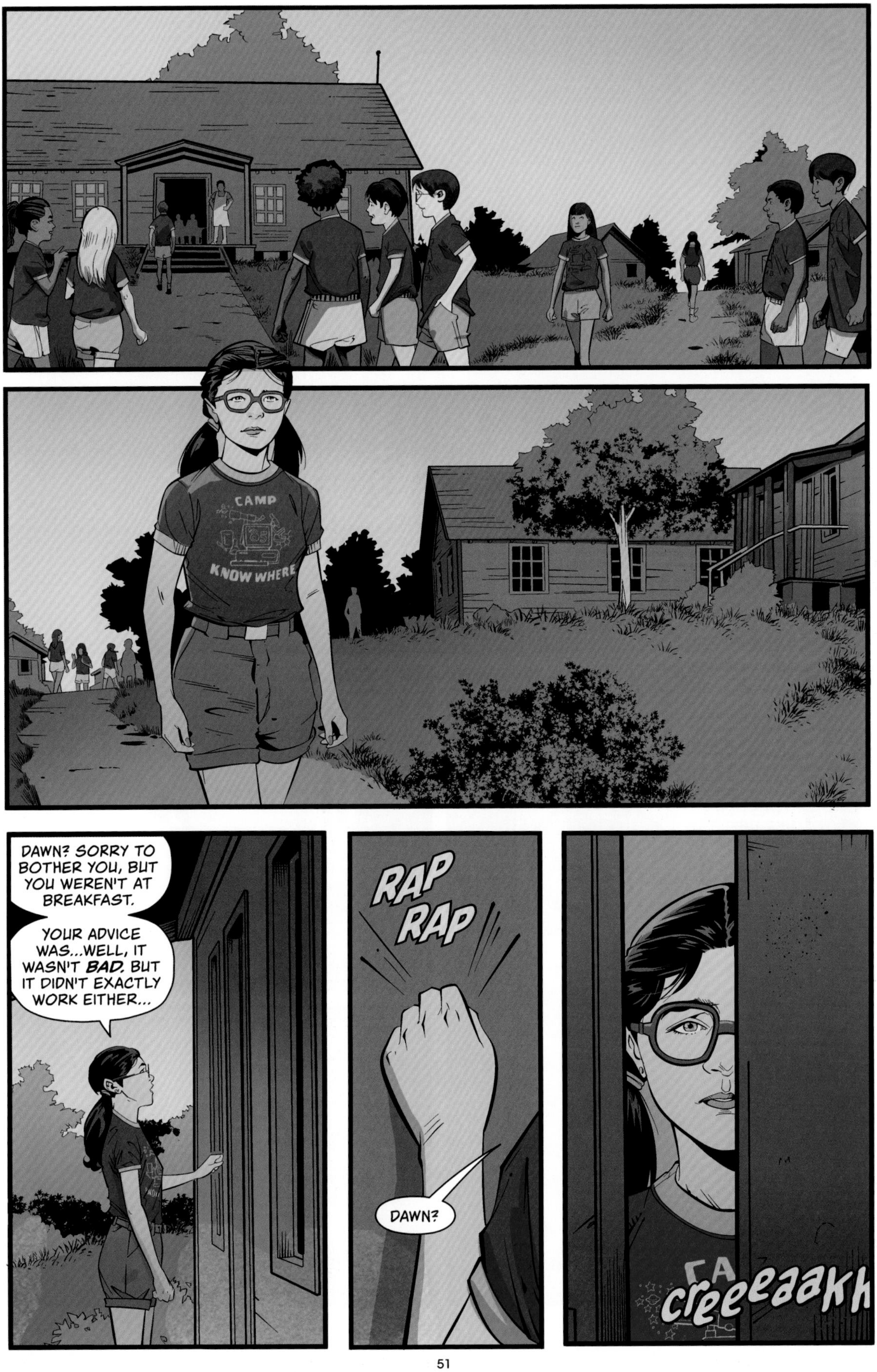
CAMP
KNOW WHERE
DAWN? SORRY TO BOTHER YOU, BUT YOU WEREN'T AT BREAKFAST.
YOUR ADVICE WAS...WELL, IT WASN'T *BAD*, BUT IT DIDN'T EXACTLY WORK EITHER...
RAP RAP
DAWN?
creeeaakh

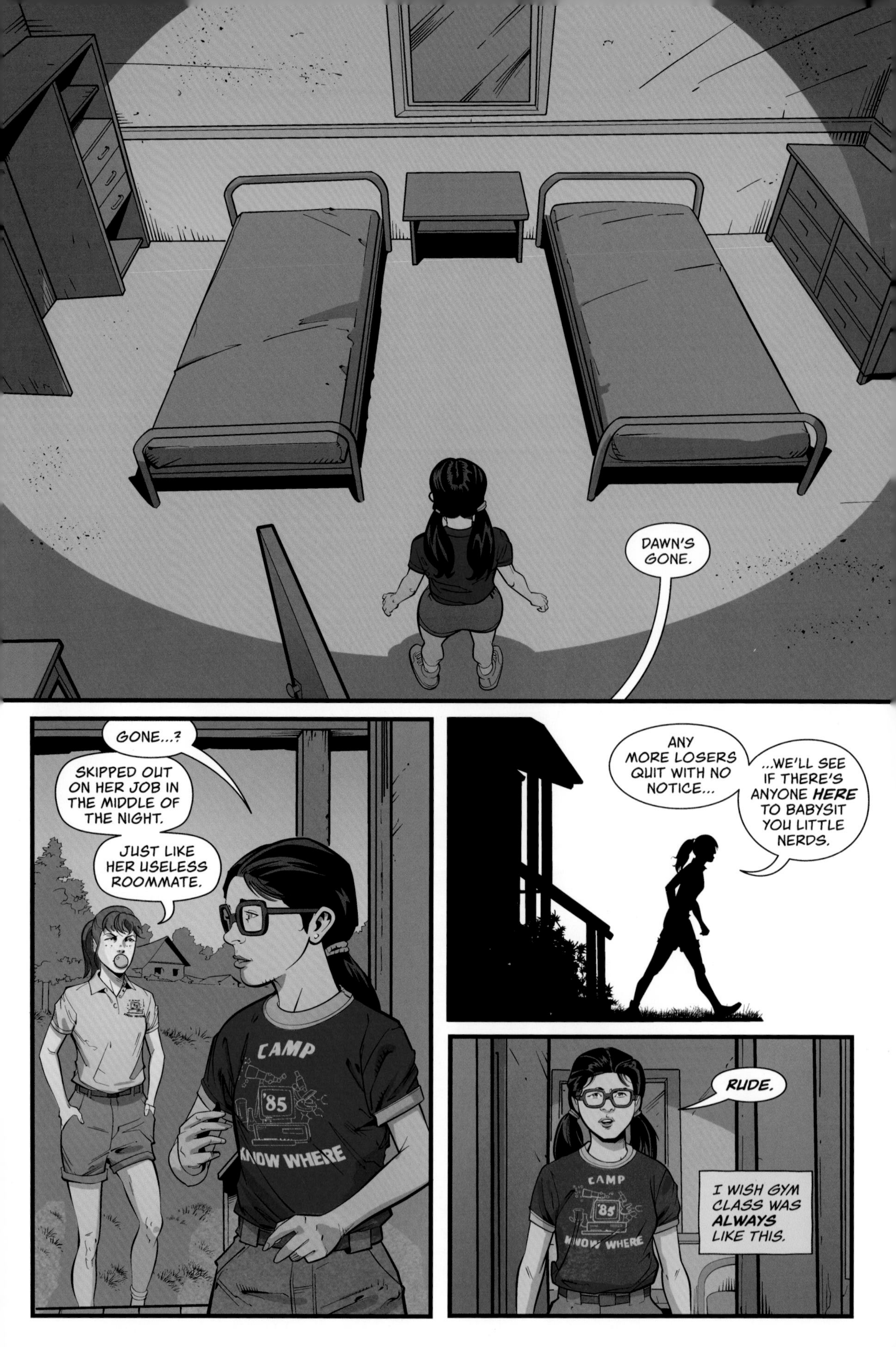
DAWN'S GONE.
GONE...?
SKIPPED OUT ON HER JOB IN THE MIDDLE OF THE NIGHT.
JUST LIKE HER USELESS ROOMMATE.
CAMP '85 KNOW WHERE
ANY MORE LOSERS QUIT WITH NO NOTICE...
...WE'LL SEE IF THERE'S ANYONE **HERE** TO BABYSIT YOU LITTLE NERDS.
RUDE.
CAMP '85 KNOW WHERE
I WISH GYM CLASS WAS **ALWAYS** LIKE THIS.

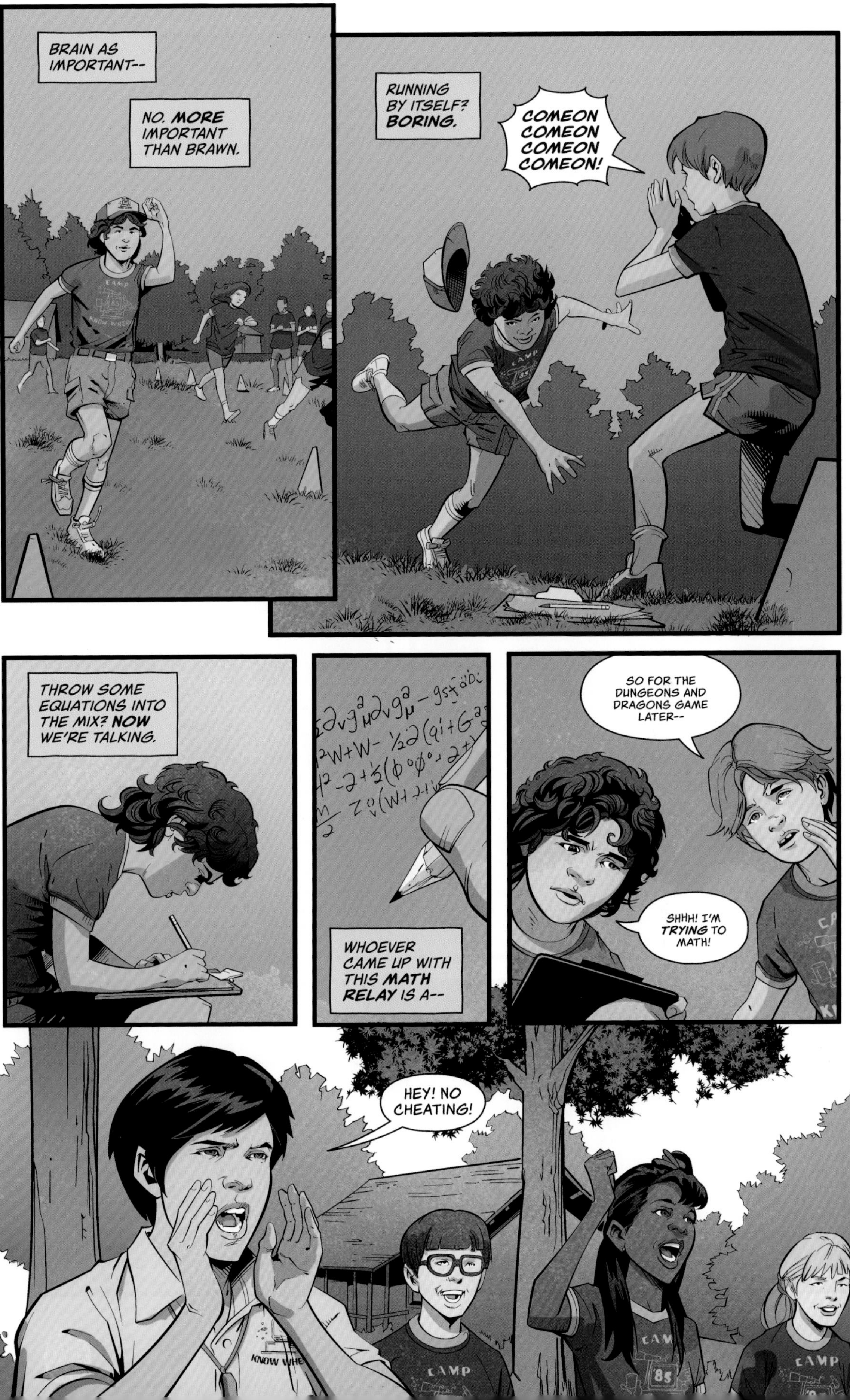
BRAIN AS IMPORTANT--
NO. MORE IMPORTANT THAN BRAWN.
RUNNING BY ITSELF? BORING.
COMEON COMEON COMEON COMEON!
THROW SOME EQUATIONS INTO THE MIX? NOW WE'RE TALKING.
WHOEVER CAME UP WITH THIS MATH RELAY IS A--
SO FOR THE DUNGEONS AND DRAGONS GAME LATER--
SHHH! I'M TRYING TO MATH!
HEY! NO CHEATING!

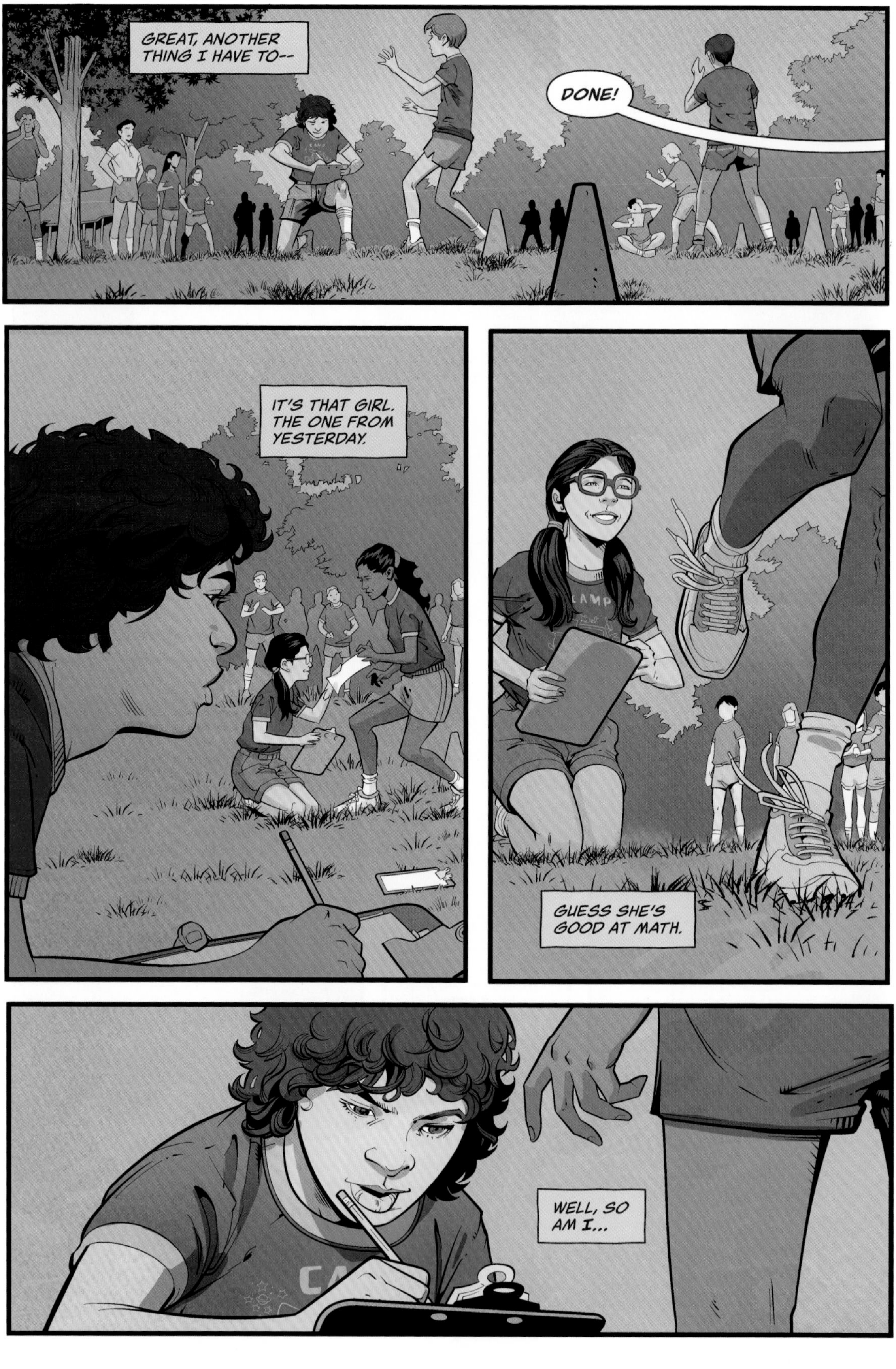
GREAT, ANOTHER THING I HAVE TO--
DONE!
IT'S THAT GIRL. THE ONE FROM YESTERDAY.
GUESS SHE'S GOOD AT MATH.
WELL, SO AM I...

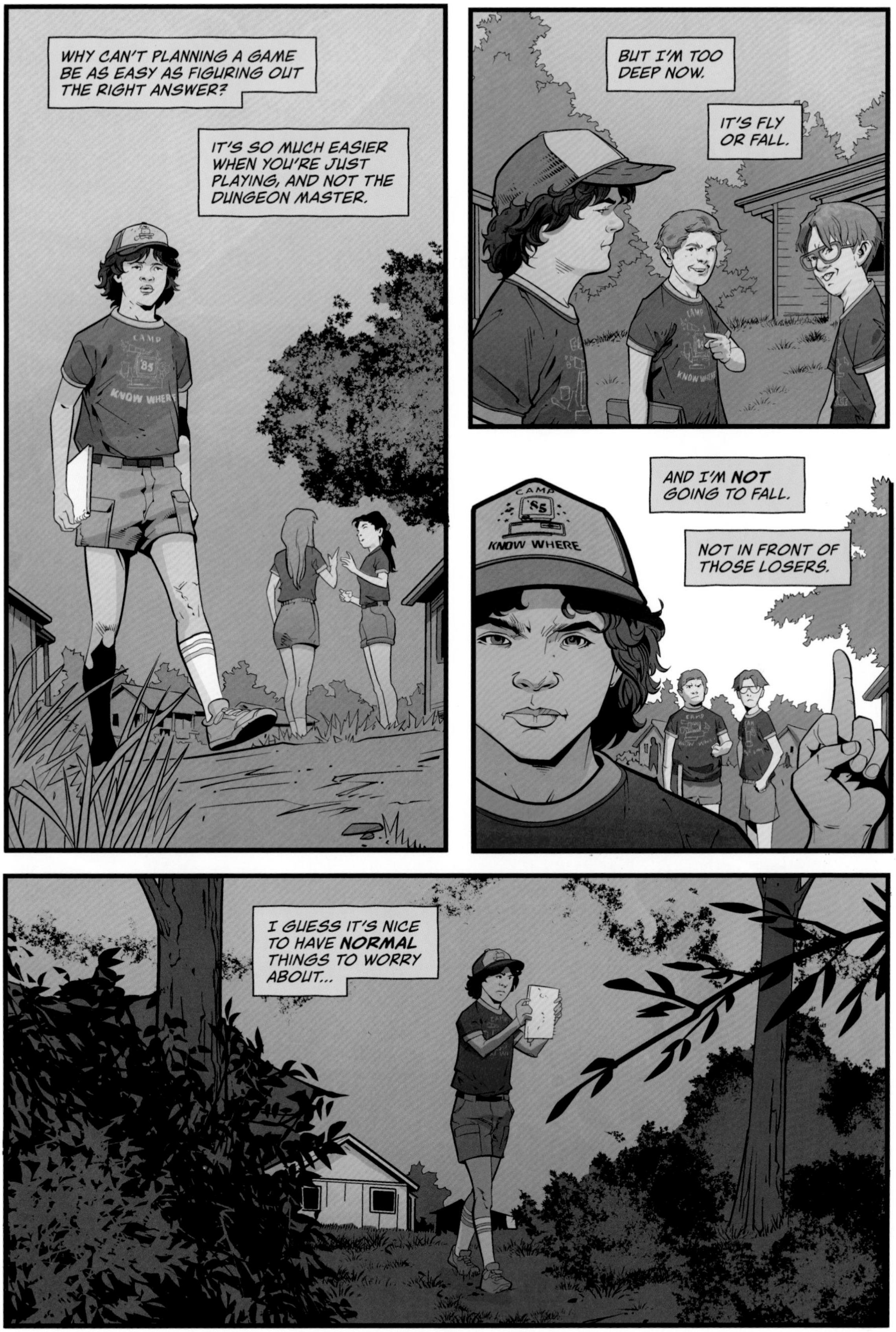
WHY CAN'T PLANNING A GAME BE AS EASY AS FIGURING OUT THE RIGHT ANSWER?
IT'S SO MUCH EASIER WHEN YOU'RE JUST PLAYING, AND NOT THE DUNGEON MASTER.
KNOW WHERE
BUT I'M TOO DEEP NOW.
IT'S FLY OR FALL.
AND I'M **NOT** GOING TO FALL.
CAMP
'85
KNOW WHERE
NOT IN FRONT OF THOSE LOSERS.
I GUESS IT'S NICE TO HAVE **NORMAL** THINGS TO WORRY ABOUT...

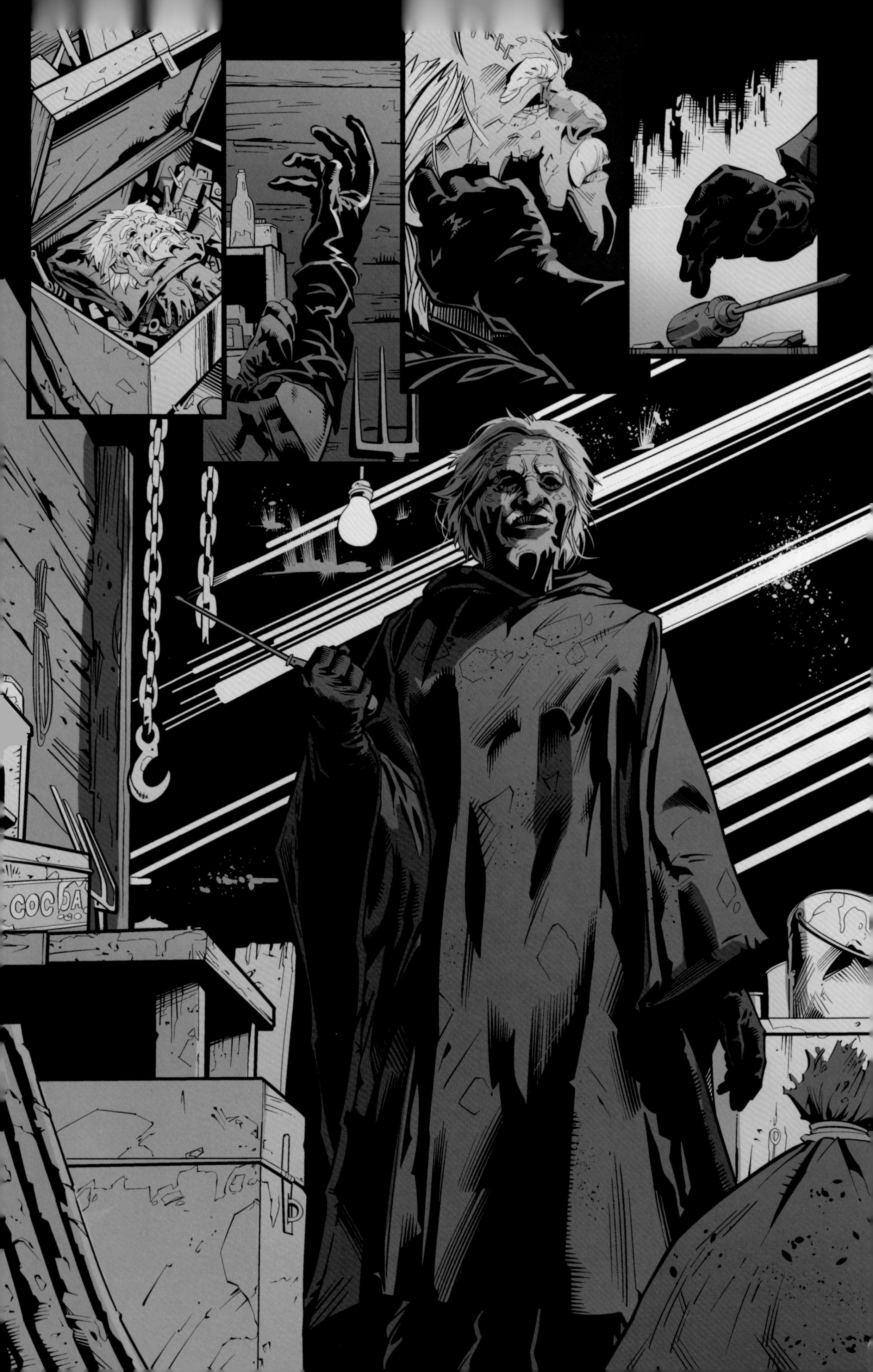
COC
DA

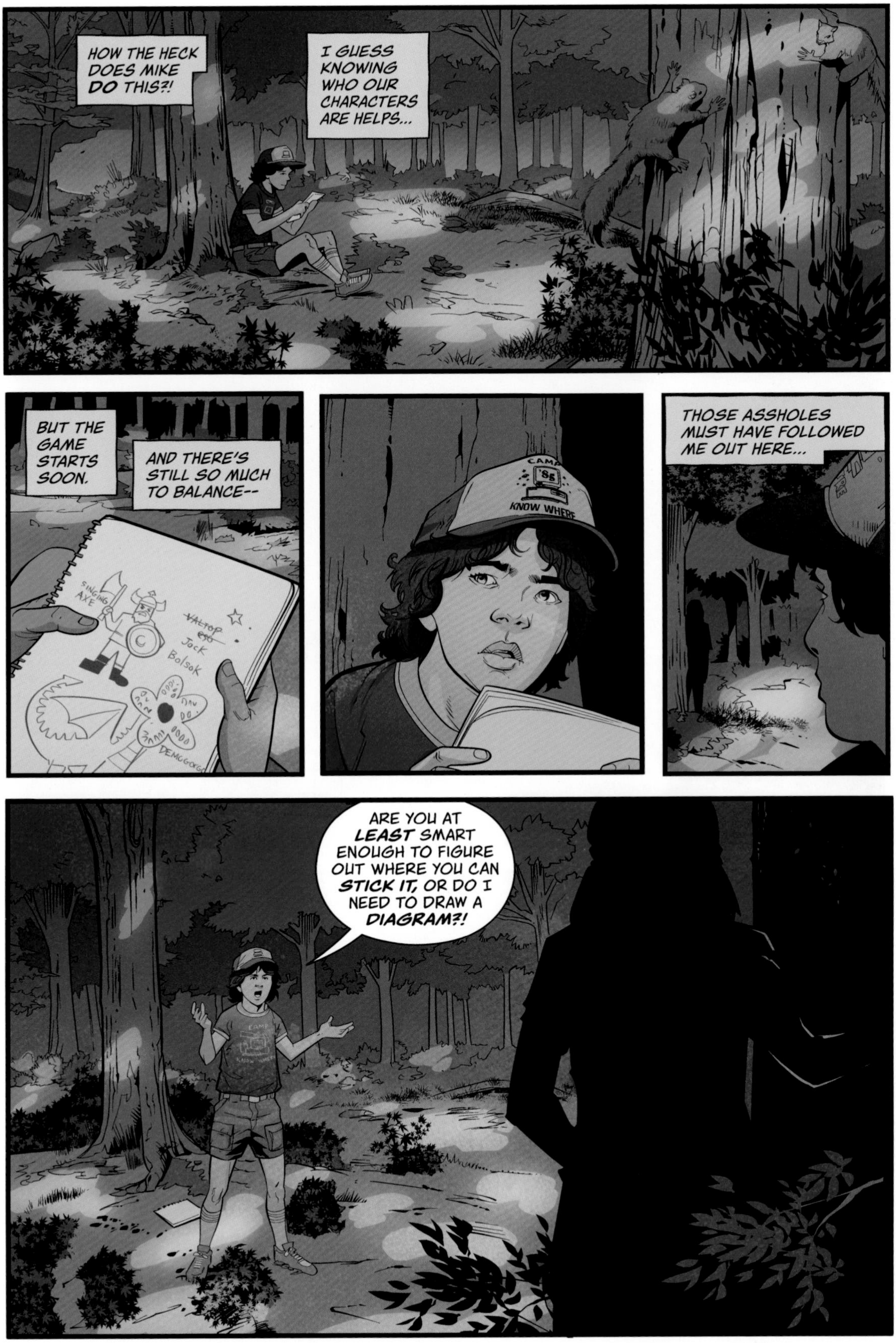
HOW THE HECK DOES MIKE DO THIS?!
I GUESS KNOWING WHO OUR CHARACTERS ARE HELPS...
BUT THE GAME STARTS SOON.
AND THERE'S STILL SO MUCH TO BALANCE--
SINGING AXE
Jack
Bolsok
THOSE ASSHOLES MUST HAVE FOLLOWED ME OUT HERE...
ARE YOU AT LEAST SMART ENOUGH TO FIGURE OUT WHERE YOU CAN STICK IT, OR DO I NEED TO DRAW A DIAGRAM?!

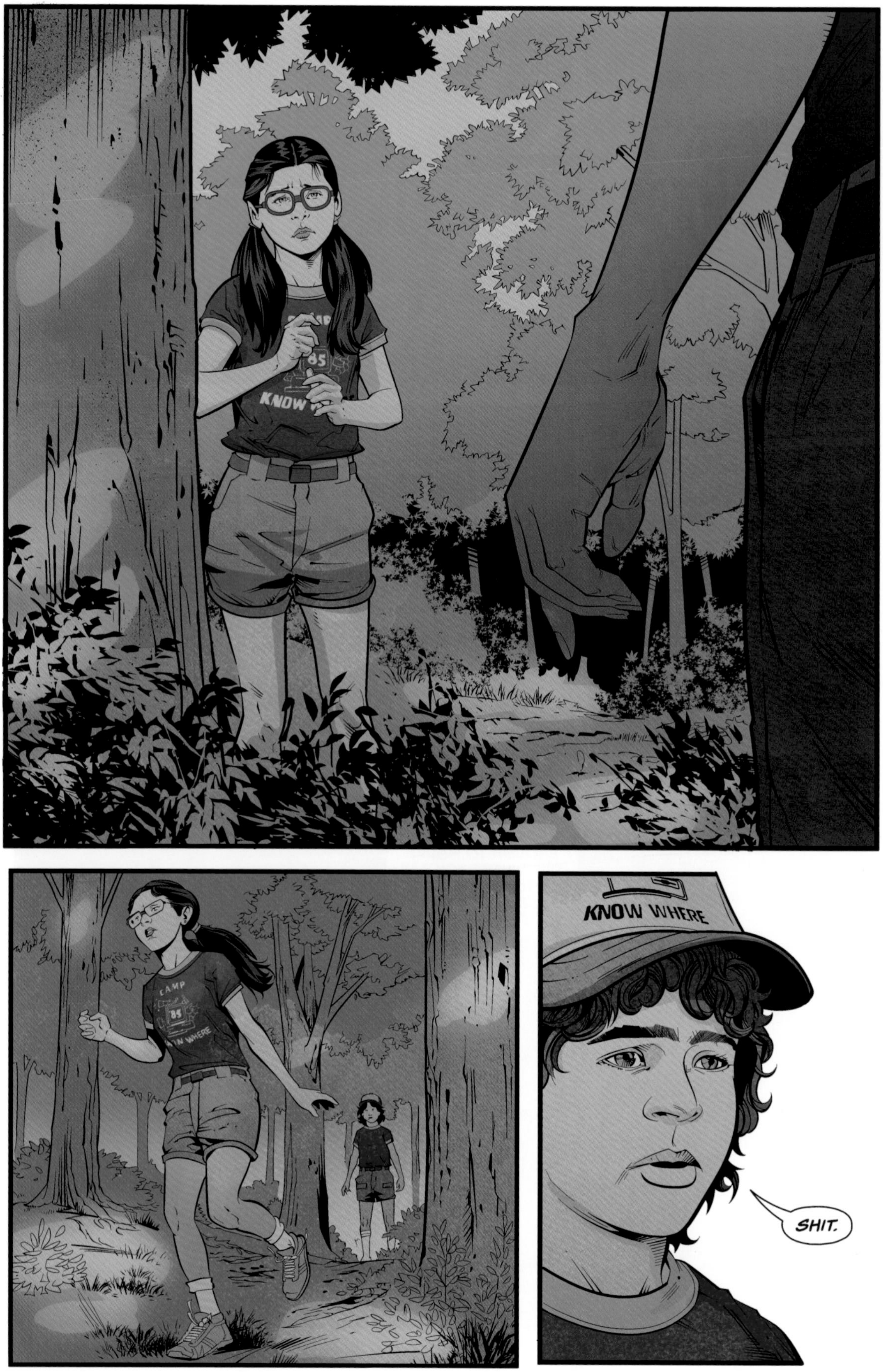
KNOW WHERE
SHIT.

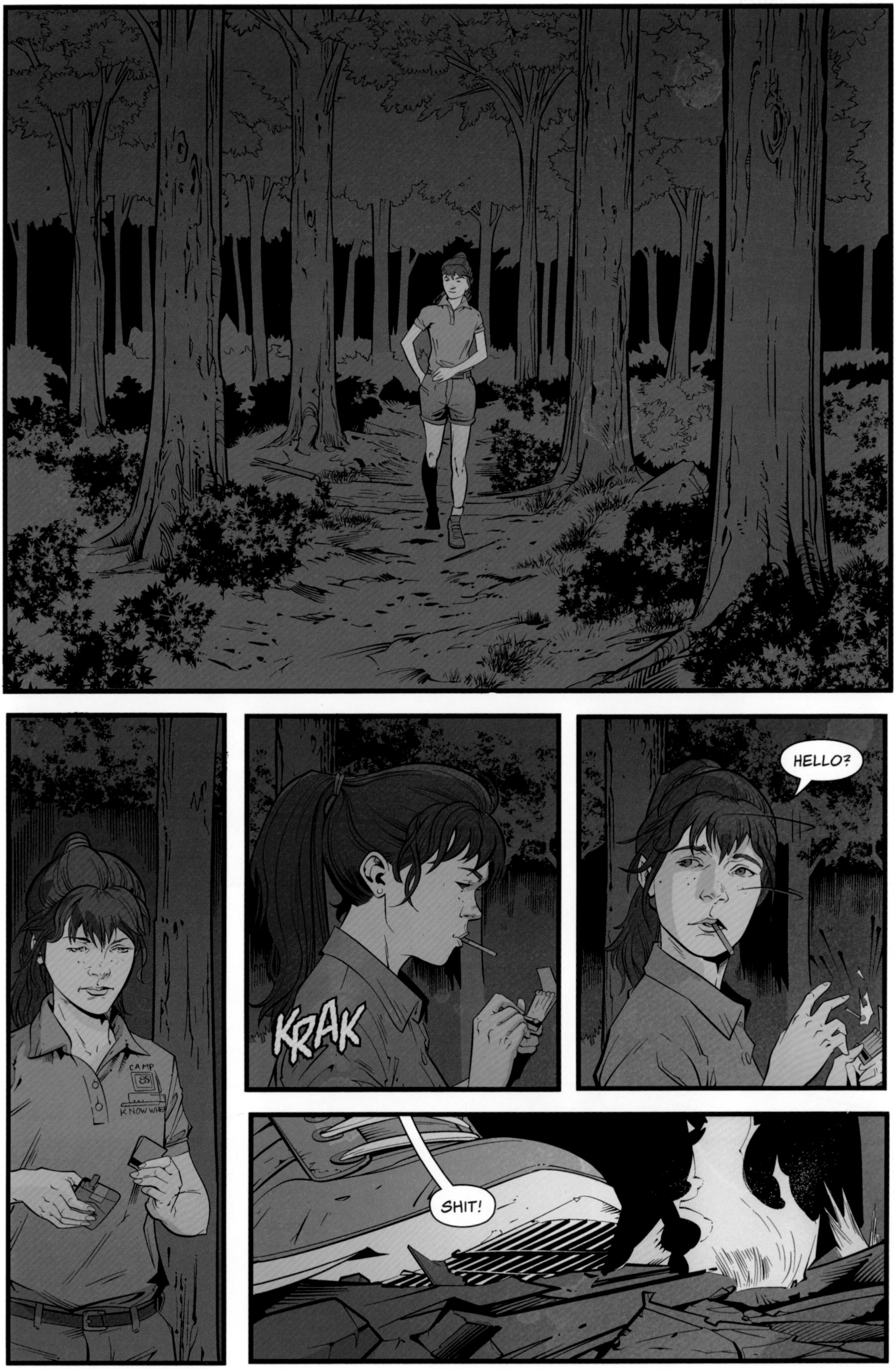
CAMP
KNOW WHE
KRAK
HELLO?
SHIT!

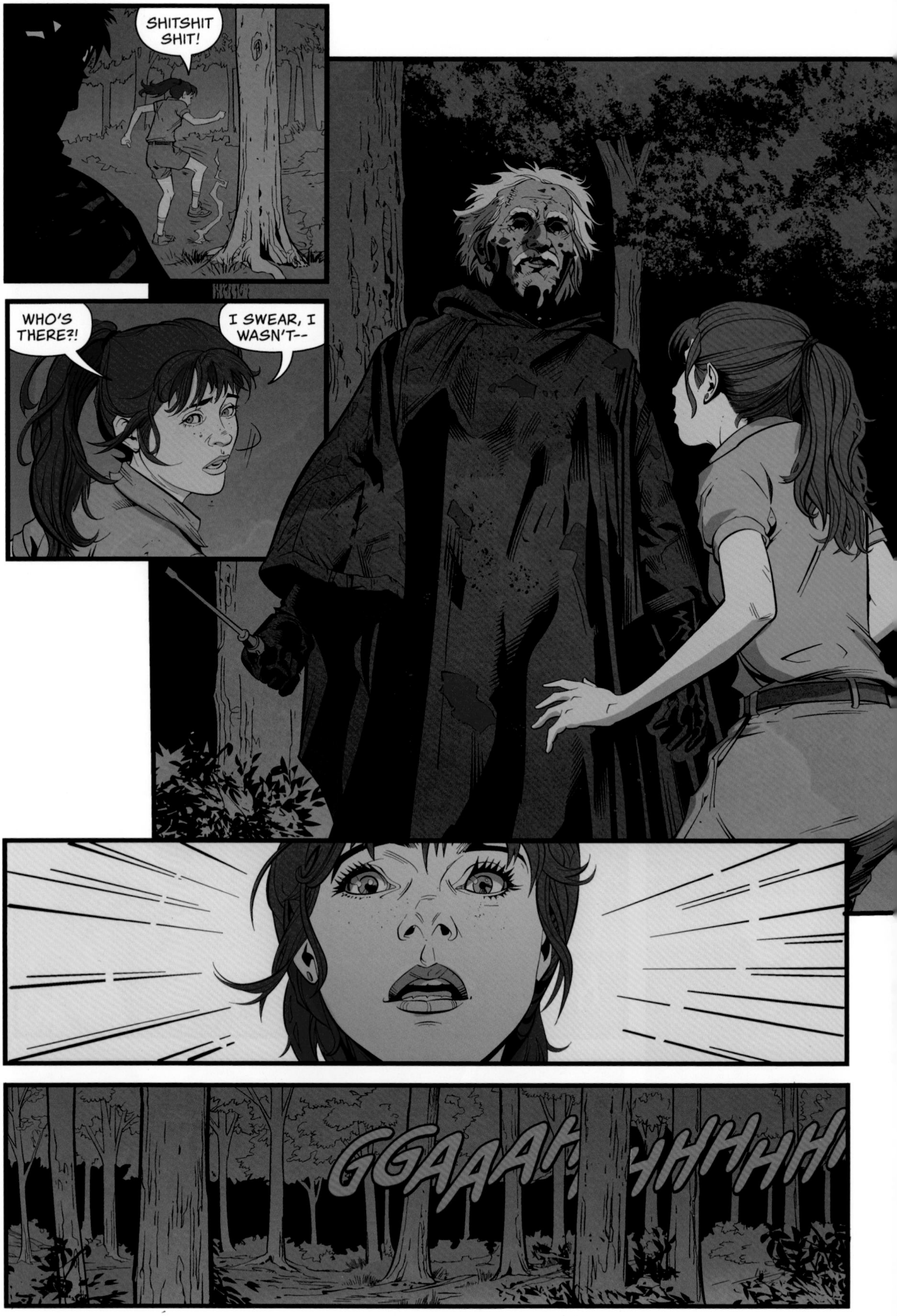
SHITSHIT SHIT!
WHO'S THERE?!
I SWEAR, I WASN'T--
GGAAAHHHHHH

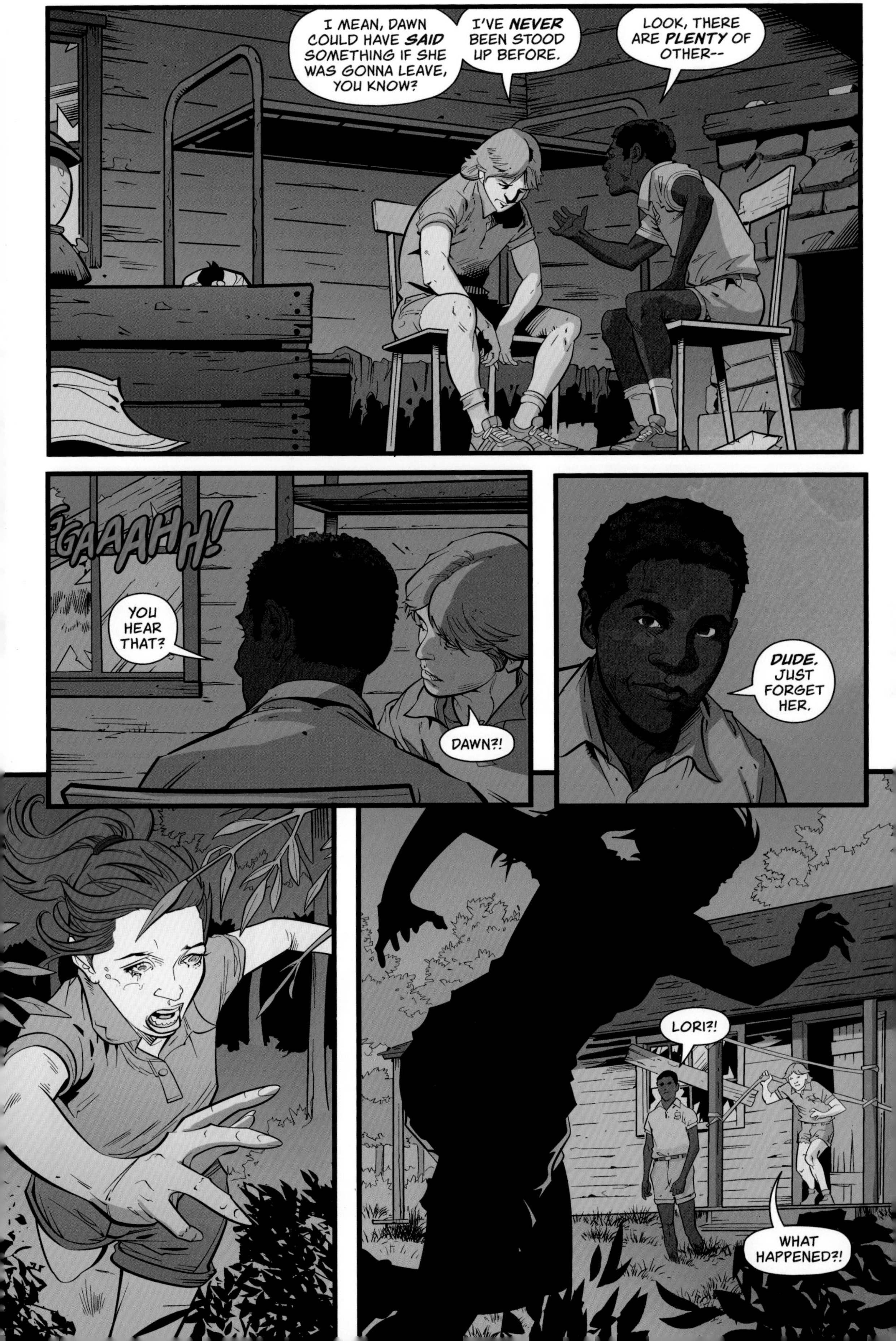
I MEAN, DAWN COULD HAVE SAID SOMETHING IF SHE WAS GONNA LEAVE, YOU KNOW?
I'VE NEVER BEEN STOOD UP BEFORE.
LOOK, THERE ARE PLENTY OF OTHER--
GAAAHH!
YOU HEAR THAT?
DAWN?!
DUDE. JUST FORGET HER.
LORI?!
WHAT HAPPENED?!

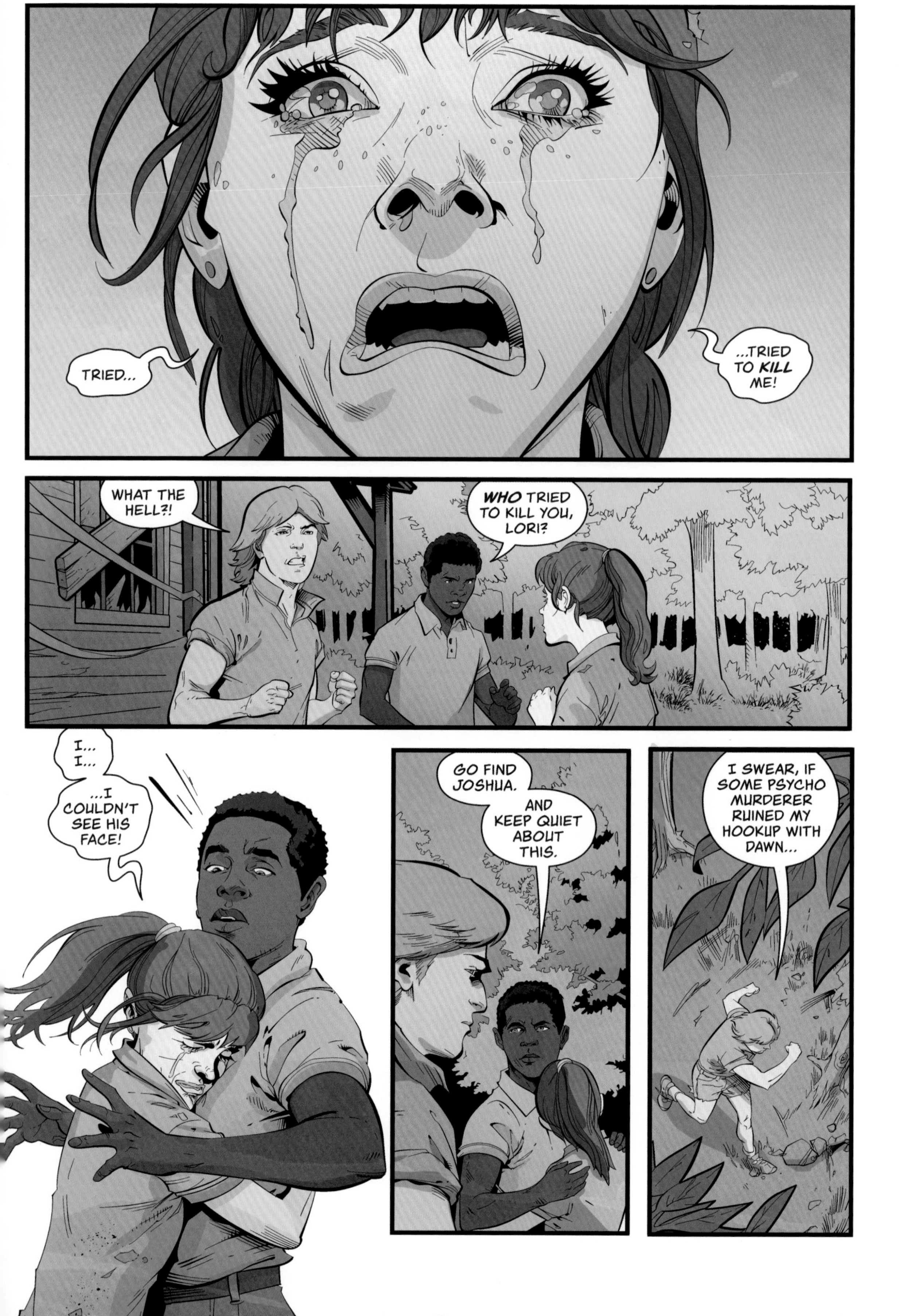
TRIED...
...TRIED TO KILL ME!
WHAT THE HELL?!
WHO TRIED TO KILL YOU, LORI?
I... I...
...I COULDN'T SEE HIS FACE!
GO FIND JOSHUA.
AND KEEP QUIET ABOUT THIS.
I SWEAR, IF SOME PSYCHO MURDERER RUINED MY HOOKUP WITH DAWN...

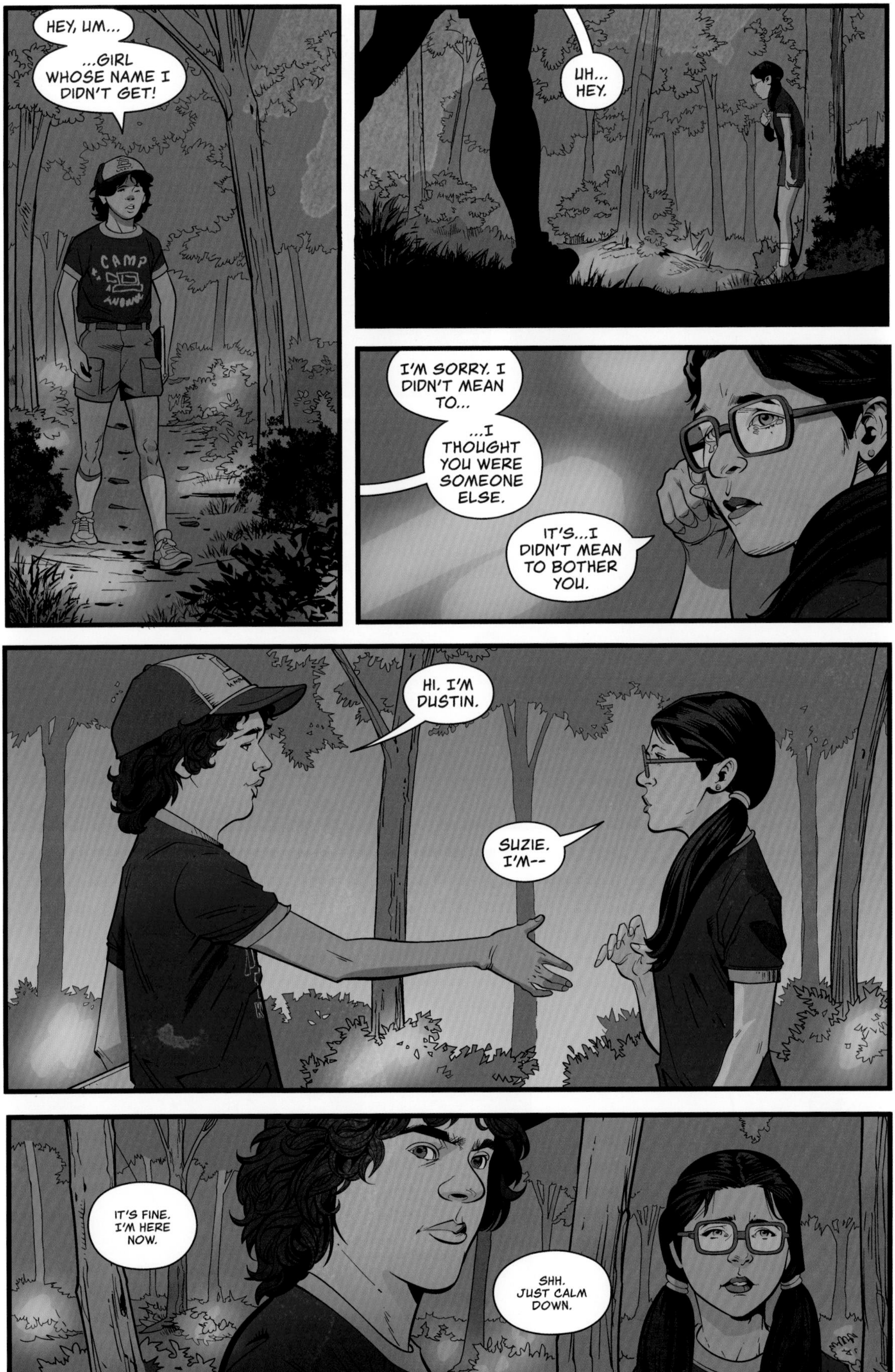
HEY, UM...
...GIRL WHOSE NAME I DIDN'T GET!
UH... HEY.
I'M SORRY. I DIDN'T MEAN TO...
...I THOUGHT YOU WERE SOMEONE ELSE.
IT'S...I DIDN'T MEAN TO BOTHER YOU.
HI. I'M DUSTIN.
SUZIE. I'M--
IT'S FINE. I'M HERE NOW.
SHH. JUST CALM DOWN.

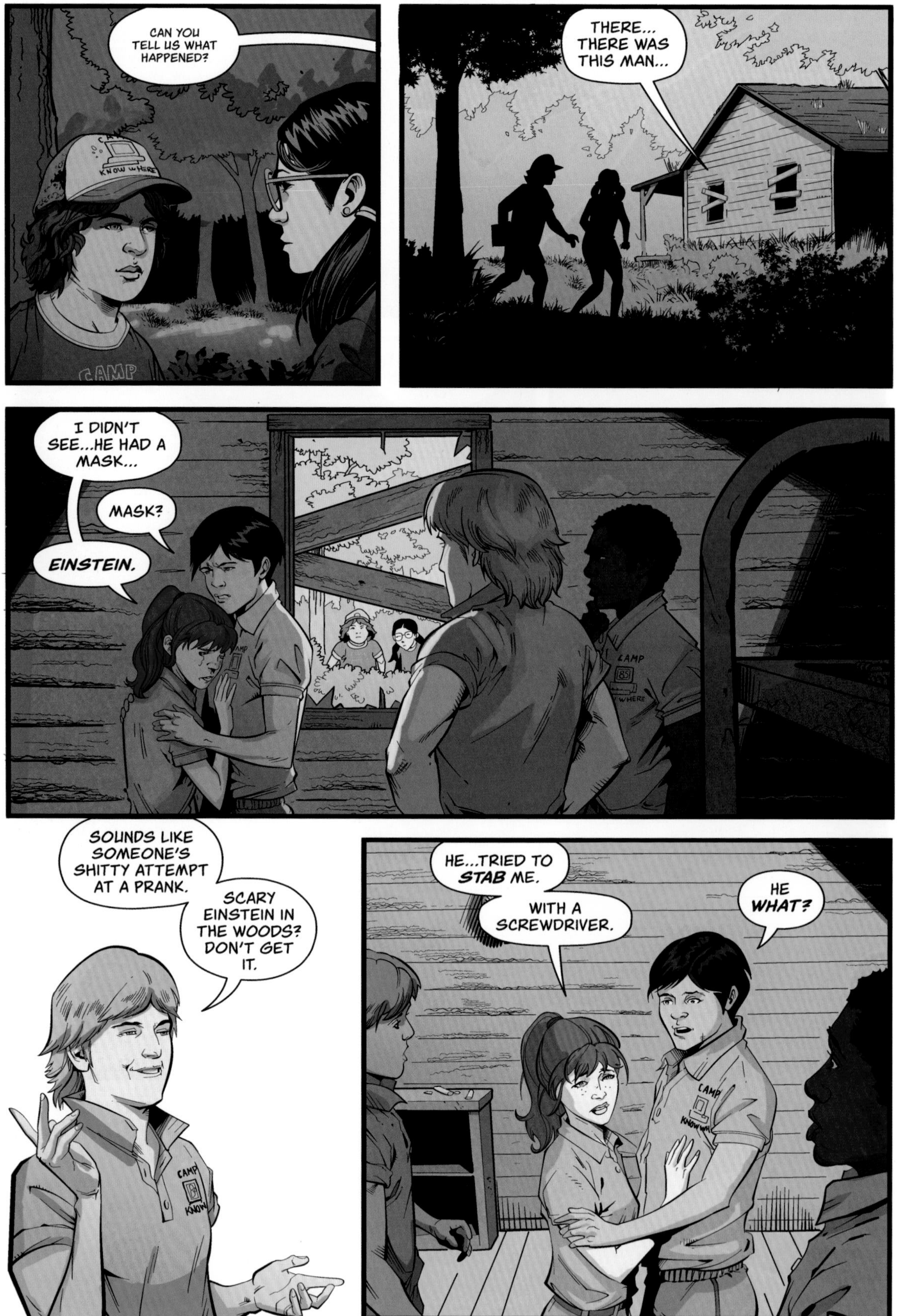
CAN YOU TELL US WHAT HAPPENED?
THERE... THERE WAS THIS MAN...
I DIDN'T SEE...HE HAD A MASK...
MASK?
EINSTEIN.
SOUNDS LIKE SOMEONE'S SHITTY ATTEMPT AT A PRANK.
SCARY EINSTEIN IN THE WOODS? DON'T GET IT.
HE...TRIED TO STAB ME.
WITH A SCREWDRIVER.
HE WHAT?

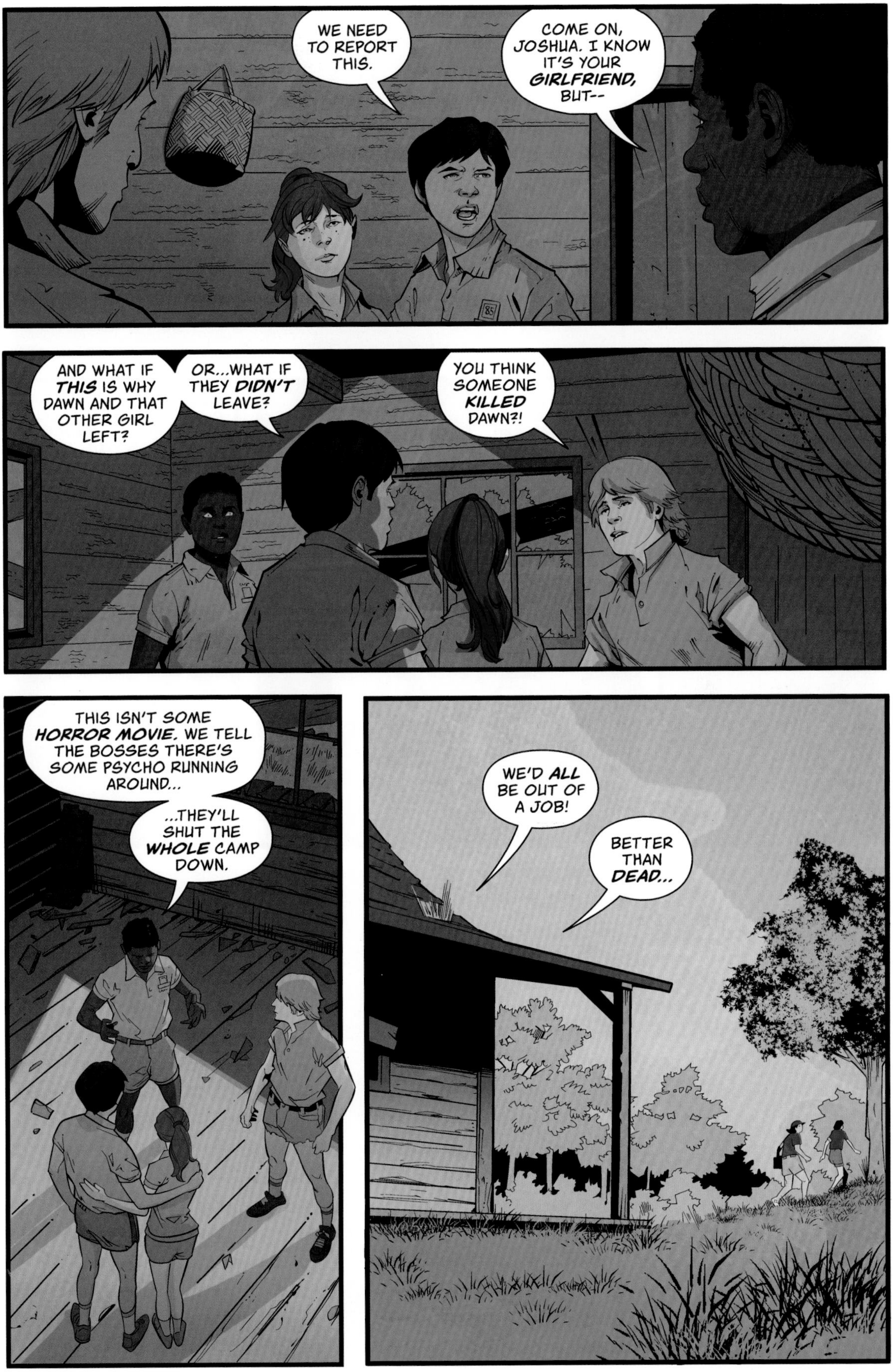
WE NEED TO REPORT THIS.
COME ON, JOSHUA. I KNOW IT'S YOUR GIRLFRIEND, BUT--
AND WHAT IF THIS IS WHY DAWN AND THAT OTHER GIRL LEFT?
OR...WHAT IF THEY DIDN'T LEAVE?
YOU THINK SOMEONE KILLED DAWN?!
THIS ISN'T SOME HORROR MOVIE. WE TELL THE BOSSES THERE'S SOME PSYCHO RUNNING AROUND...
...THEY'LL SHUT THE WHOLE CAMP DOWN.
WE'D ALL BE OUT OF A JOB!
BETTER THAN DEAD...

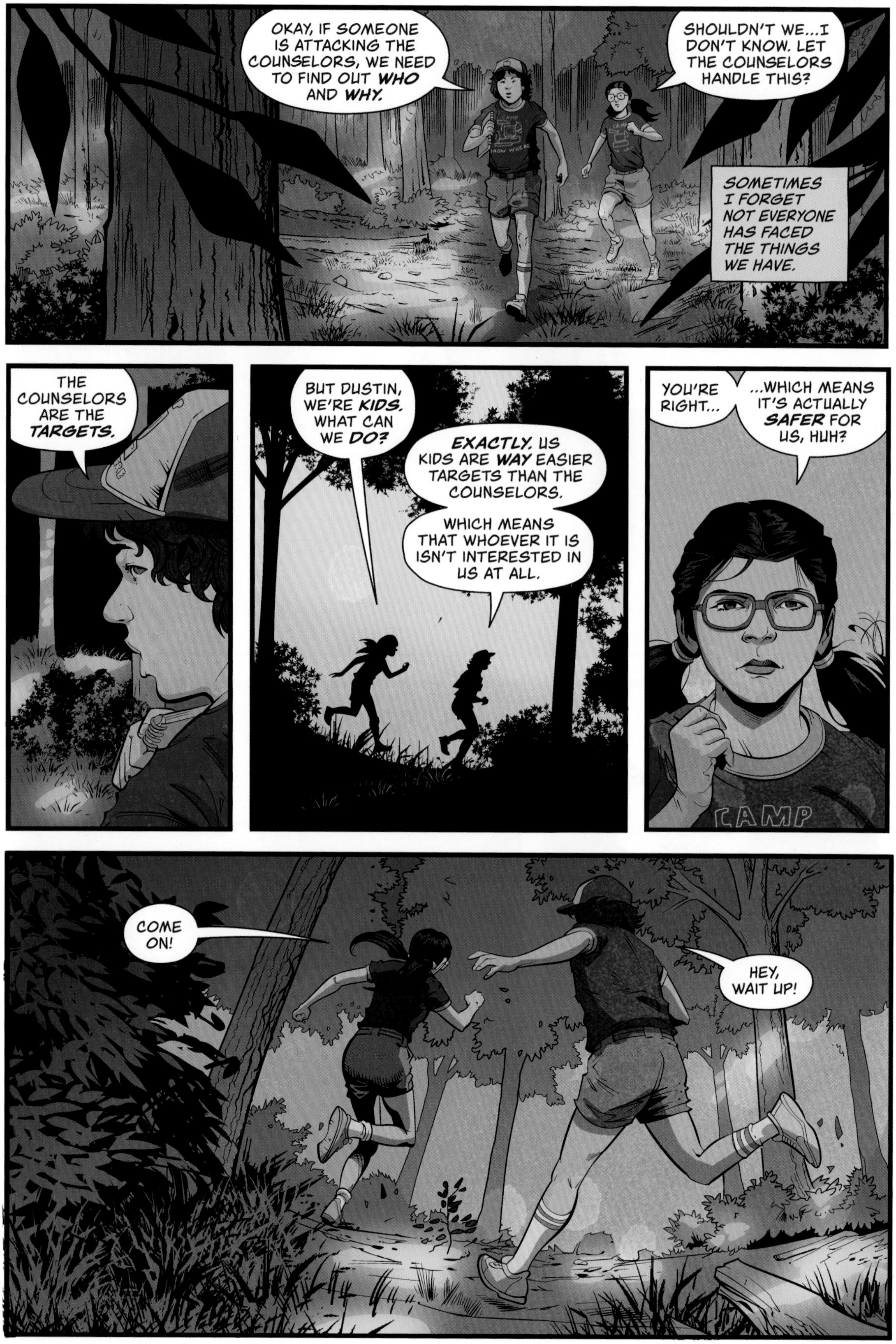
OKAY, IF SOMEONE IS ATTACKING THE COUNSELORS, WE NEED TO FIND OUT WHO AND WHY.
SHOULDN'T WE...I DON'T KNOW. LET THE COUNSELORS HANDLE THIS?
SOMETIMES I FORGET NOT EVERYONE HAS FACED THE THINGS WE HAVE.
THE COUNSELORS ARE THE TARGETS.
BUT DUSTIN, WE'RE KIDS. WHAT CAN WE DO?
EXACTLY. US KIDS ARE WAY EASIER TARGETS THAN THE COUNSELORS.
WHICH MEANS THAT WHOEVER IT IS ISN'T INTERESTED IN US AT ALL.
YOU'RE RIGHT...
...WHICH MEANS IT'S ACTUALLY SAFER FOR US, HUH?
CAMP
COME ON!
HEY, WAIT UP!

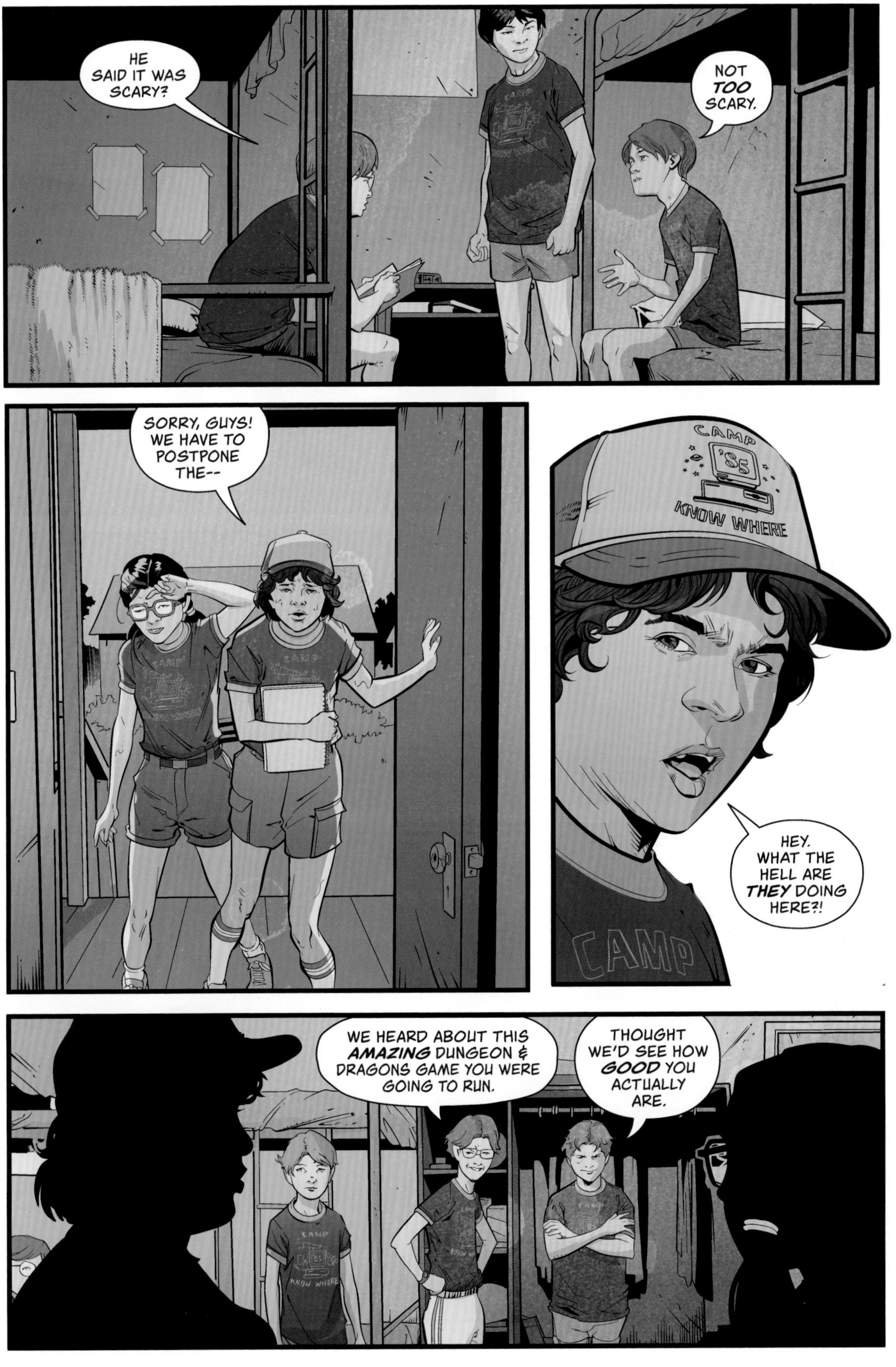
HE SAID IT WAS SCARY?
NOT TOO SCARY.
SORRY, GUYS! WE HAVE TO POSTPONE THE--
CAMP '85 KNOW WHERE
HEY. WHAT THE HELL ARE THEY DOING HERE?!
CAMP
WE HEARD ABOUT THIS AMAZING DUNGEON & DRAGONS GAME YOU WERE GOING TO RUN.
THOUGHT WE'D SEE HOW GOOD YOU ACTUALLY ARE.

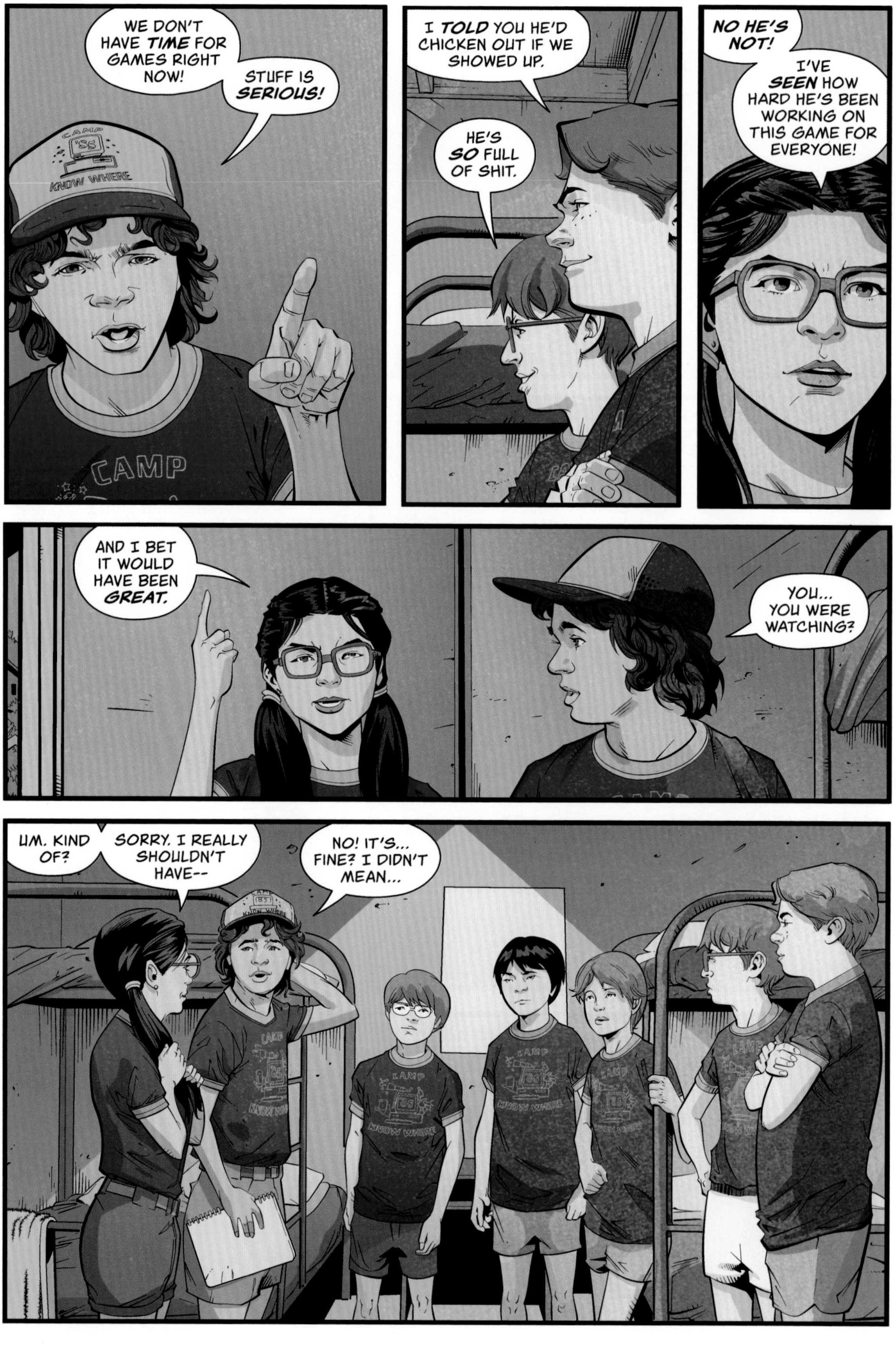
WE DON'T HAVE *TIME* FOR GAMES RIGHT NOW!
STUFF IS *SERIOUS!*
CAMP '85 KNOW WHERE
CAMP
I *TOLD* YOU HE'D CHICKEN OUT IF WE SHOWED UP.
HE'S *SO* FULL OF SHIT.
NO HE'S NOT!
I'VE *SEEN* HOW HARD HE'S BEEN WORKING ON THIS GAME FOR EVERYONE!
AND I BET IT WOULD HAVE BEEN *GREAT.*
YOU... YOU WERE WATCHING?
UM. KIND OF?
SORRY. I REALLY SHOULDN'T HAVE--
NO! IT'S... FINE? I DIDN'T MEAN...

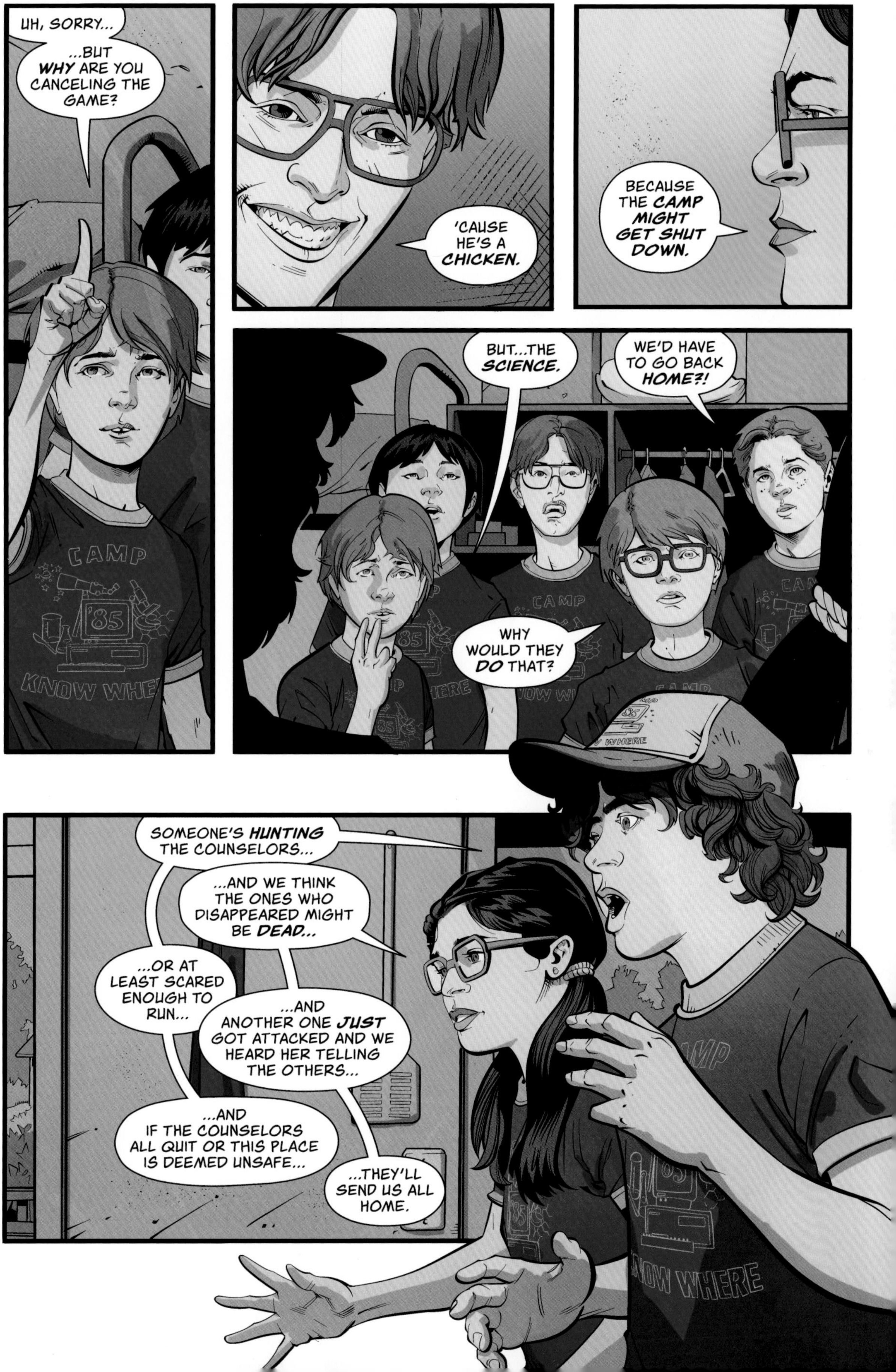
UH, SORRY...
...BUT WHY ARE YOU CANCELING THE GAME?
'CAUSE HE'S A CHICKEN.
BECAUSE THE CAMP MIGHT GET SHUT DOWN.
BUT...THE SCIENCE.
WE'D HAVE TO GO BACK HOME?!
WHY WOULD THEY DO THAT?
SOMEONE'S HUNTING THE COUNSELORS...
...AND WE THINK THE ONES WHO DISAPPEARED MIGHT BE DEAD...
...OR AT LEAST SCARED ENOUGH TO RUN...
...AND ANOTHER ONE JUST GOT ATTACKED AND WE HEARD HER TELLING THE OTHERS...
...AND IF THE COUNSELORS ALL QUIT OR THIS PLACE IS DEEMED UNSAFE...
...THEY'LL SEND US ALL HOME.

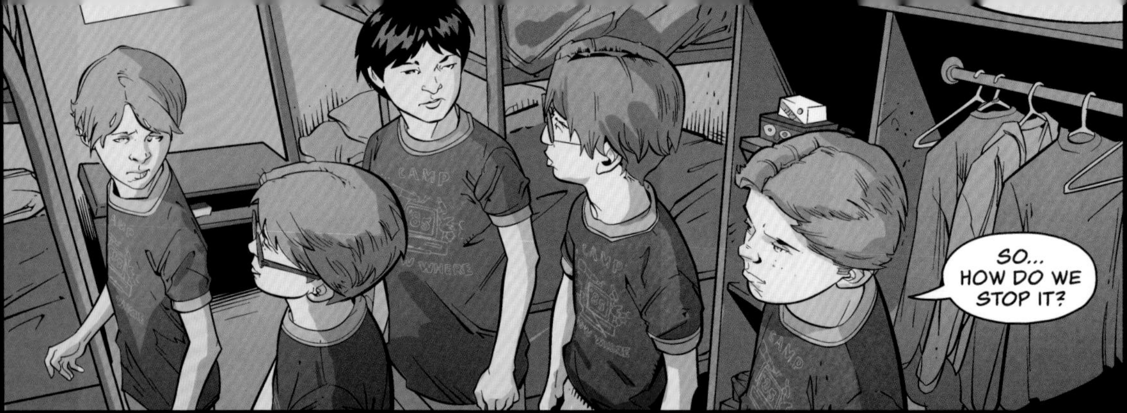
SO... HOW DO WE STOP IT?

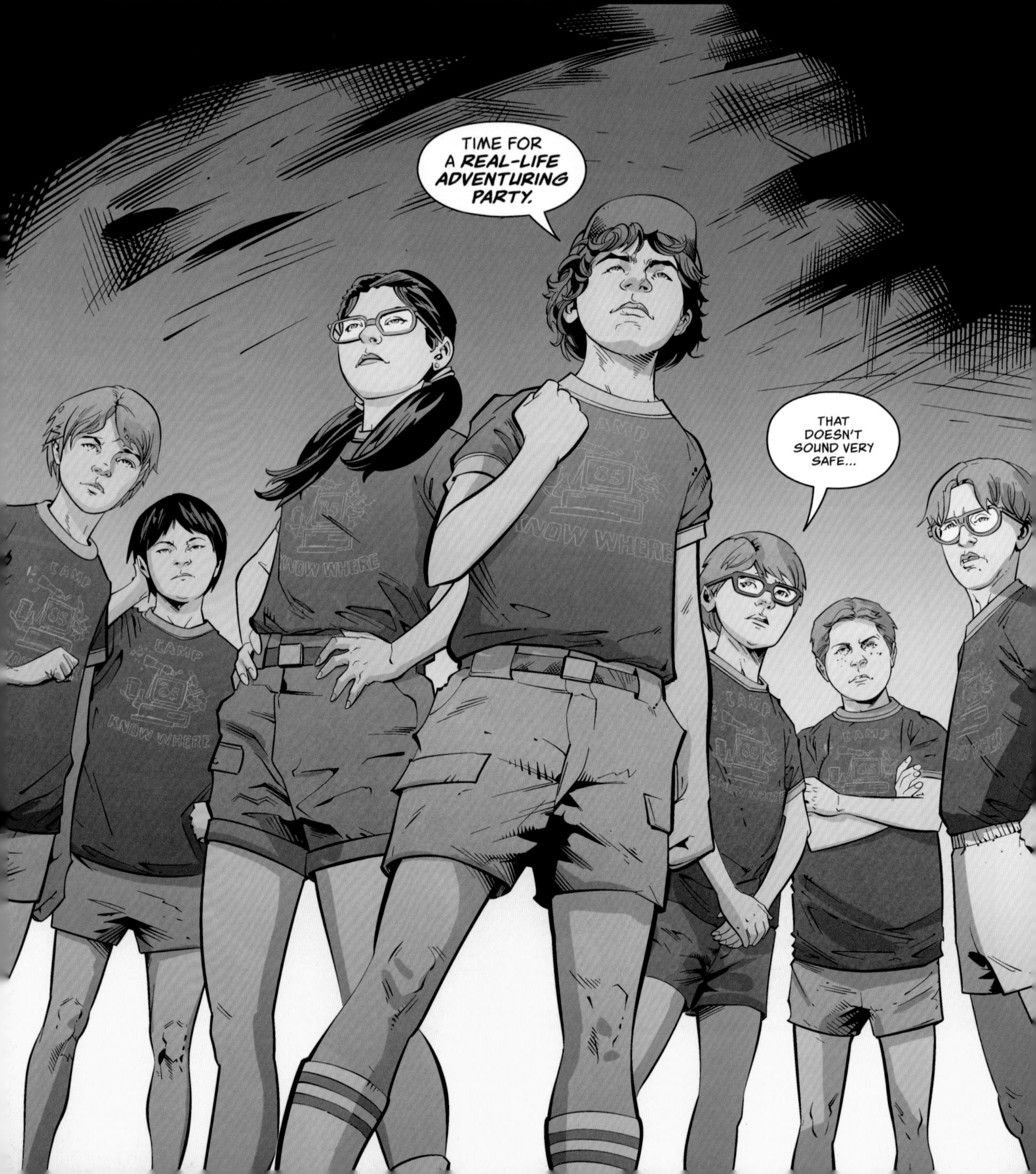
TIME FOR A REAL-LIFE ADVENTURING PARTY.
THAT DOESN'T SOUND VERY SAFE...

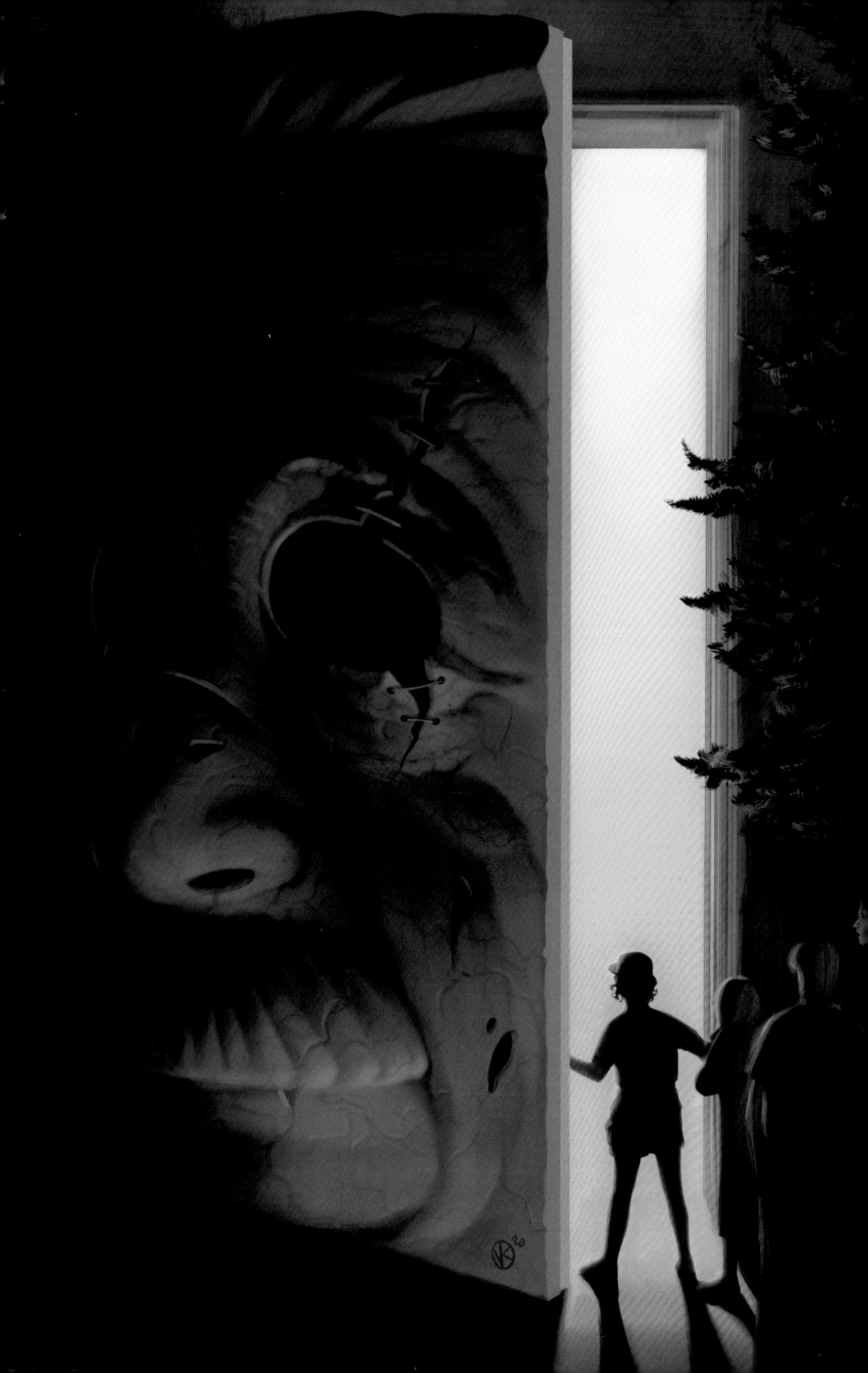

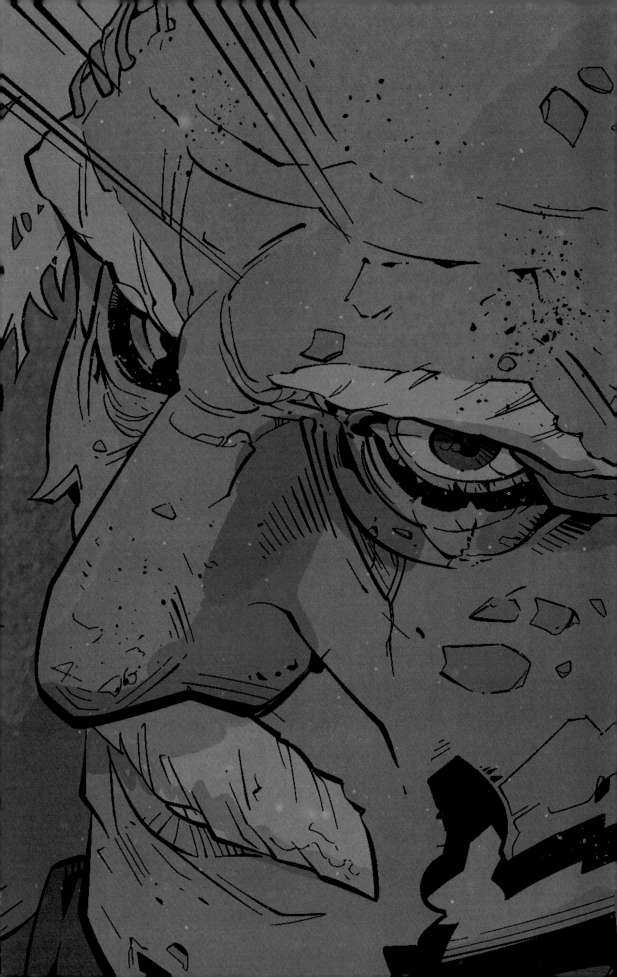

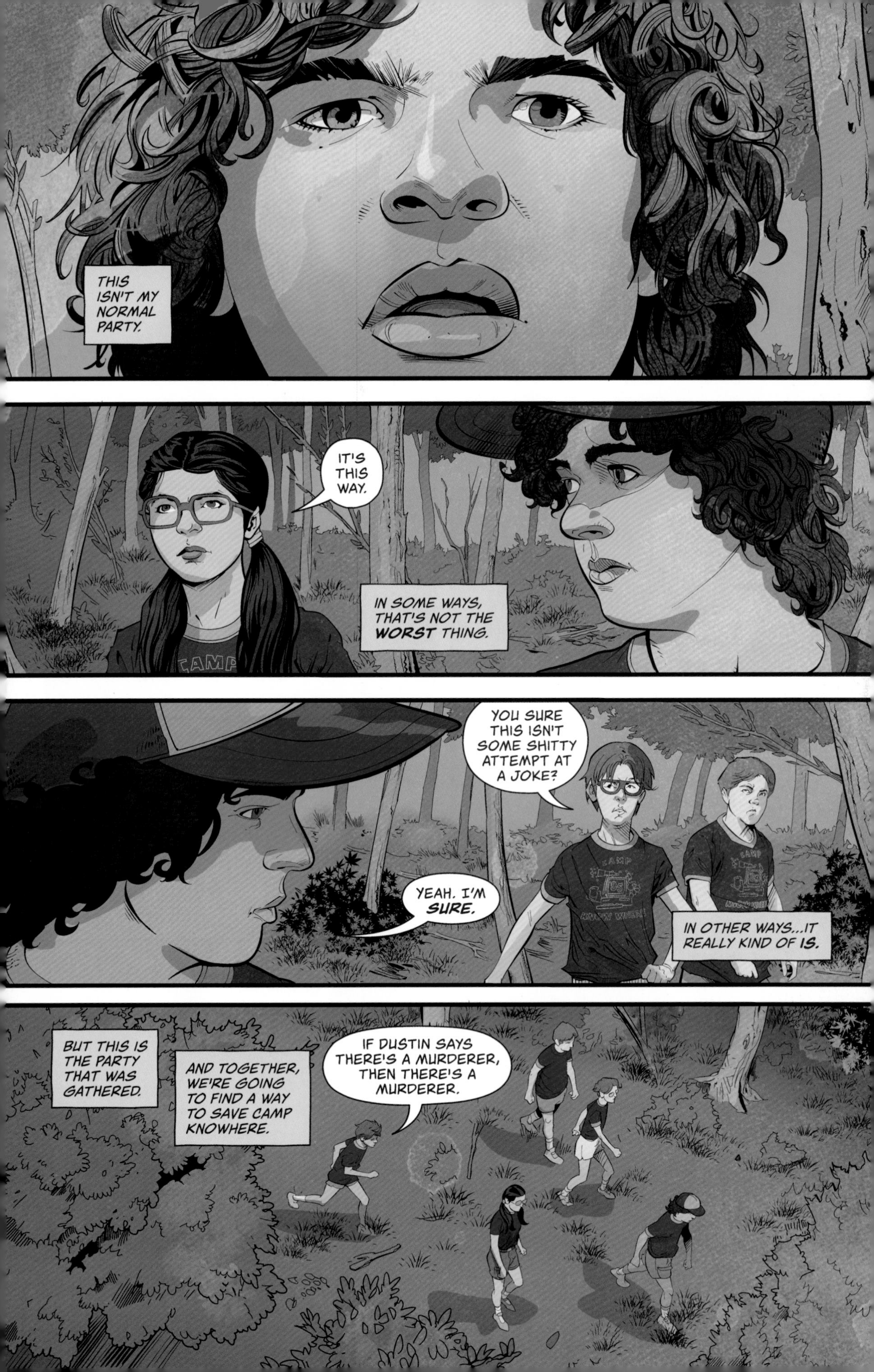
THIS ISN'T MY NORMAL PARTY.
IT'S THIS WAY.
IN SOME WAYS, THAT'S NOT THE WORST THING.
YOU SURE THIS ISN'T SOME SHITTY ATTEMPT AT A JOKE?
YEAH. I'M SURE.
IN OTHER WAYS...IT REALLY KIND OF IS.
BUT THIS IS THE PARTY THAT WAS GATHERED.
AND TOGETHER, WE'RE GOING TO FIND A WAY TO SAVE CAMP KNOWHERE.
IF DUSTIN SAYS THERE'S A MURDERER, THEN THERE'S A MURDERER.

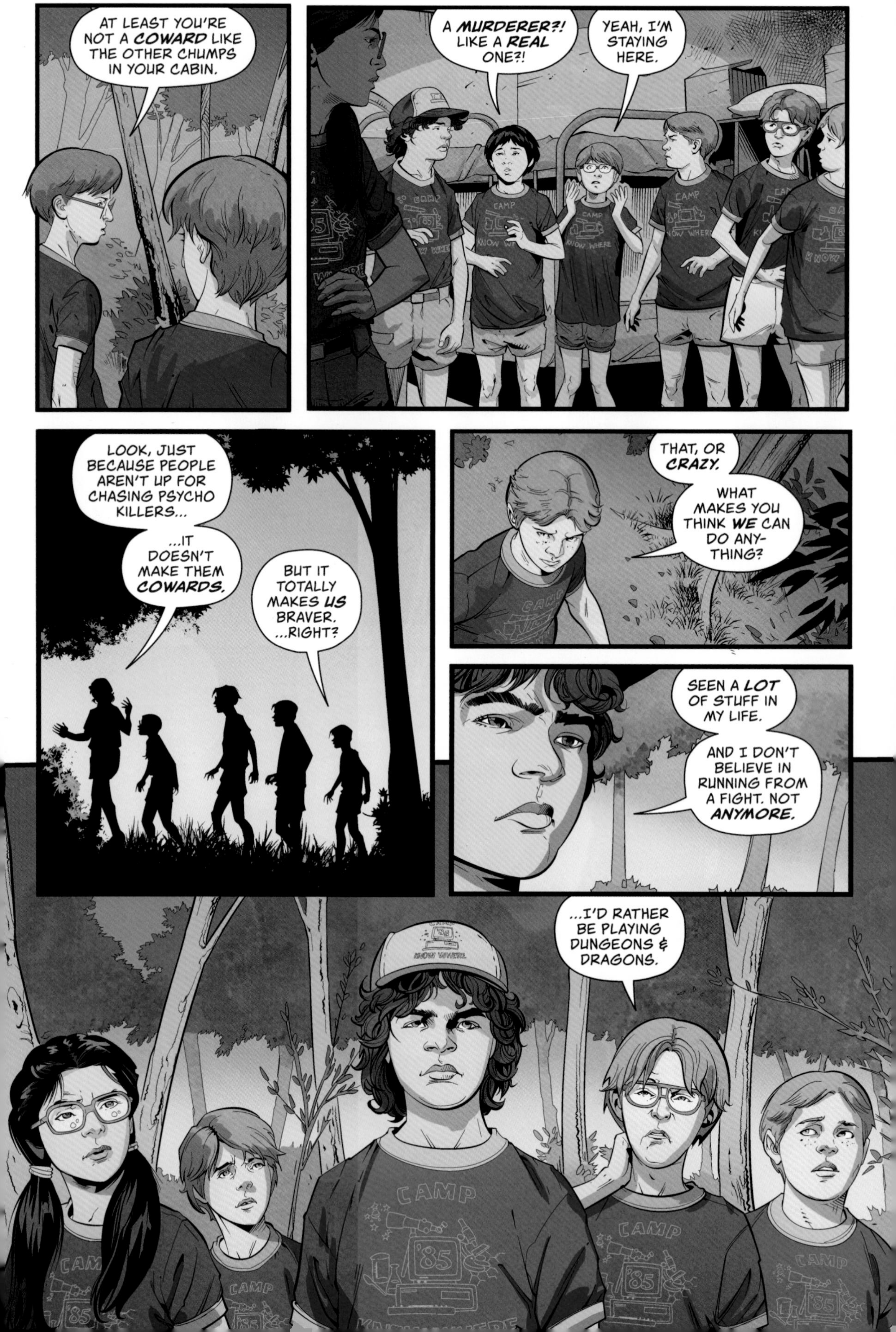
AT LEAST YOU'RE NOT A COWARD LIKE THE OTHER CHUMPS IN YOUR CABIN.
A MURDERER?! LIKE A REAL ONE?!
YEAH, I'M STAYING HERE.
LOOK, JUST BECAUSE PEOPLE AREN'T UP FOR CHASING PSYCHO KILLERS...
...IT DOESN'T MAKE THEM COWARDS.
BUT IT TOTALLY MAKES US BRAVER. ...RIGHT?
THAT, OR CRAZY.
WHAT MAKES YOU THINK WE CAN DO ANY-THING?
SEEN A LOT OF STUFF IN MY LIFE.
AND I DON'T BELIEVE IN RUNNING FROM A FIGHT. NOT ANYMORE.
...I'D RATHER BE PLAYING DUNGEONS & DRAGONS.

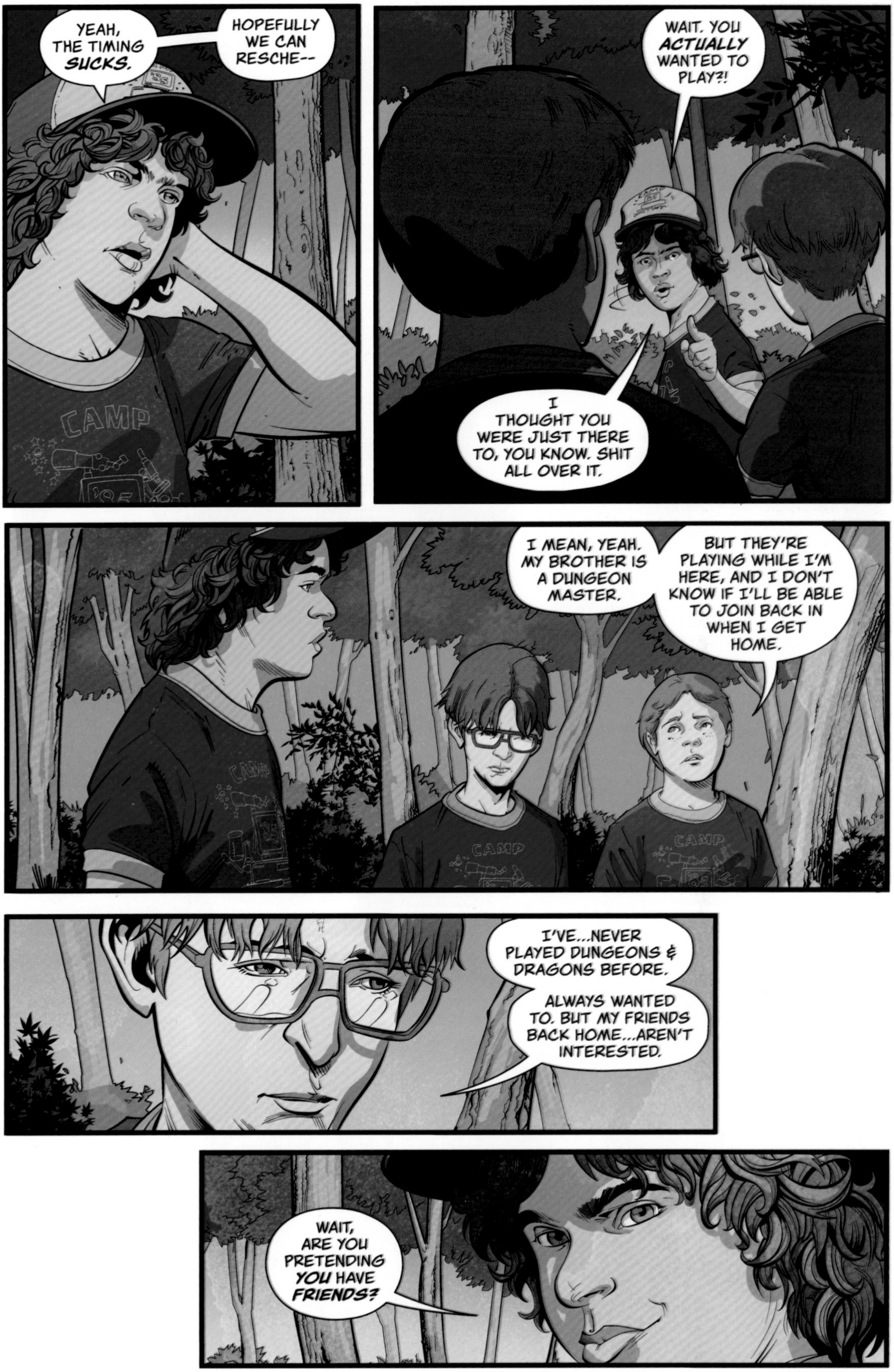
YEAH, THE TIMING SUCKS.
HOPEFULLY WE CAN RESCHE--
WAIT. YOU ACTUALLY WANTED TO PLAY?!
I THOUGHT YOU WERE JUST THERE TO, YOU KNOW. SHIT ALL OVER IT.
I MEAN, YEAH. MY BROTHER IS A DUNGEON MASTER.
BUT THEY'RE PLAYING WHILE I'M HERE, AND I DON'T KNOW IF I'LL BE ABLE TO JOIN BACK IN WHEN I GET HOME.
I'VE...NEVER PLAYED DUNGEONS & DRAGONS BEFORE.
ALWAYS WANTED TO. BUT MY FRIENDS BACK HOME...AREN'T INTERESTED.
WAIT, ARE YOU PRETENDING YOU HAVE FRIENDS?

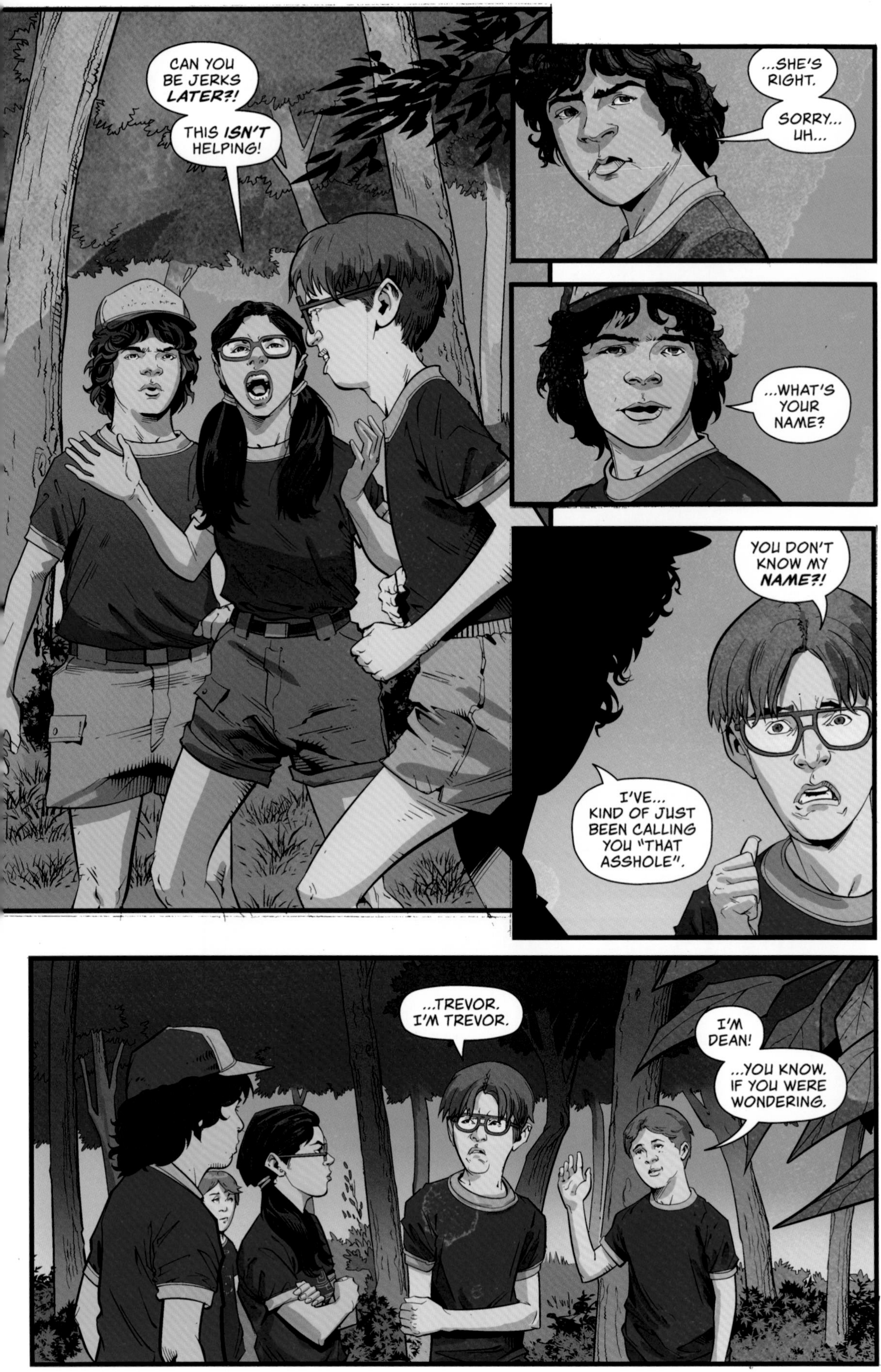
CAN YOU BE JERKS *LATER?!*
THIS *ISN'T* HELPING!
...SHE'S RIGHT.
SORRY... UH...
...WHAT'S YOUR NAME?
YOU DON'T KNOW MY *NAME?!*
I'VE... KIND OF JUST BEEN CALLING YOU "THAT ASSHOLE".
...TREVOR. I'M TREVOR.
I'M DEAN!
...YOU KNOW. IF YOU WERE WONDERING.

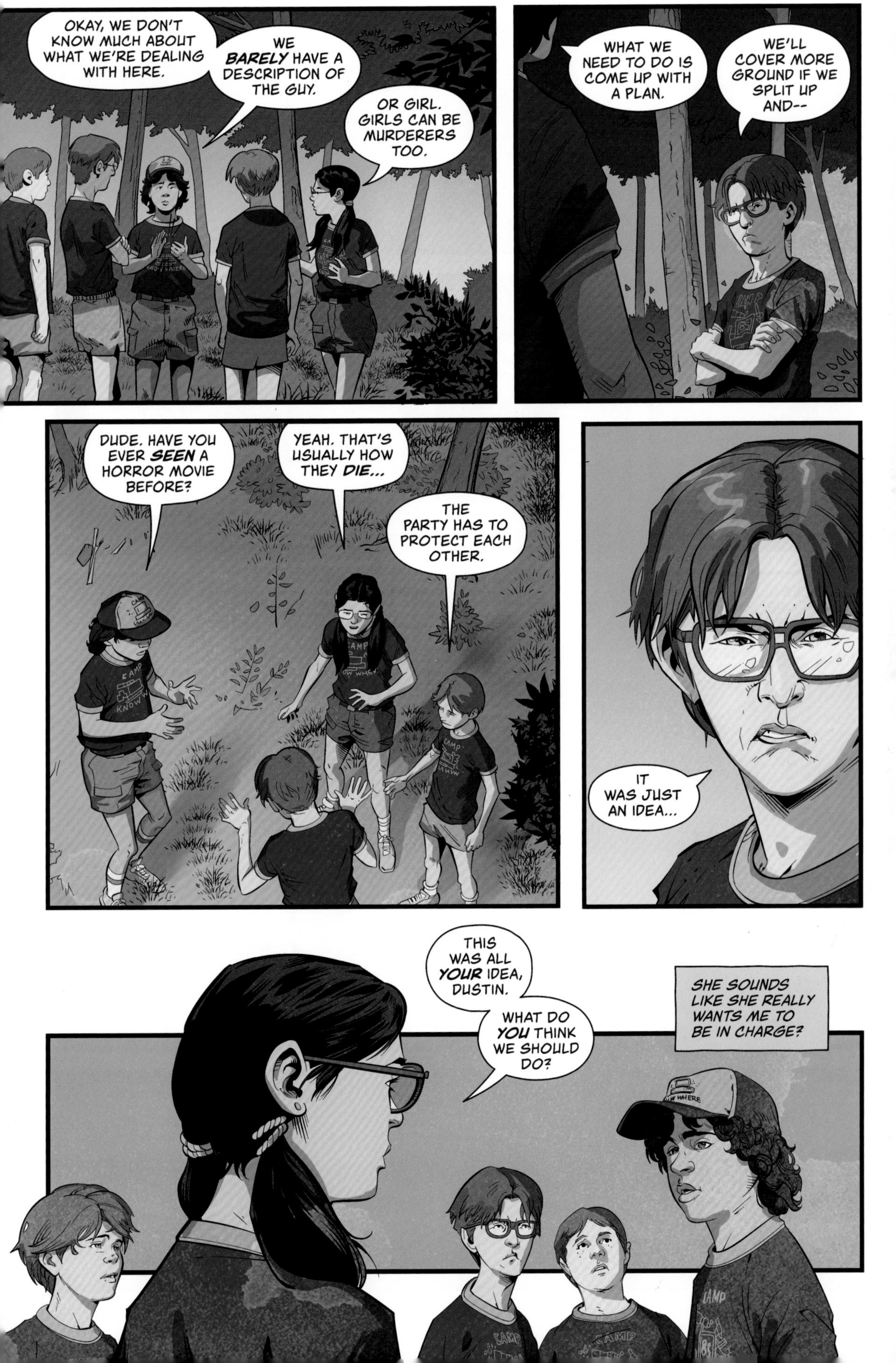
OKAY, WE DON'T KNOW MUCH ABOUT WHAT WE'RE DEALING WITH HERE.
WE *BARELY* HAVE A DESCRIPTION OF THE GUY.
OR GIRL. GIRLS CAN BE MURDERERS TOO.
WHAT WE NEED TO DO IS COME UP WITH A PLAN.
WE'LL COVER MORE GROUND IF WE SPLIT UP AND--
DUDE. HAVE YOU EVER *SEEN* A HORROR MOVIE BEFORE?
YEAH. THAT'S USUALLY HOW THEY *DIE*...
THE PARTY HAS TO PROTECT EACH OTHER.
IT WAS JUST AN IDEA...
THIS WAS ALL *YOUR* IDEA, DUSTIN.
WHAT DO *YOU* THINK WE SHOULD DO?
SHE SOUNDS LIKE SHE REALLY WANTS ME TO BE IN CHARGE?

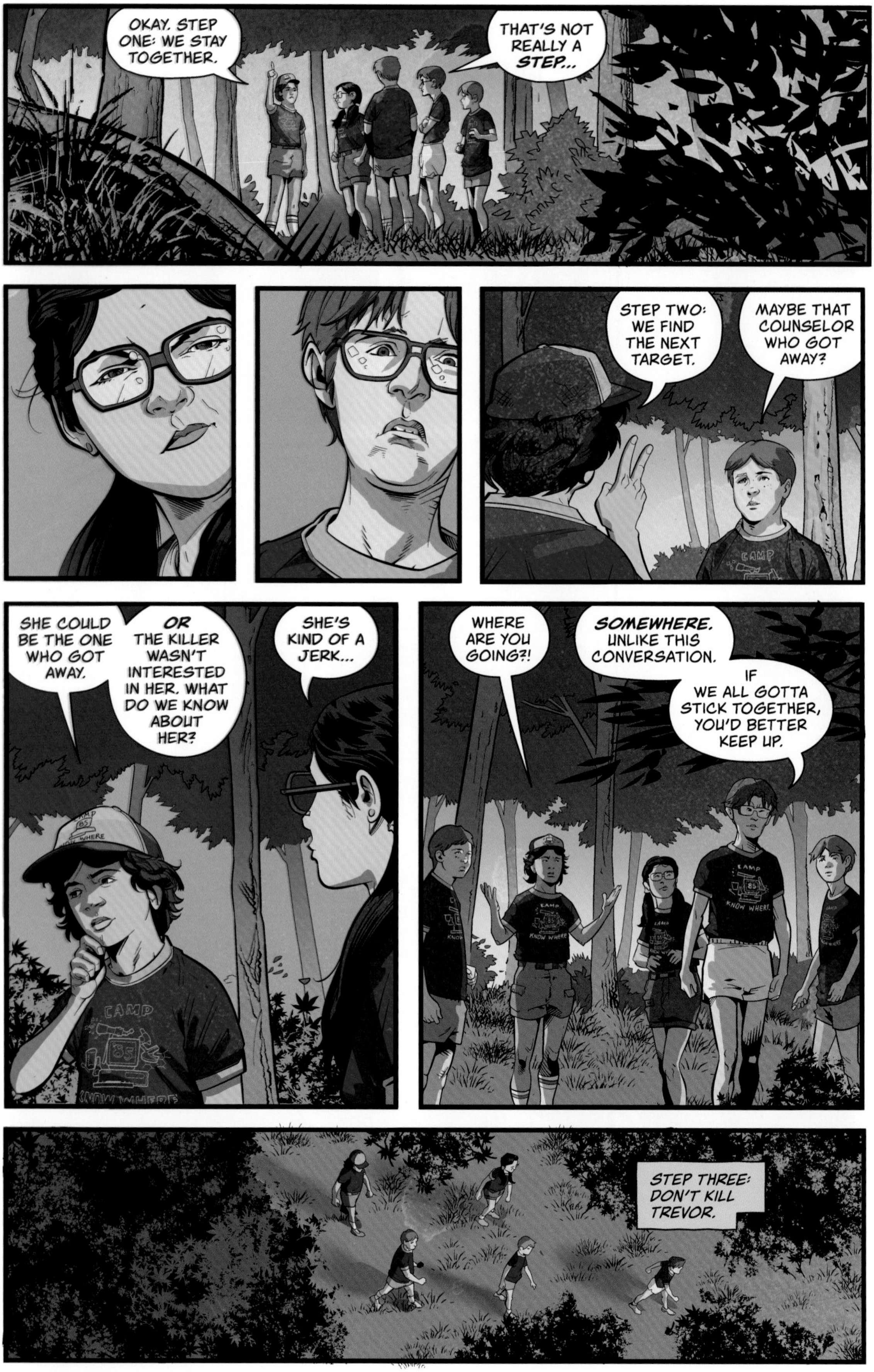
OKAY. STEP ONE: WE STAY TOGETHER.
THAT'S NOT REALLY A STEP...
STEP TWO: WE FIND THE NEXT TARGET.
MAYBE THAT COUNSELOR WHO GOT AWAY?
SHE COULD BE THE ONE WHO GOT AWAY.
OR THE KILLER WASN'T INTERESTED IN HER. WHAT DO WE KNOW ABOUT HER?
SHE'S KIND OF A JERK...
WHERE ARE YOU GOING?!
SOMEWHERE. UNLIKE THIS CONVERSATION.
IF WE ALL GOTTA STICK TOGETHER, YOU'D BETTER KEEP UP.
STEP THREE: DON'T KILL TREVOR.

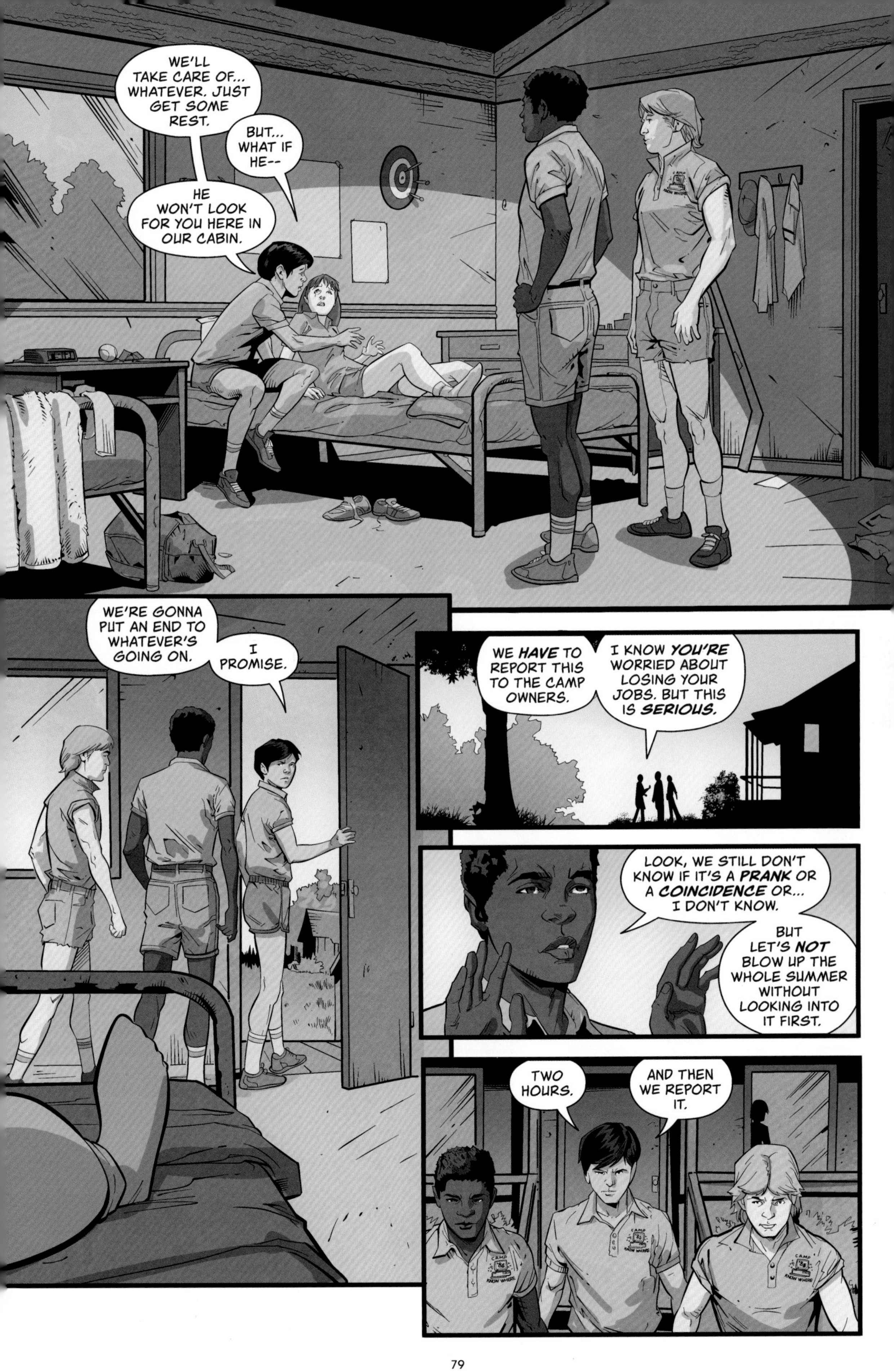
WE'LL TAKE CARE OF... WHATEVER. JUST GET SOME REST.
BUT... WHAT IF HE--
HE WON'T LOOK FOR YOU HERE IN OUR CABIN.
WE'RE GONNA PUT AN END TO WHATEVER'S GOING ON.
I PROMISE.
WE HAVE TO REPORT THIS TO THE CAMP OWNERS.
I KNOW YOU'RE WORRIED ABOUT LOSING YOUR JOBS. BUT THIS IS SERIOUS.
LOOK, WE STILL DON'T KNOW IF IT'S A PRANK OR A COINCIDENCE OR... I DON'T KNOW.
BUT LET'S NOT BLOW UP THE WHOLE SUMMER WITHOUT LOOKING INTO IT FIRST.
TWO HOURS.
AND THEN WE REPORT IT.

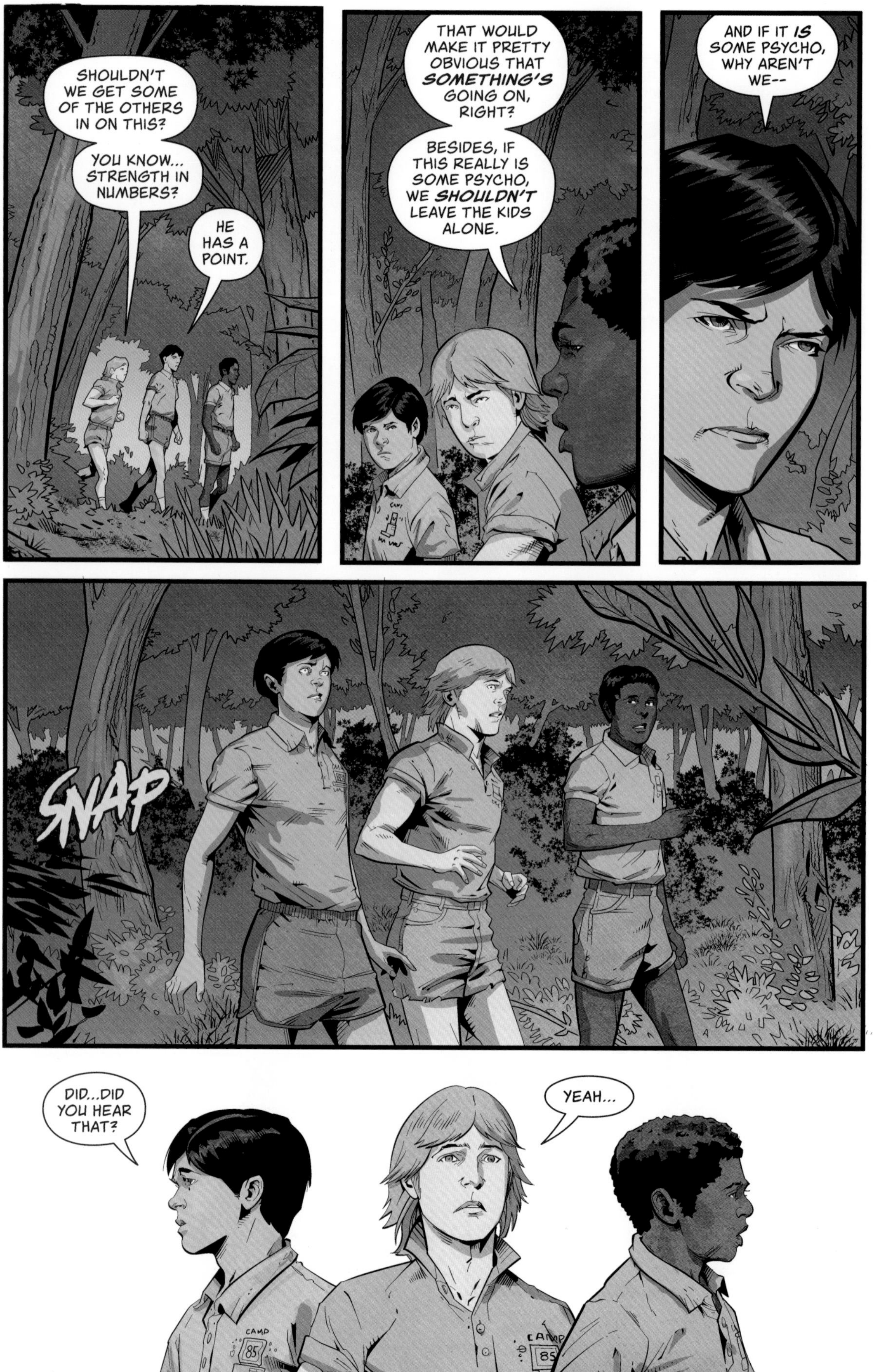
SHOULDN'T WE GET SOME OF THE OTHERS IN ON THIS?
YOU KNOW... STRENGTH IN NUMBERS?
HE HAS A POINT.
THAT WOULD MAKE IT PRETTY OBVIOUS THAT SOMETHING'S GOING ON, RIGHT?
BESIDES, IF THIS REALLY IS SOME PSYCHO, WE SHOULDN'T LEAVE THE KIDS ALONE.
AND IF IT IS SOME PSYCHO, WHY AREN'T WE--
SNAP
DID...DID YOU HEAR THAT?
YEAH...
CAMP
85
KNOWHERE

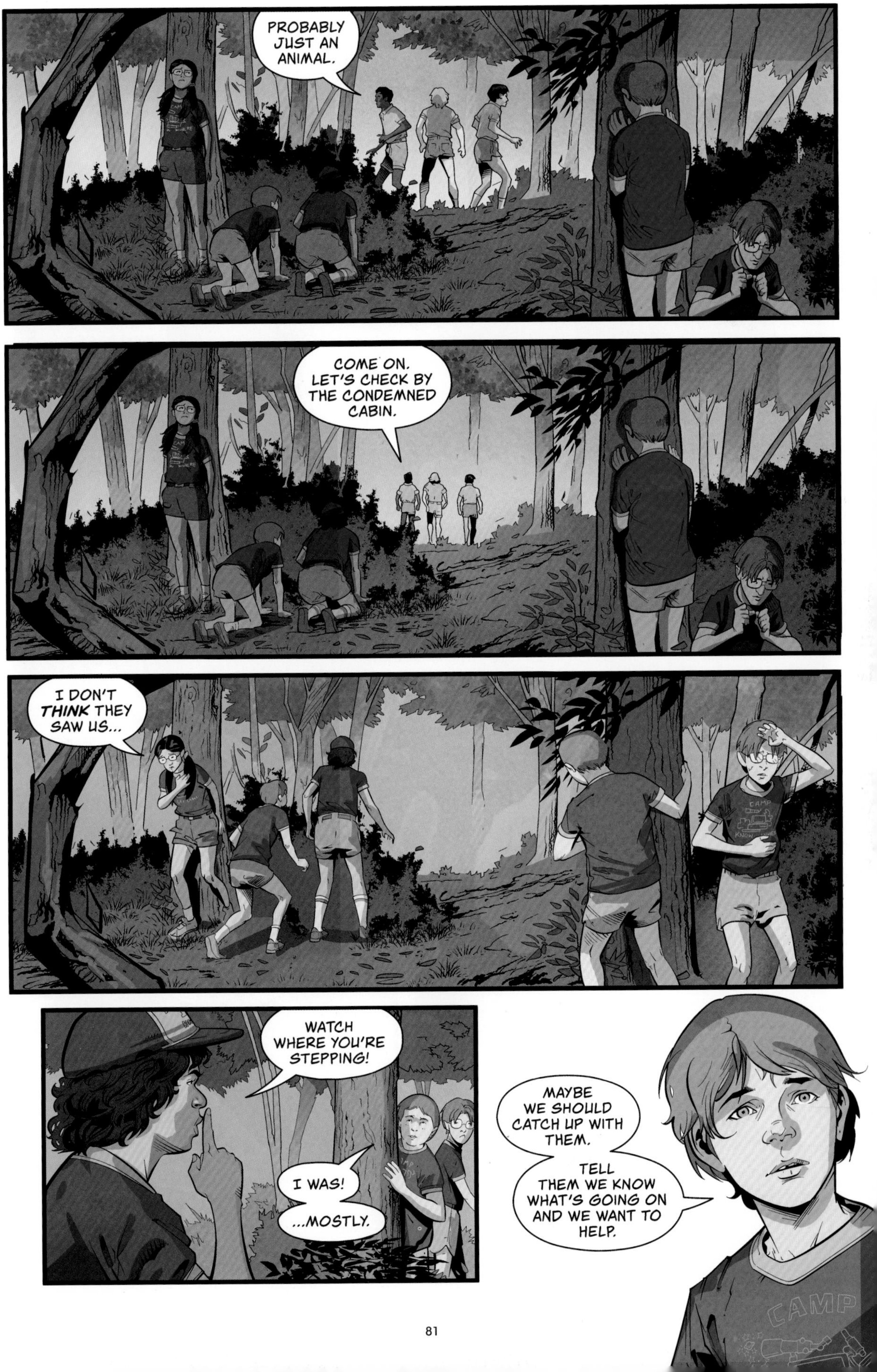

PROBABLY JUST AN ANIMAL.
COME ON. LET'S CHECK BY THE CONDEMNED CABIN.
I DON'T *THINK* THEY SAW US...
WATCH WHERE YOU'RE STEPPING!
I WAS!
...MOSTLY.
MAYBE WE SHOULD CATCH UP WITH THEM.
TELL THEM WE KNOW WHAT'S GOING ON AND WE WANT TO HELP.
CAMP

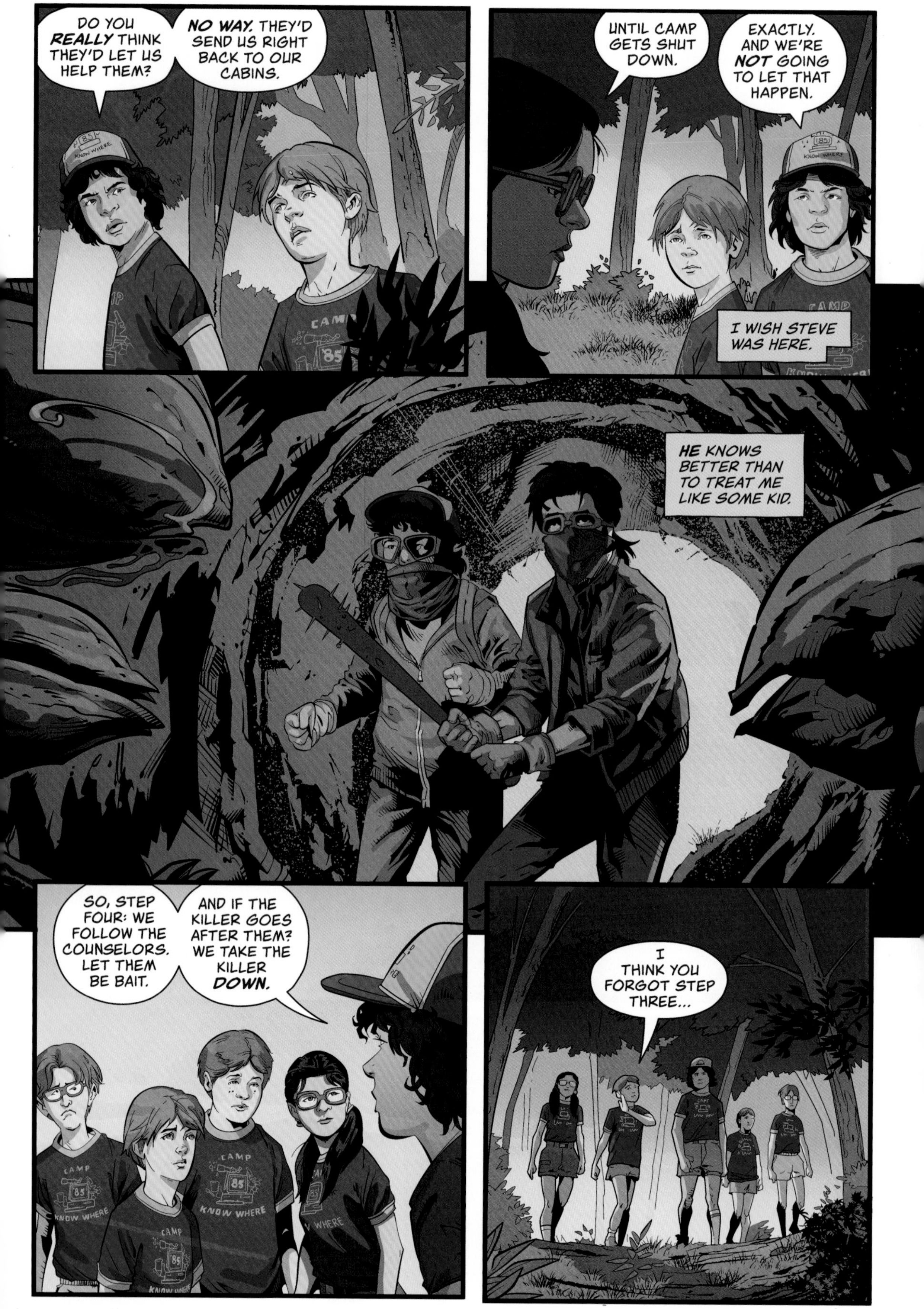
DO YOU REALLY THINK THEY'D LET US HELP THEM?
NO WAY. THEY'D SEND US RIGHT BACK TO OUR CABINS.
UNTIL CAMP GETS SHUT DOWN.
EXACTLY. AND WE'RE NOT GOING TO LET THAT HAPPEN.
I WISH STEVE WAS HERE.
HE KNOWS BETTER THAN TO TREAT ME LIKE SOME KID.
SO, STEP FOUR: WE FOLLOW THE COUNSELORS. LET THEM BE BAIT.
AND IF THE KILLER GOES AFTER THEM? WE TAKE THE KILLER DOWN.
I THINK YOU FORGOT STEP THREE...

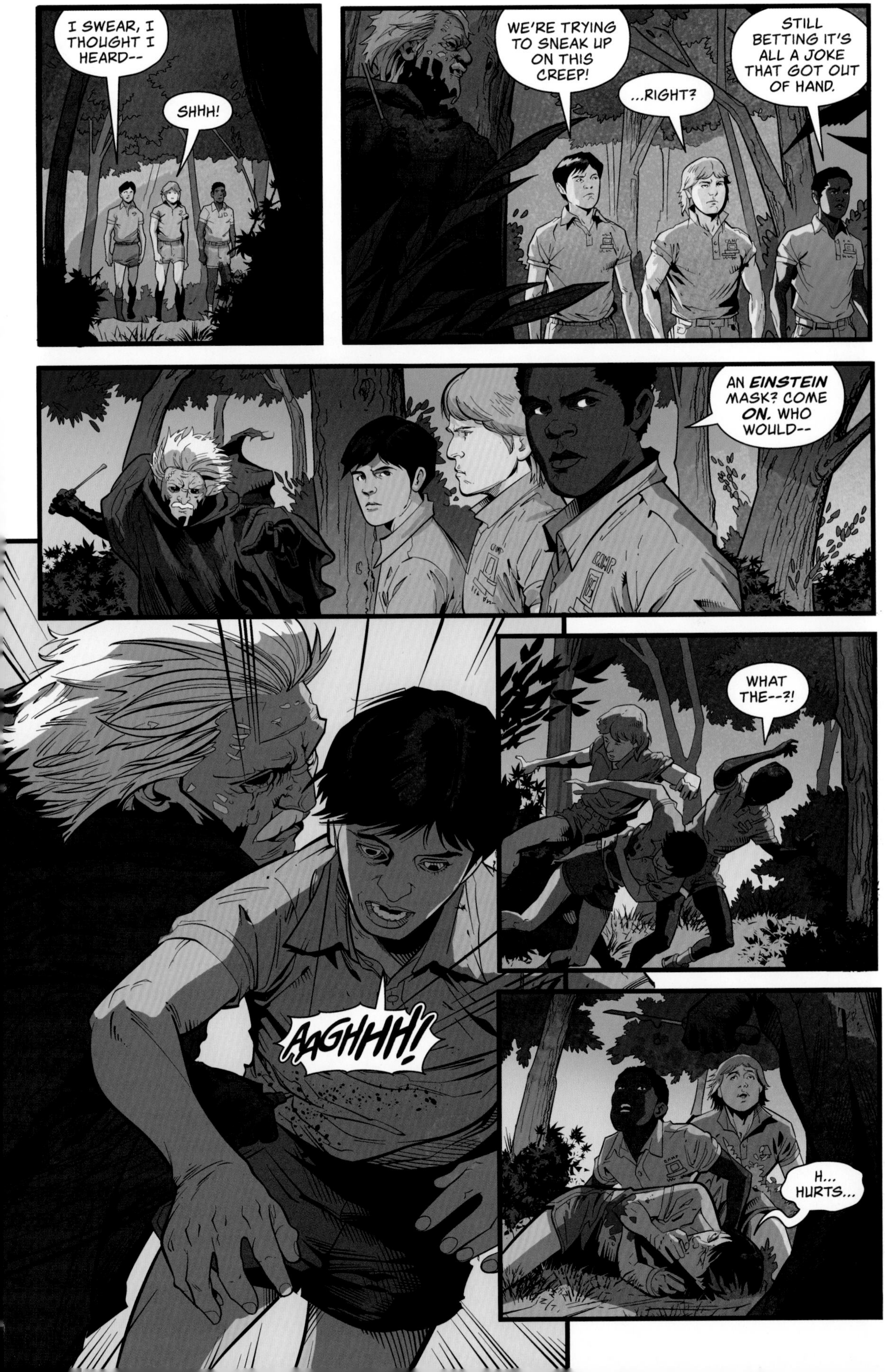
I SWEAR, I THOUGHT I HEARD--
SHHH!
WE'RE TRYING TO SNEAK UP ON THIS CREEP!
...RIGHT?
STILL BETTING IT'S ALL A JOKE THAT GOT OUT OF HAND.
AN EINSTEIN MASK? COME ON. WHO WOULD--
AAGHHH!
WHAT THE--?!
H... HURTS...

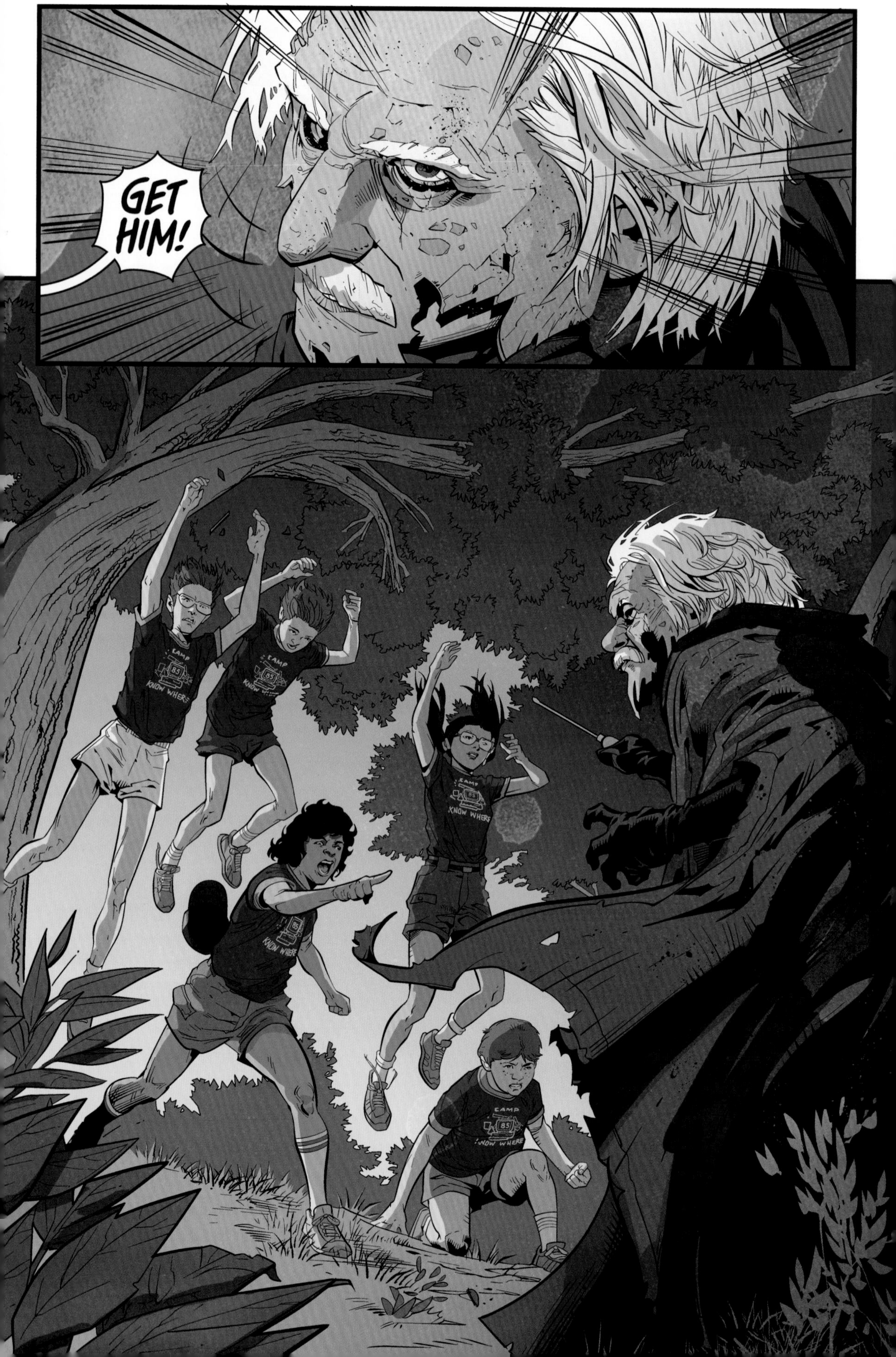
GET HIM!

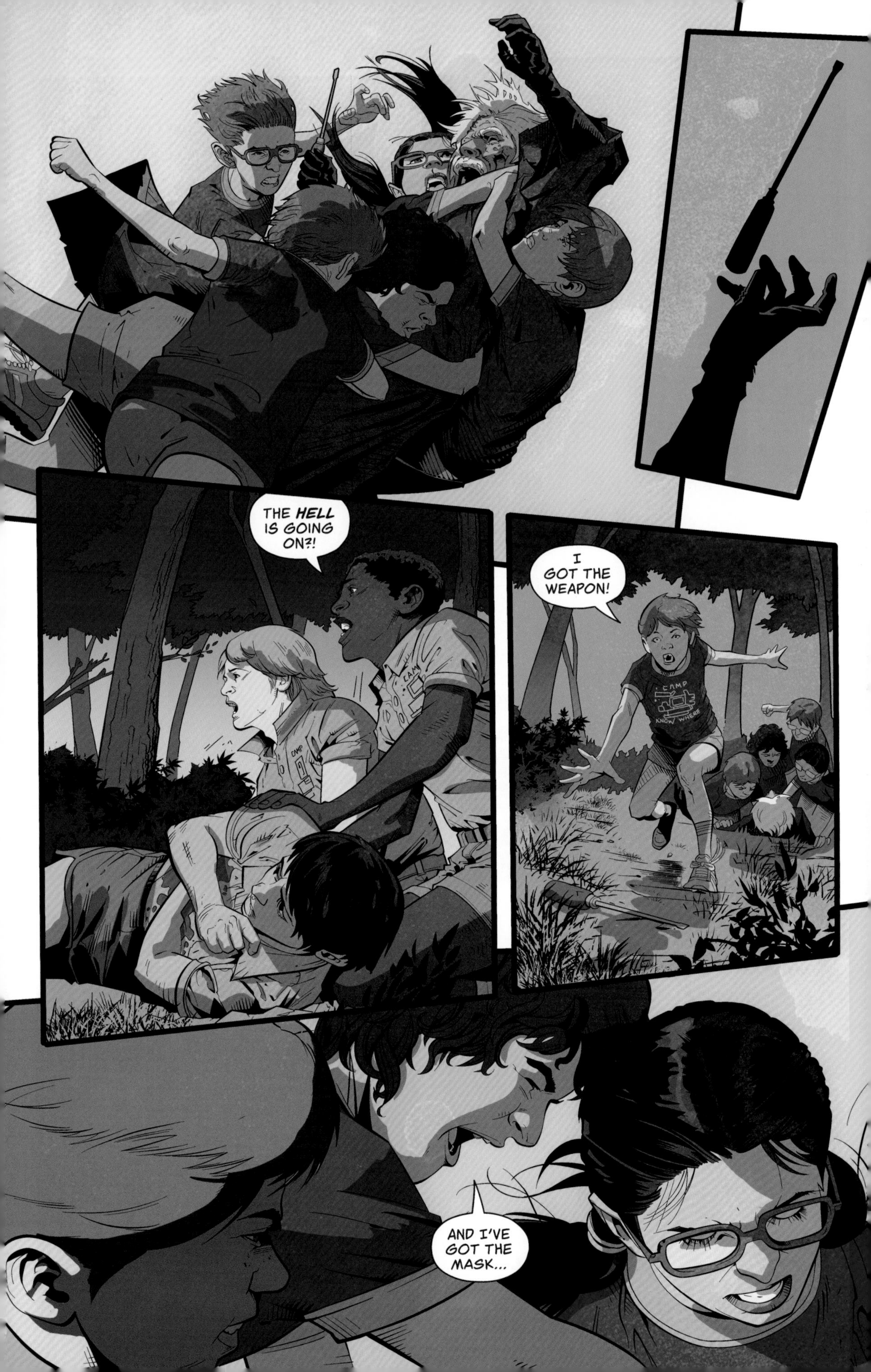
THE **HELL** IS GOING ON?!
I GOT THE WEAPON!
CAMP KNOW WHERE
AND I'VE GOT THE MASK...

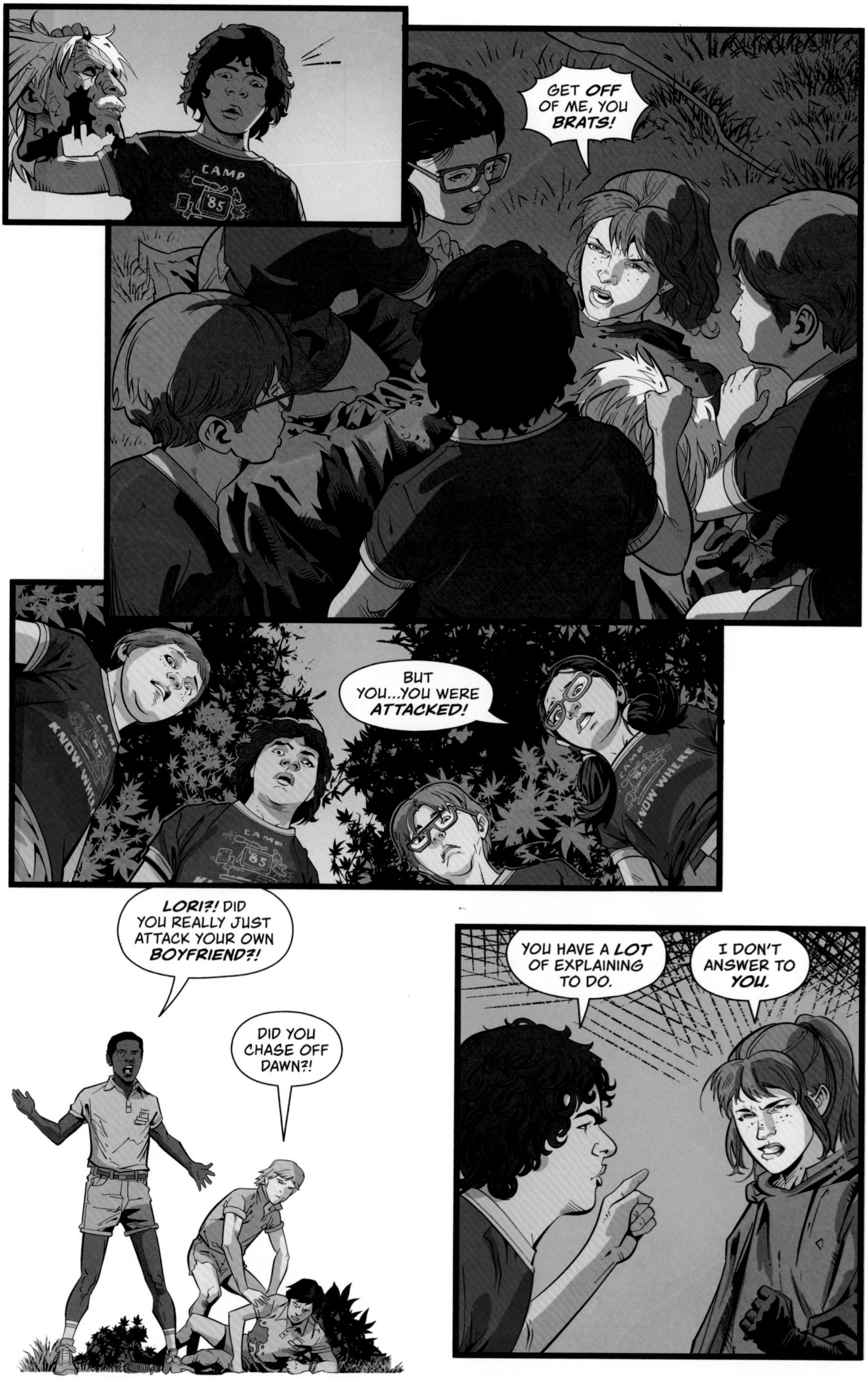
GET OFF OF ME, YOU BRATS!
BUT YOU...YOU WERE ATTACKED!
LORI?! DID YOU REALLY JUST ATTACK YOUR OWN BOYFRIEND?!
DID YOU CHASE OFF DAWN?!
YOU HAVE A LOT OF EXPLAINING TO DO.
I DON'T ANSWER TO YOU.

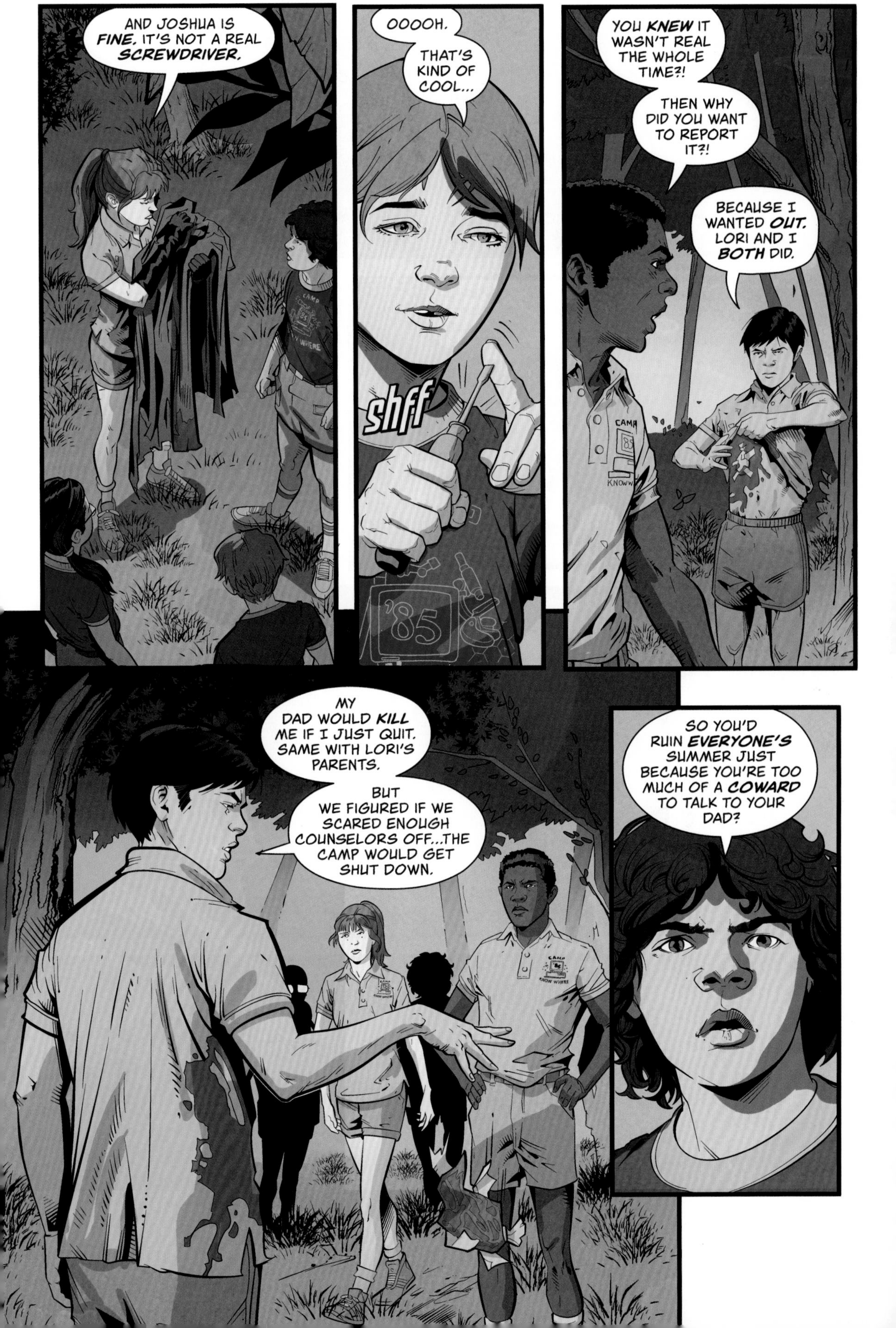

AND JOSHUA IS FINE. IT'S NOT A REAL SCREWDRIVER.
OOOOH.
THAT'S KIND OF COOL...
shff
YOU KNEW IT WASN'T REAL THE WHOLE TIME?!
THEN WHY DID YOU WANT TO REPORT IT?!
BECAUSE I WANTED OUT. LORI AND I BOTH DID.
MY DAD WOULD KILL ME IF I JUST QUIT. SAME WITH LORI'S PARENTS.
BUT WE FIGURED IF WE SCARED ENOUGH COUNSELORS OFF...THE CAMP WOULD GET SHUT DOWN.
SO YOU'D RUIN EVERYONE'S SUMMER JUST BECAUSE YOU'RE TOO MUCH OF A COWARD TO TALK TO YOUR DAD?

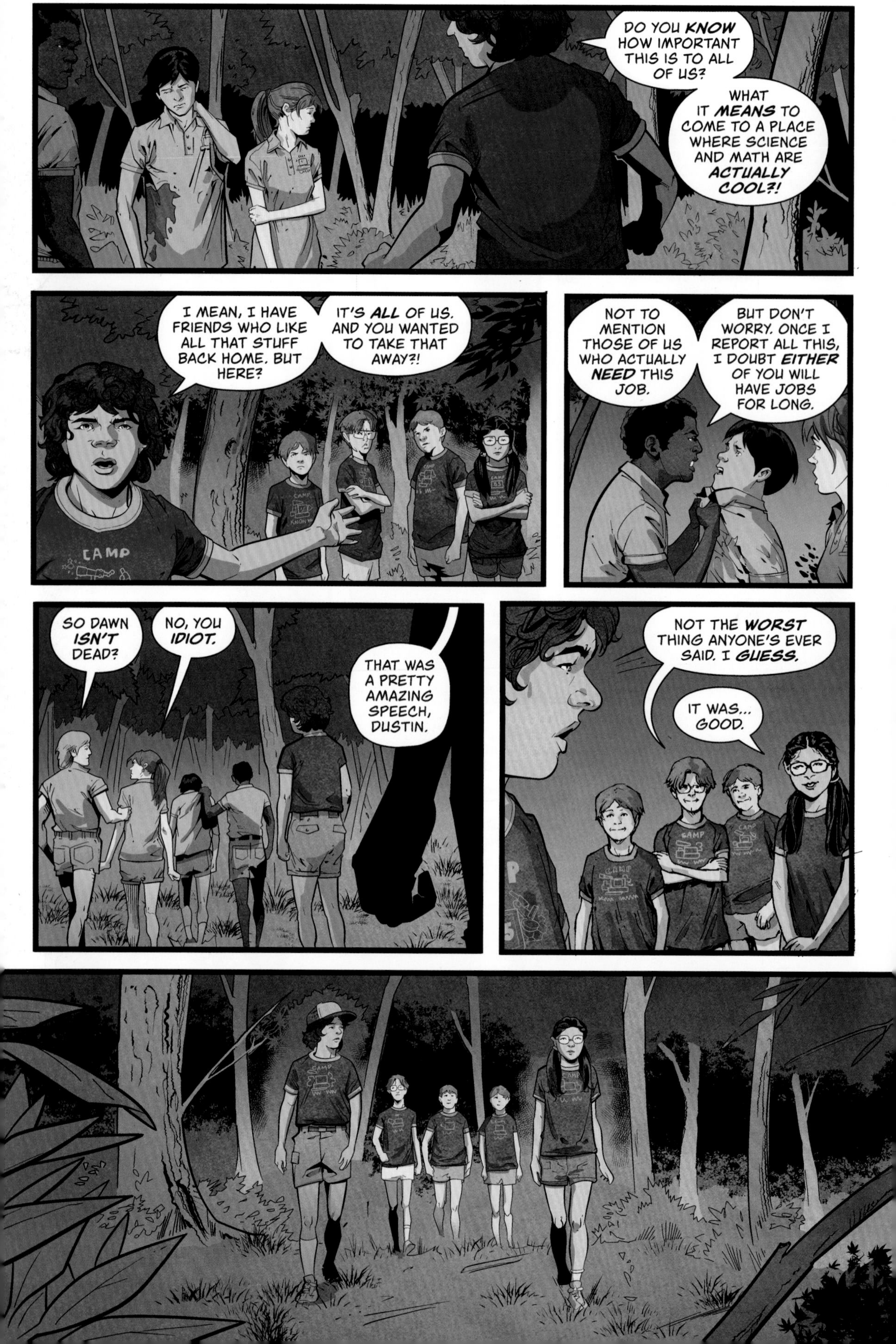
DO YOU **KNOW** HOW IMPORTANT THIS IS TO ALL OF US?
WHAT IT **MEANS** TO COME TO A PLACE WHERE SCIENCE AND MATH ARE **ACTUALLY COOL?!**
I MEAN, I HAVE FRIENDS WHO LIKE ALL THAT STUFF BACK HOME. BUT HERE?
IT'S **ALL** OF US. AND YOU WANTED TO TAKE THAT AWAY?!
NOT TO MENTION THOSE OF US WHO ACTUALLY **NEED** THIS JOB.
BUT DON'T WORRY. ONCE I REPORT ALL THIS, I DOUBT **EITHER** OF YOU WILL HAVE JOBS FOR LONG.
SO DAWN **ISN'T** DEAD?
NO, YOU **IDIOT.**
THAT WAS A PRETTY AMAZING SPEECH, DUSTIN.
NOT THE **WORST** THING ANYONE'S EVER SAID. I **GUESS.**
IT WAS... GOOD.

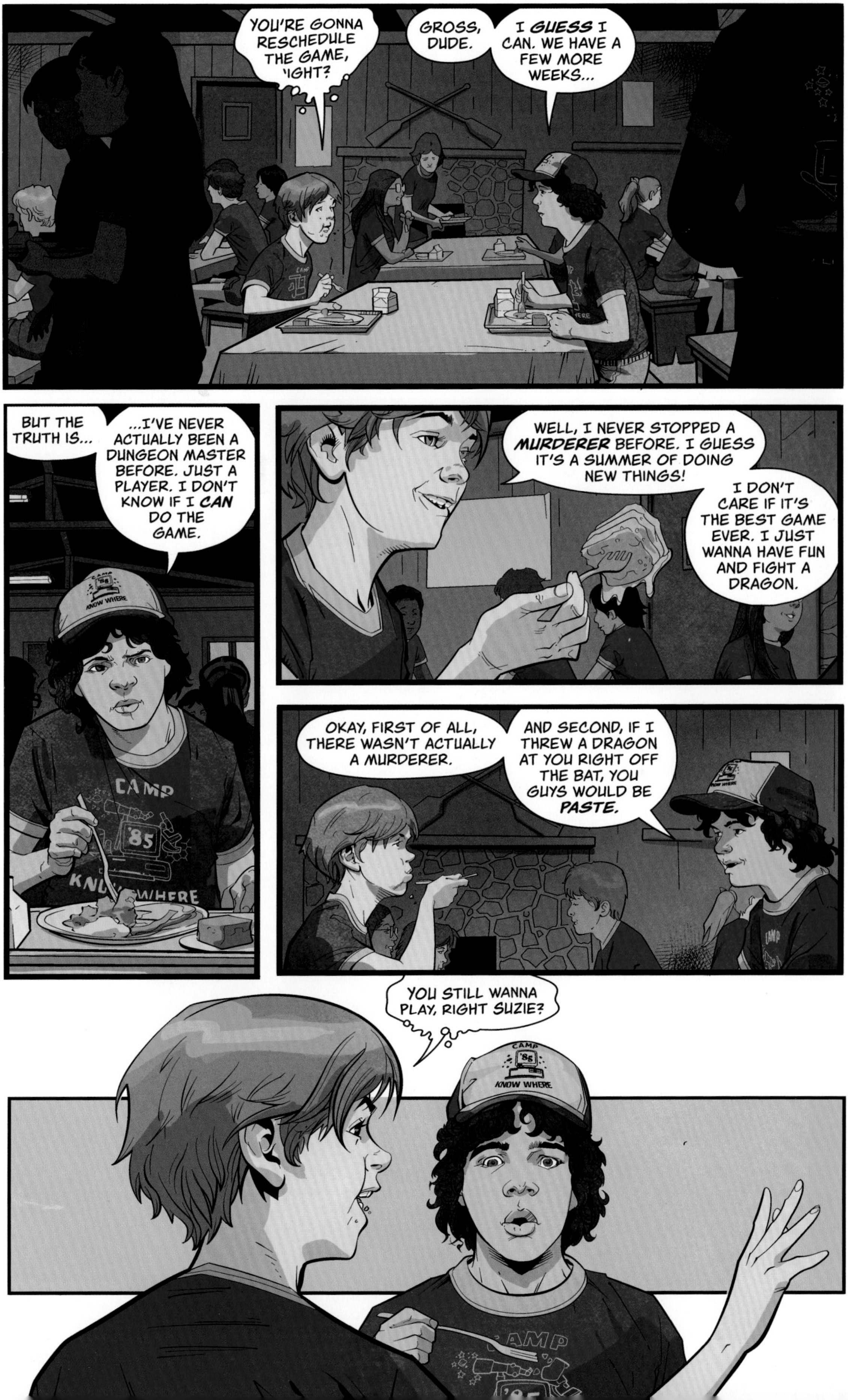
YOU'RE GONNA RESCHEDULE THE GAME, 'IGHT?
GROSS, DUDE.
I GUESS I CAN. WE HAVE A FEW MORE WEEKS...
BUT THE TRUTH IS...
...I'VE NEVER ACTUALLY BEEN A DUNGEON MASTER BEFORE. JUST A PLAYER. I DON'T KNOW IF I CAN DO THE GAME.
WELL, I NEVER STOPPED A MURDERER BEFORE. I GUESS IT'S A SUMMER OF DOING NEW THINGS!
I DON'T CARE IF IT'S THE BEST GAME EVER. I JUST WANNA HAVE FUN AND FIGHT A DRAGON.
OKAY, FIRST OF ALL, THERE WASN'T ACTUALLY A MURDERER.
AND SECOND, IF I THREW A DRAGON AT YOU RIGHT OFF THE BAT, YOU GUYS WOULD BE PASTE.
YOU STILL WANNA PLAY, RIGHT SUZIE?

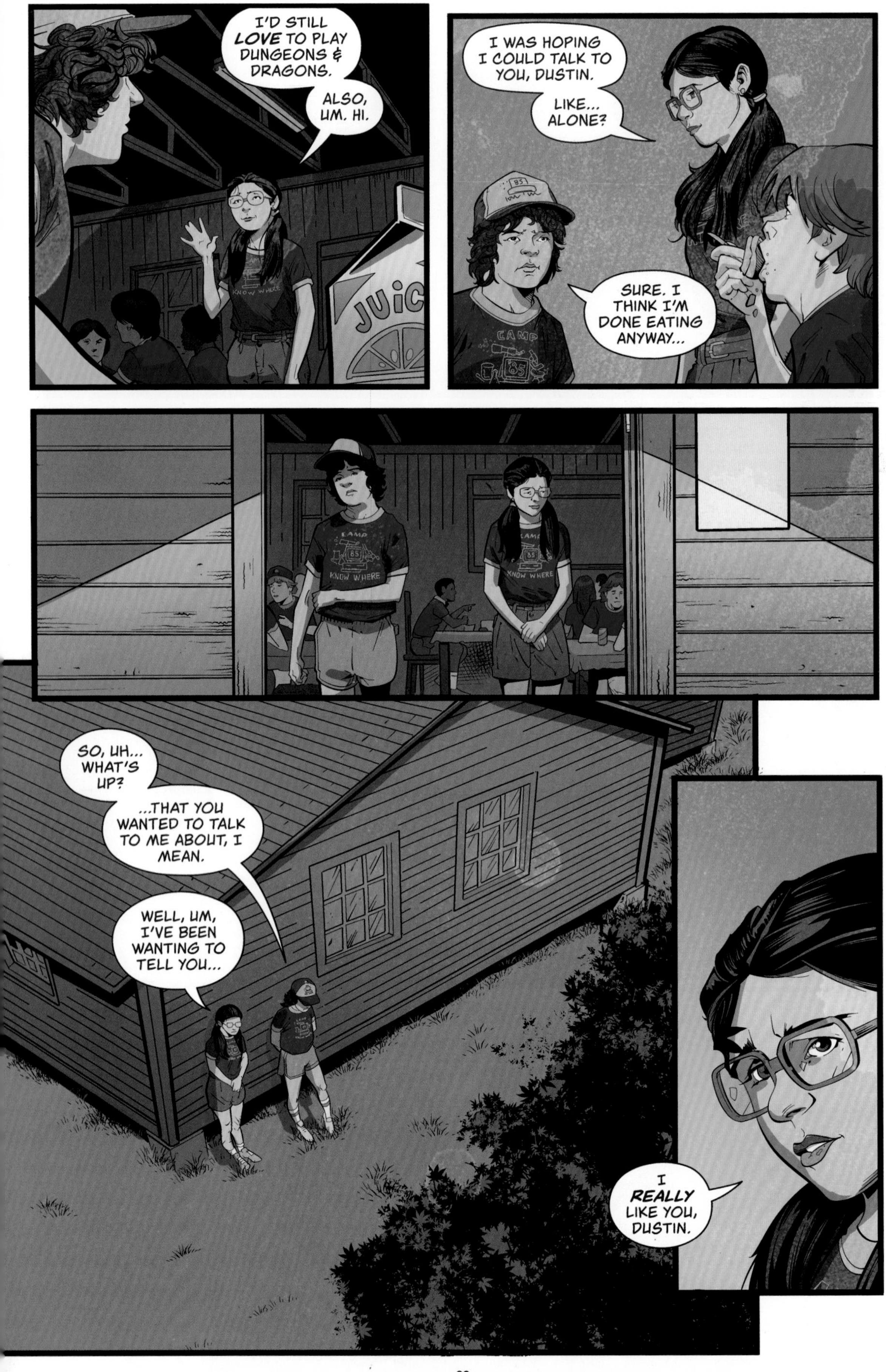
I'D STILL **LOVE** TO PLAY DUNGEONS & DRAGONS.
ALSO, UM. HI.
JUIC
I WAS HOPING I COULD TALK TO YOU, DUSTIN.
LIKE... ALONE?
SURE. I THINK I'M DONE EATING ANYWAY...
CAMP
KNOW WHERE
SO, UH... WHAT'S UP?
...THAT YOU WANTED TO TALK TO ME ABOUT, I MEAN.
WELL, UM, I'VE BEEN WANTING TO TELL YOU...
I **REALLY** LIKE YOU, DUSTIN.

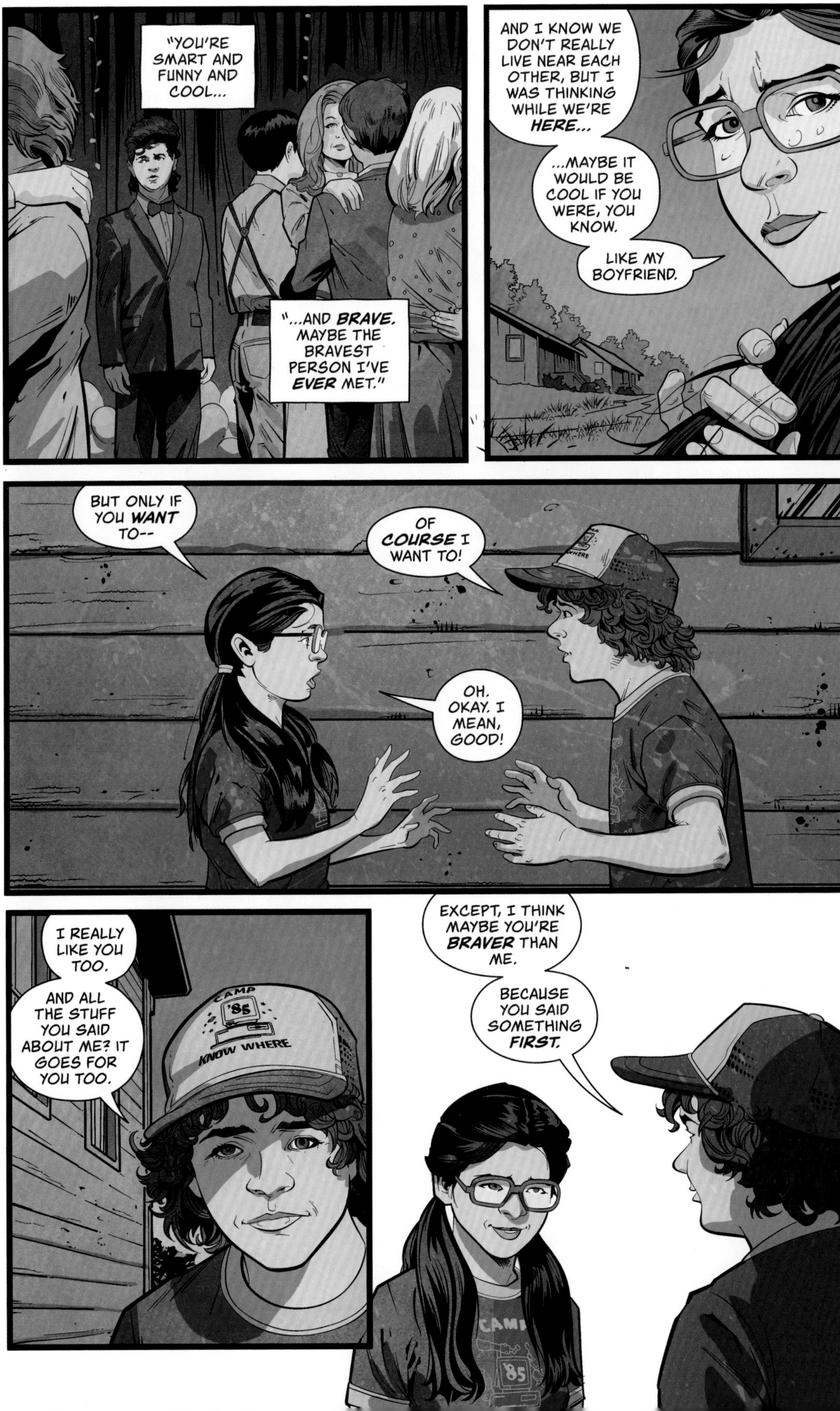
"YOU'RE SMART AND FUNNY AND COOL...
"...AND BRAVE. MAYBE THE BRAVEST PERSON I'VE EVER MET."
AND I KNOW WE DON'T REALLY LIVE NEAR EACH OTHER, BUT I WAS THINKING WHILE WE'RE HERE...
...MAYBE IT WOULD BE COOL IF YOU WERE, YOU KNOW.
LIKE MY BOYFRIEND.
BUT ONLY IF YOU WANT TO--
OF COURSE I WANT TO!
OH. OKAY. I MEAN, GOOD!
I REALLY LIKE YOU TOO.
AND ALL THE STUFF YOU SAID ABOUT ME? IT GOES FOR YOU TOO.
CAMP '85 KNOW WHERE
EXCEPT, I THINK MAYBE YOU'RE BRAVER THAN ME.
BECAUSE YOU SAID SOMETHING FIRST.

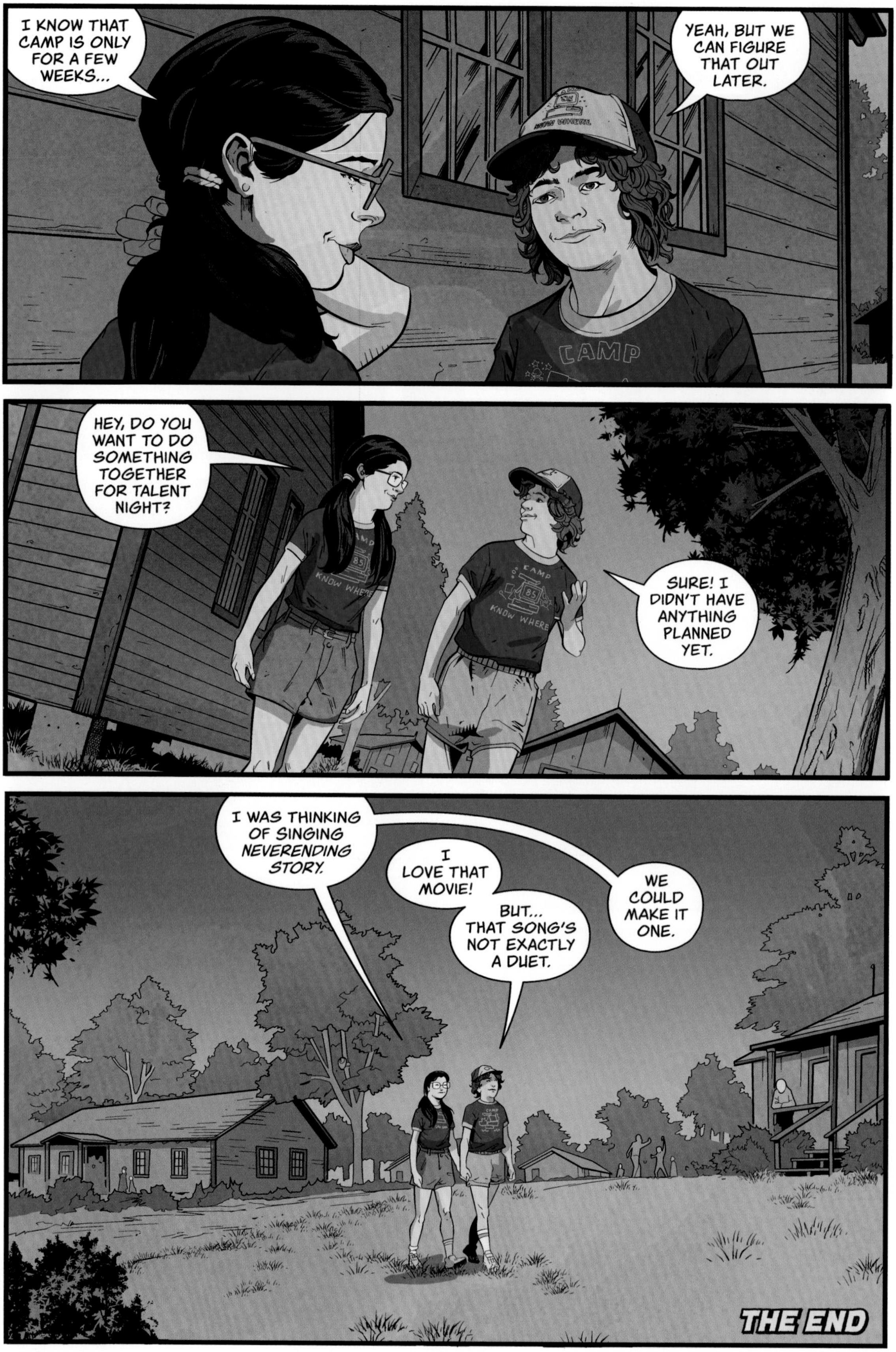
I KNOW THAT CAMP IS ONLY FOR A FEW WEEKS...
YEAH, BUT WE CAN FIGURE THAT OUT LATER.
HEY, DO YOU WANT TO DO SOMETHING TOGETHER FOR TALENT NIGHT?
SURE! I DIDN'T HAVE ANYTHING PLANNED YET.
I WAS THINKING OF SINGING NEVERENDING STORY.
I LOVE THAT MOVIE!
BUT... THAT SONG'S NOT EXACTLY A DUET.
WE COULD MAKE IT ONE.
THE END

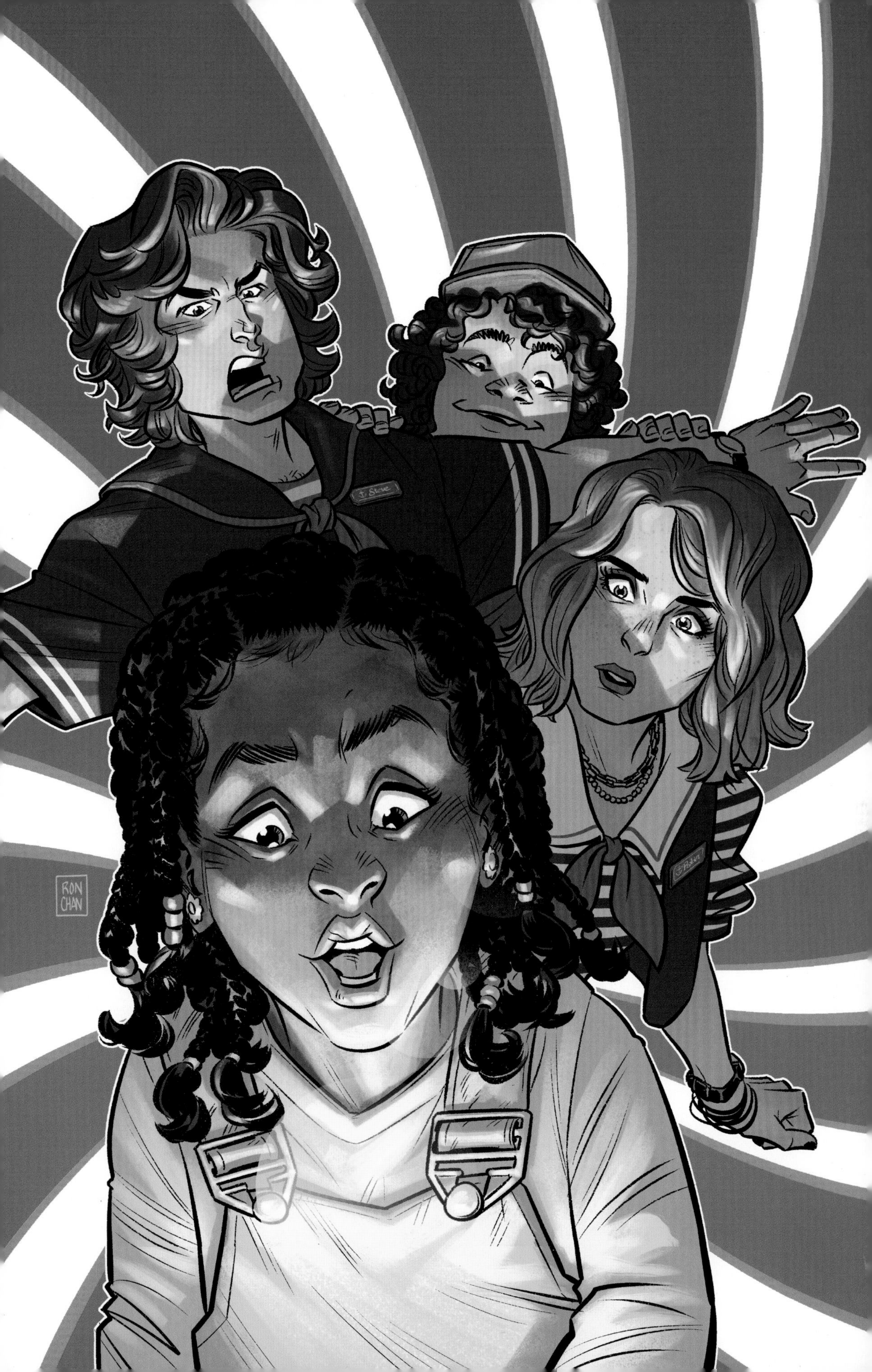
Steve
RON CHAN

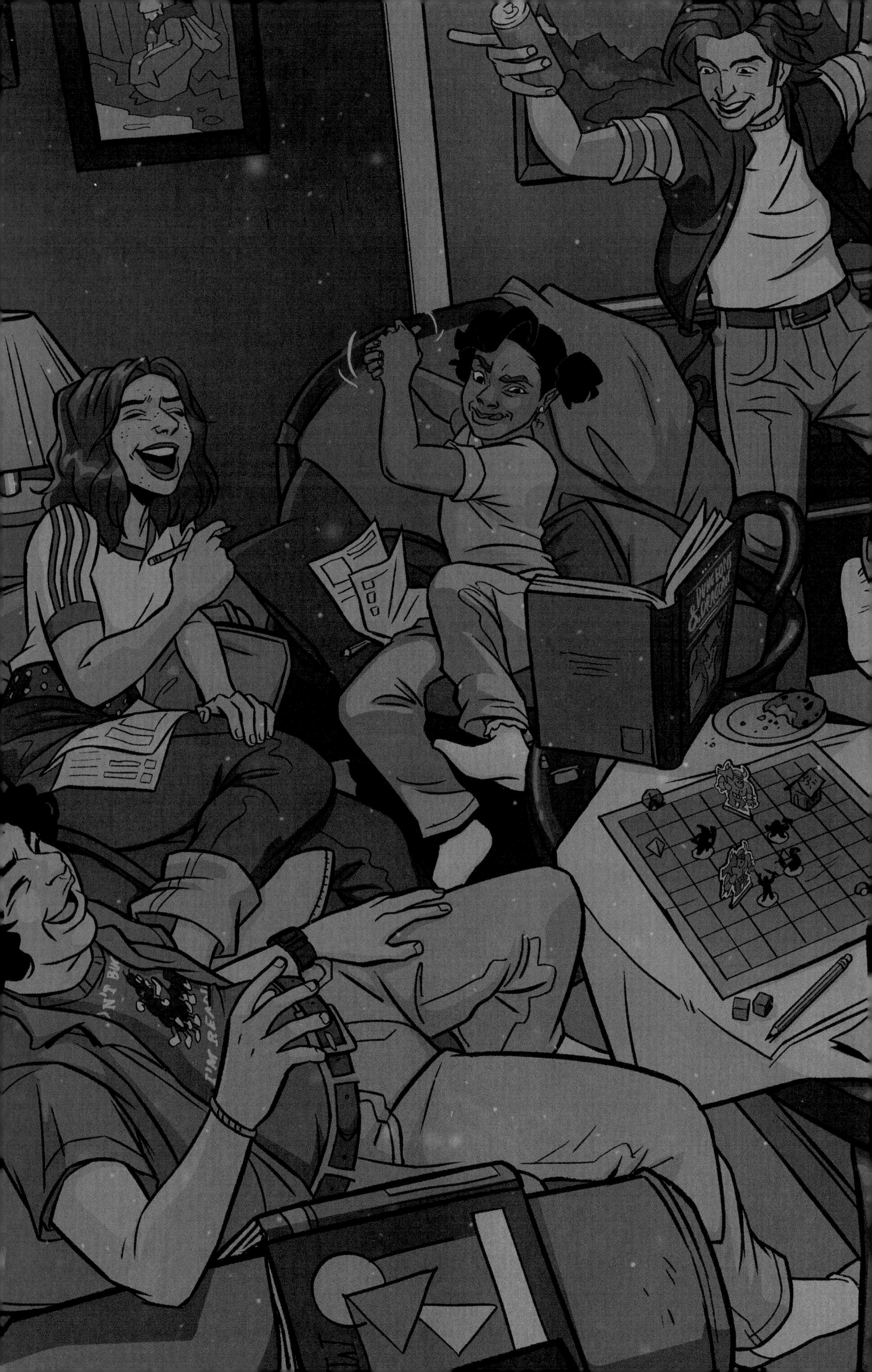

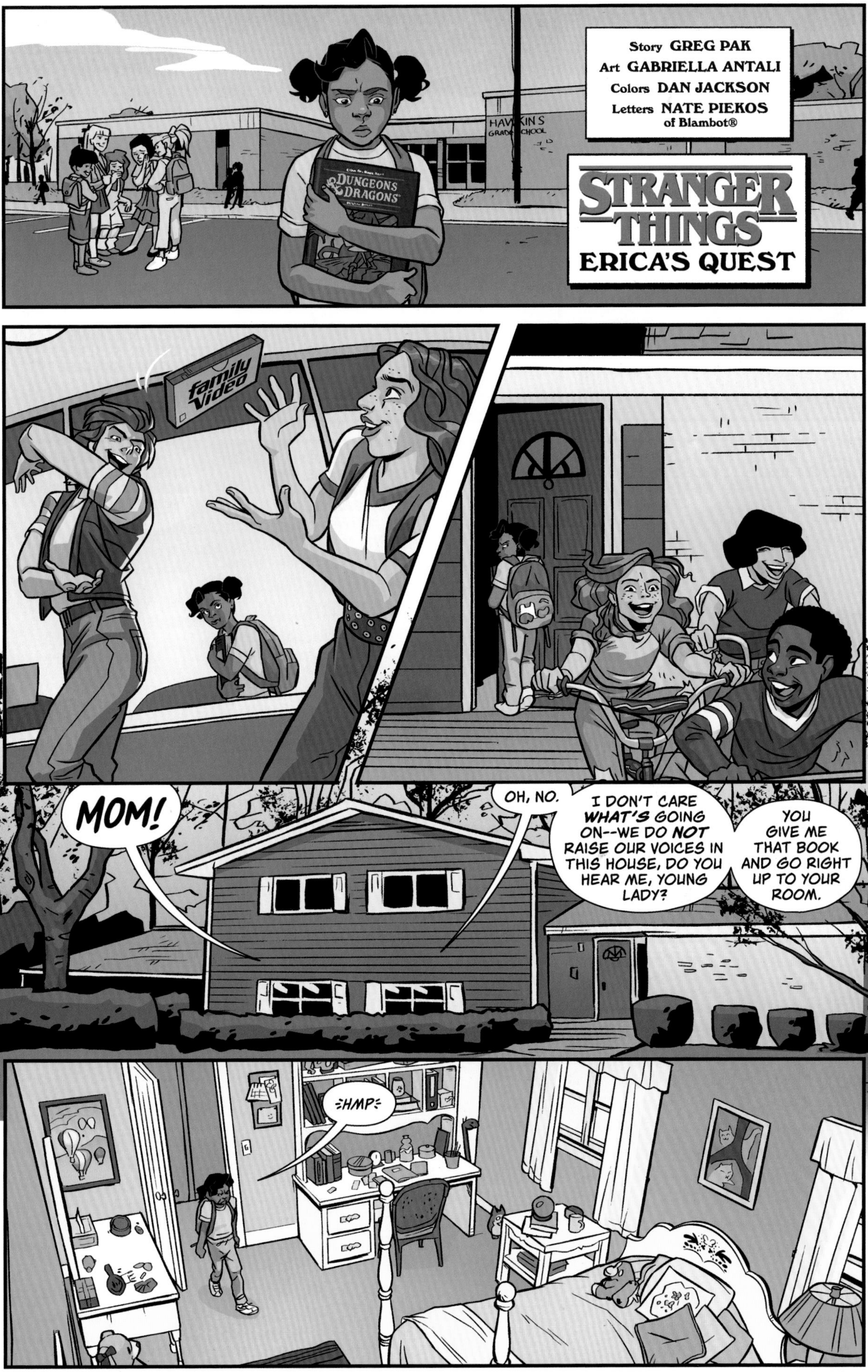

Story GREG PAK
Art GABRIELLA ANTALI
Colors DAN JACKSON
Letters NATE PIEKOS of Blambot®
STRANGER THINGS
ERICA'S QUEST
HAWKINS GRADE SCHOOL
DUNGEONS & DRAGONS
family video
MOM!
OH, NO.
I DON'T CARE WHAT'S GOING ON--WE DO NOT RAISE OUR VOICES IN THIS HOUSE, DO YOU HEAR ME, YOUNG LADY?
YOU GIVE ME THAT BOOK AND GO RIGHT UP TO YOUR ROOM.
HMP

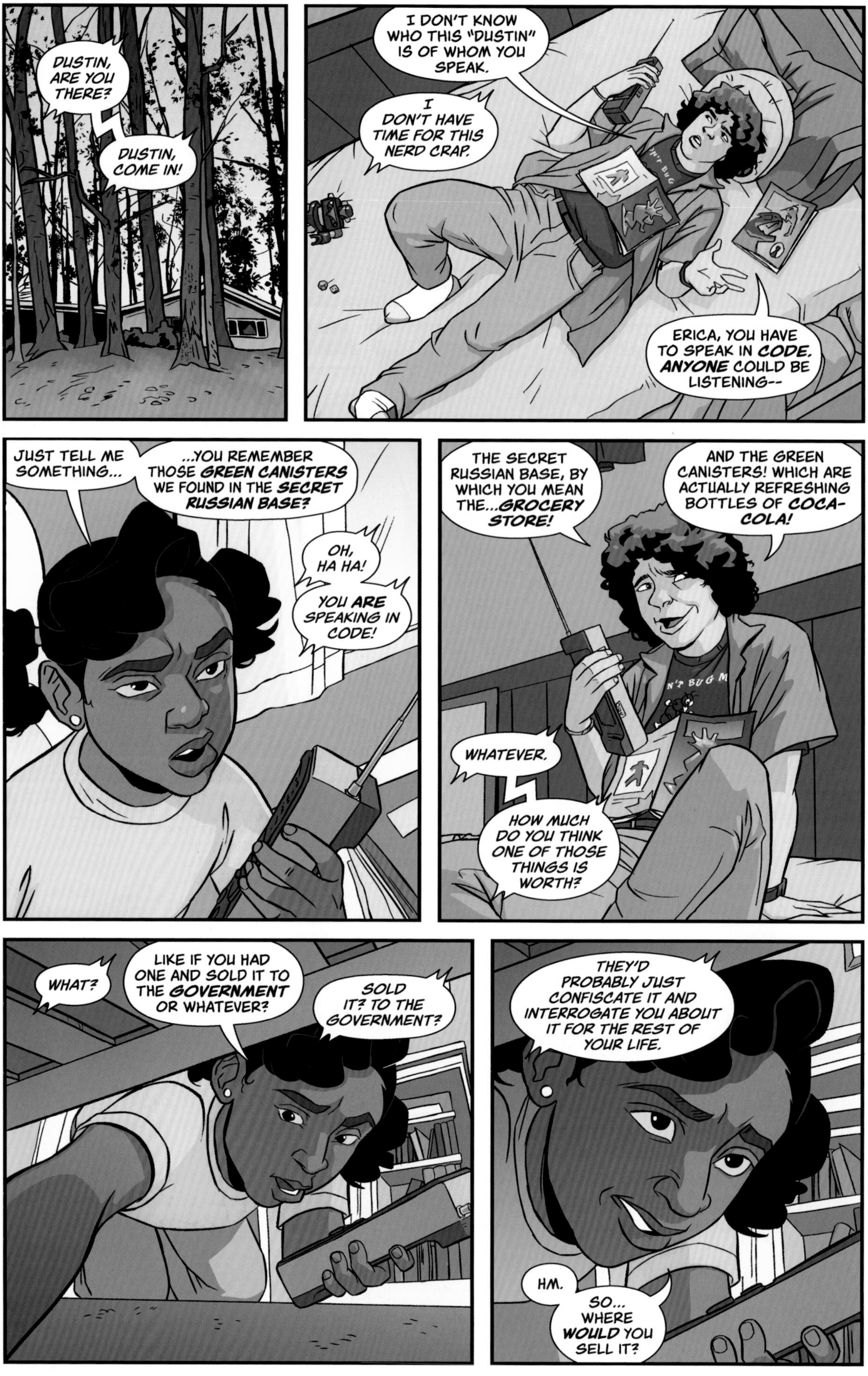
DUSTIN, ARE YOU THERE?
DUSTIN, COME IN!
I DON'T KNOW WHO THIS "DUSTIN" IS OF WHOM YOU SPEAK.
I DON'T HAVE TIME FOR THIS NERD CRAP.
ERICA, YOU HAVE TO SPEAK IN CODE. ANYONE COULD BE LISTENING--
JUST TELL ME SOMETHING...
...YOU REMEMBER THOSE GREEN CANISTERS WE FOUND IN THE SECRET RUSSIAN BASE?
OH, HA HA!
YOU ARE SPEAKING IN CODE!
THE SECRET RUSSIAN BASE, BY WHICH YOU MEAN THE...GROCERY STORE!
AND THE GREEN CANISTERS! WHICH ARE ACTUALLY REFRESHING BOTTLES OF COCA-COLA!
WHATEVER.
HOW MUCH DO YOU THINK ONE OF THOSE THINGS IS WORTH?
WHAT?
LIKE IF YOU HAD ONE AND SOLD IT TO THE GOVERNMENT OR WHATEVER?
SOLD IT? TO THE GOVERNMENT?
THEY'D PROBABLY JUST CONFISCATE IT AND INTERROGATE YOU ABOUT IT FOR THE REST OF YOUR LIFE.
HM.
SO... WHERE WOULD YOU SELL IT?

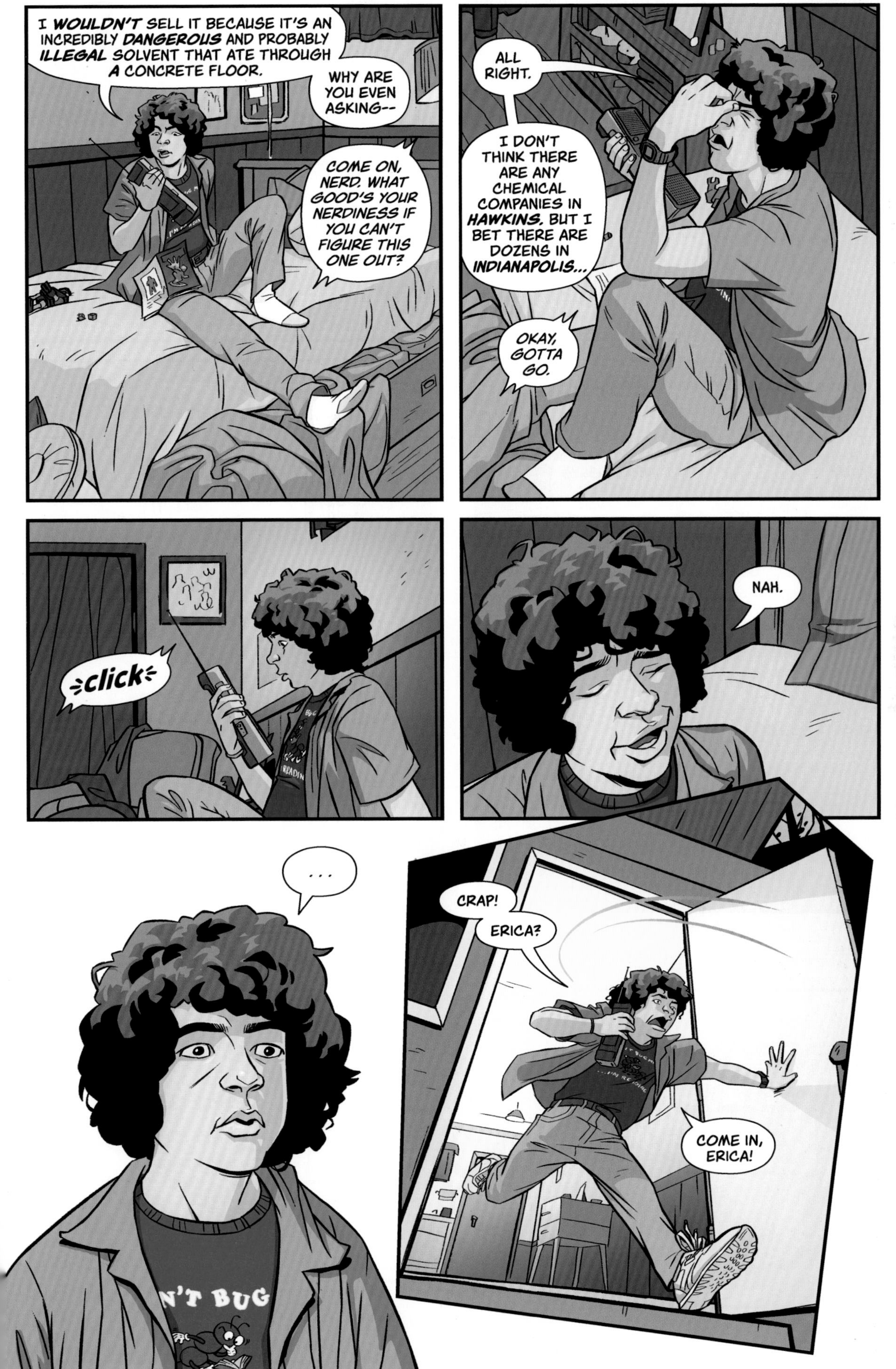
I WOULDN'T SELL IT BECAUSE IT'S AN INCREDIBLY DANGEROUS AND PROBABLY ILLEGAL SOLVENT THAT ATE THROUGH A CONCRETE FLOOR.
WHY ARE YOU EVEN ASKING--
COME ON, NERD. WHAT GOOD'S YOUR NERDINESS IF YOU CAN'T FIGURE THIS ONE OUT?
ALL RIGHT.
I DON'T THINK THERE ARE ANY CHEMICAL COMPANIES IN HAWKINS. BUT I BET THERE ARE DOZENS IN INDIANAPOLIS...
OKAY, GOTTA GO.
click
NAH.
...
CRAP!
ERICA?
COME IN, ERICA!

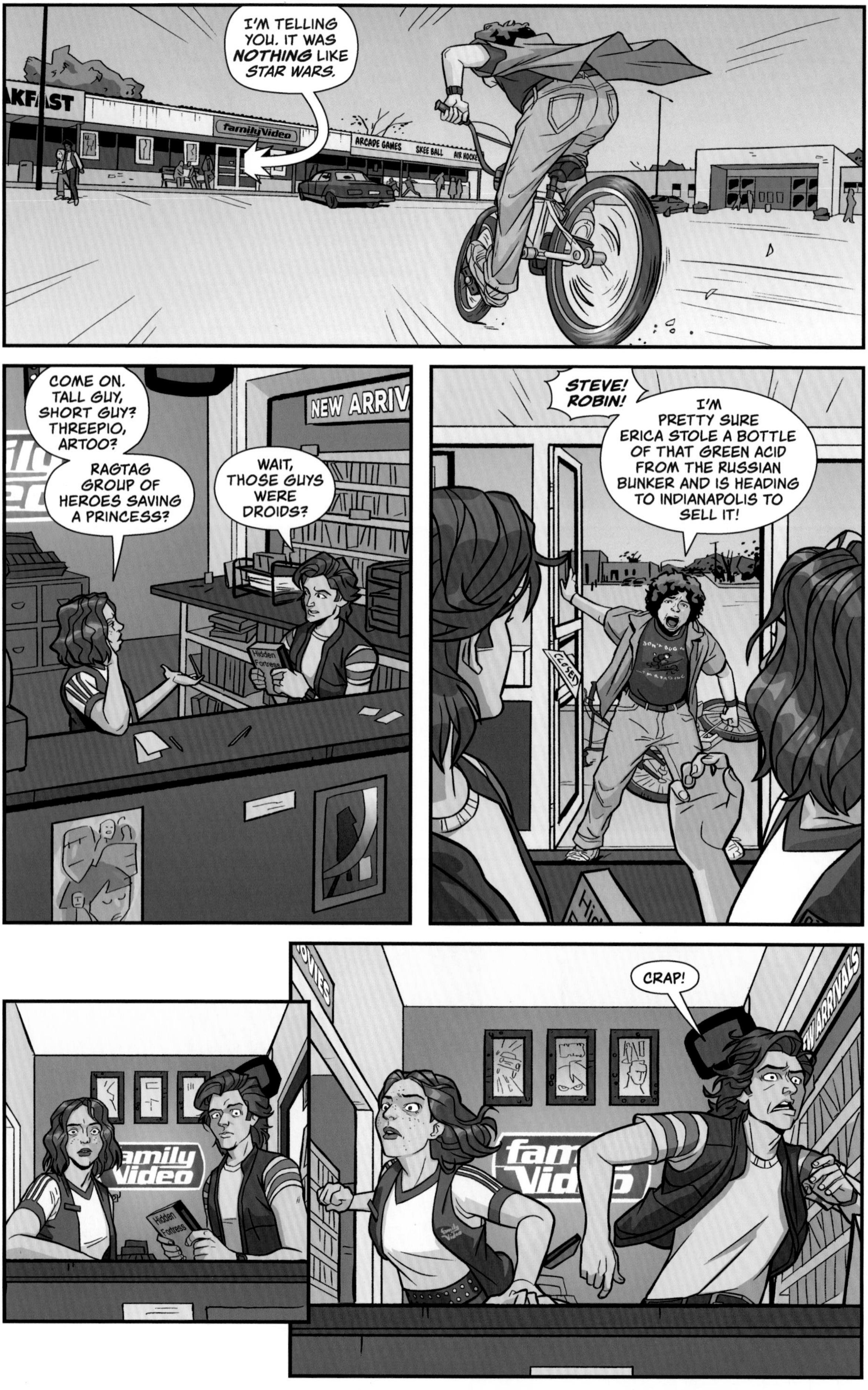
I'M TELLING YOU. IT WAS NOTHING LIKE STAR WARS.
family Video
ARCADE GAMES
SKEE BALL
COME ON. TALL GUY, SHORT GUY? THREEPIO, ARTOO?
RAGTAG GROUP OF HEROES SAVING A PRINCESS?
WAIT, THOSE GUYS WERE DROIDS?
Hidden Fortress
STEVE! ROBIN!
I'M PRETTY SURE ERICA STOLE A BOTTLE OF THAT GREEN ACID FROM THE RUSSIAN BUNKER AND IS HEADING TO INDIANAPOLIS TO SELL IT!
CLOSED
family Video
Hidden Fortress
CRAP!
family Video

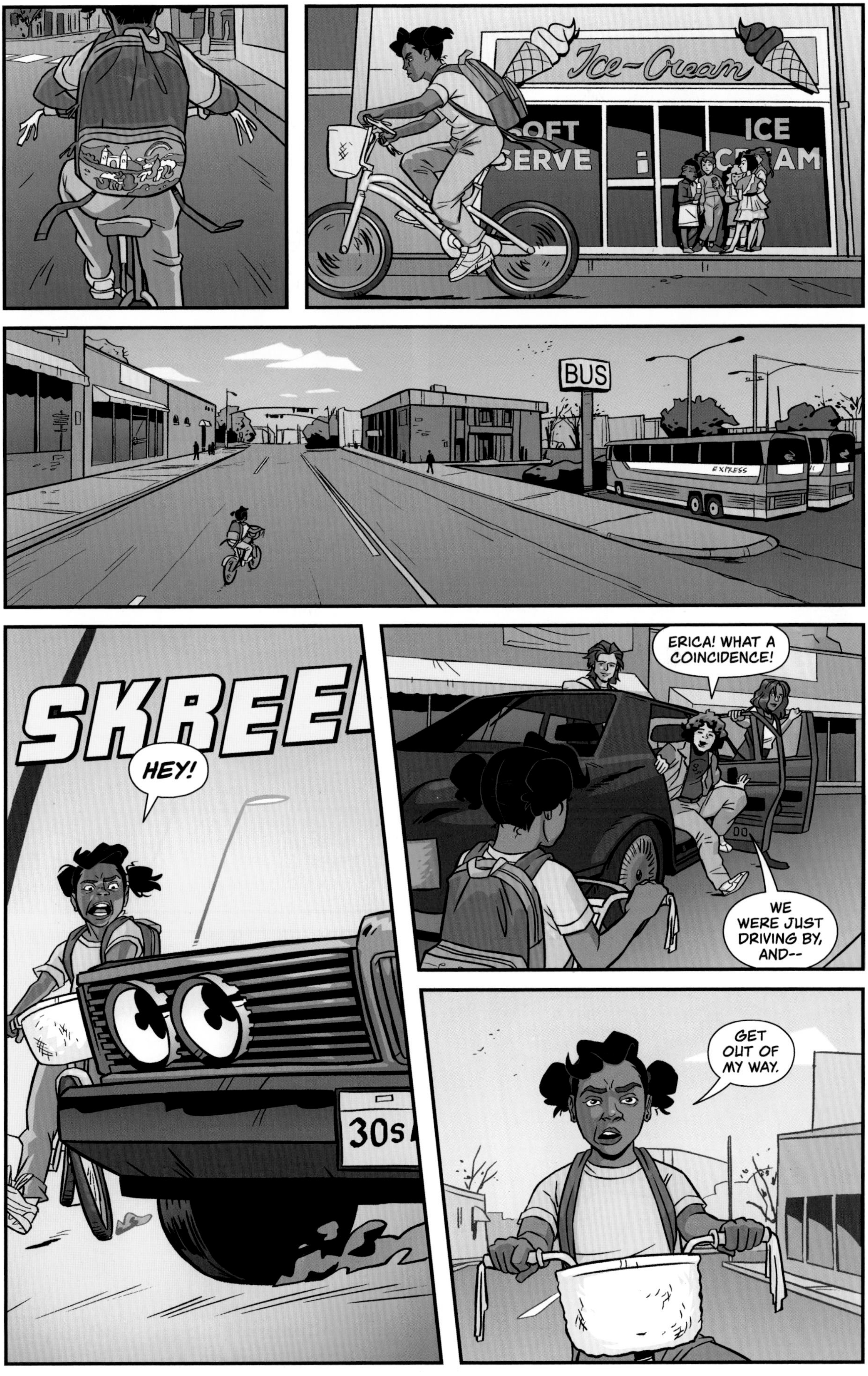
Ice-Cream
SOFT SERVE
ICE CREAM
BUS
EXPRESS
SKREE
HEY!
30S
ERICA! WHAT A COINCIDENCE!
WE WERE JUST DRIVING BY, AND--
GET OUT OF MY WAY.

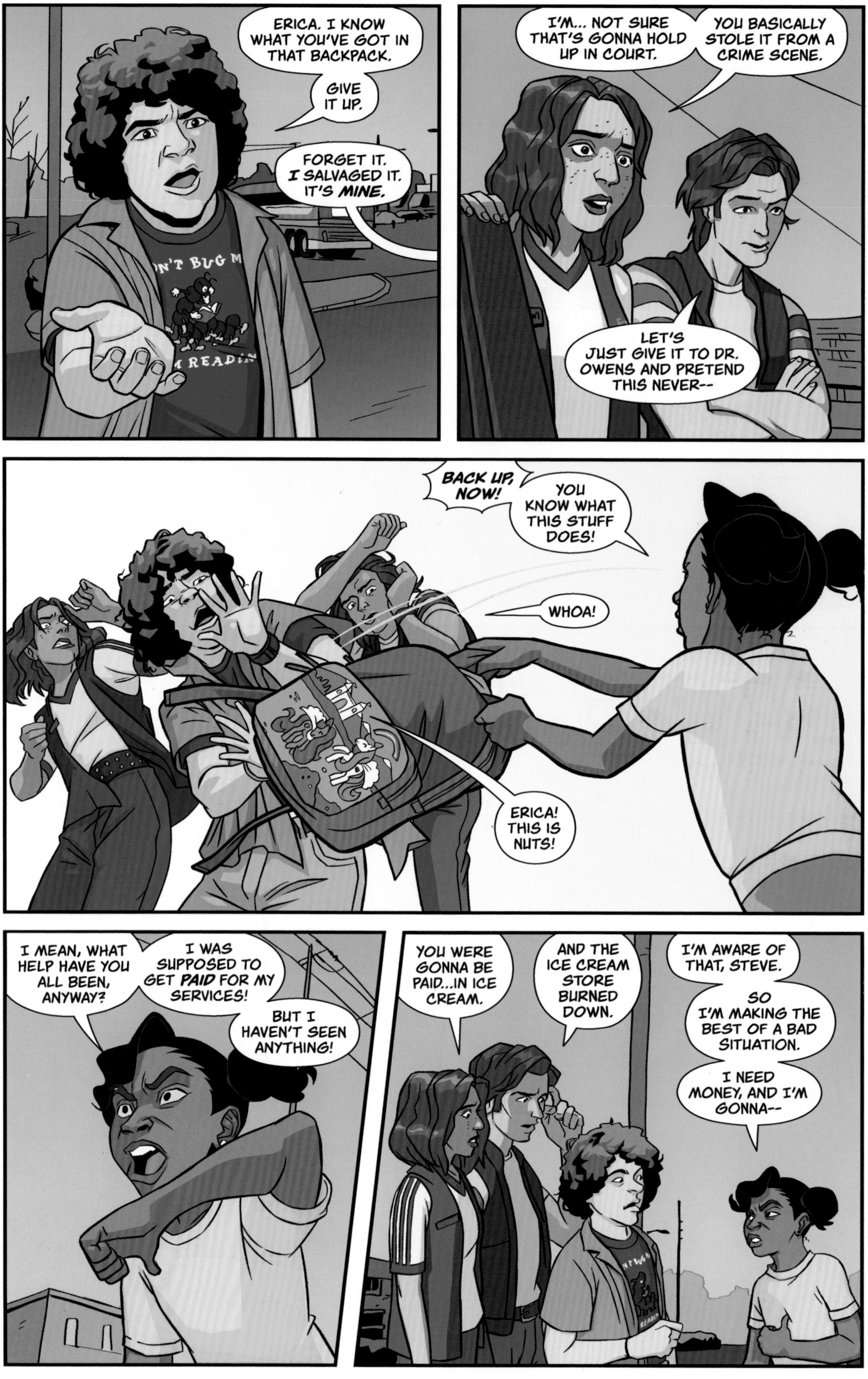
ERICA. I KNOW WHAT YOU'VE GOT IN THAT BACKPACK.
GIVE IT UP.
FORGET IT. I SALVAGED IT. IT'S MINE.
I'M... NOT SURE THAT'S GONNA HOLD UP IN COURT.
YOU BASICALLY STOLE IT FROM A CRIME SCENE.
LET'S JUST GIVE IT TO DR. OWENS AND PRETEND THIS NEVER--
BACK UP, NOW!
YOU KNOW WHAT THIS STUFF DOES!
WHOA!
ERICA! THIS IS NUTS!
I MEAN, WHAT HELP HAVE YOU ALL BEEN, ANYWAY?
I WAS SUPPOSED TO GET PAID FOR MY SERVICES!
BUT I HAVEN'T SEEN ANYTHING!
YOU WERE GONNA BE PAID...IN ICE CREAM.
AND THE ICE CREAM STORE BURNED DOWN.
I'M AWARE OF THAT, STEVE.
SO I'M MAKING THE BEST OF A BAD SITUATION.
I NEED MONEY, AND I'M GONNA--

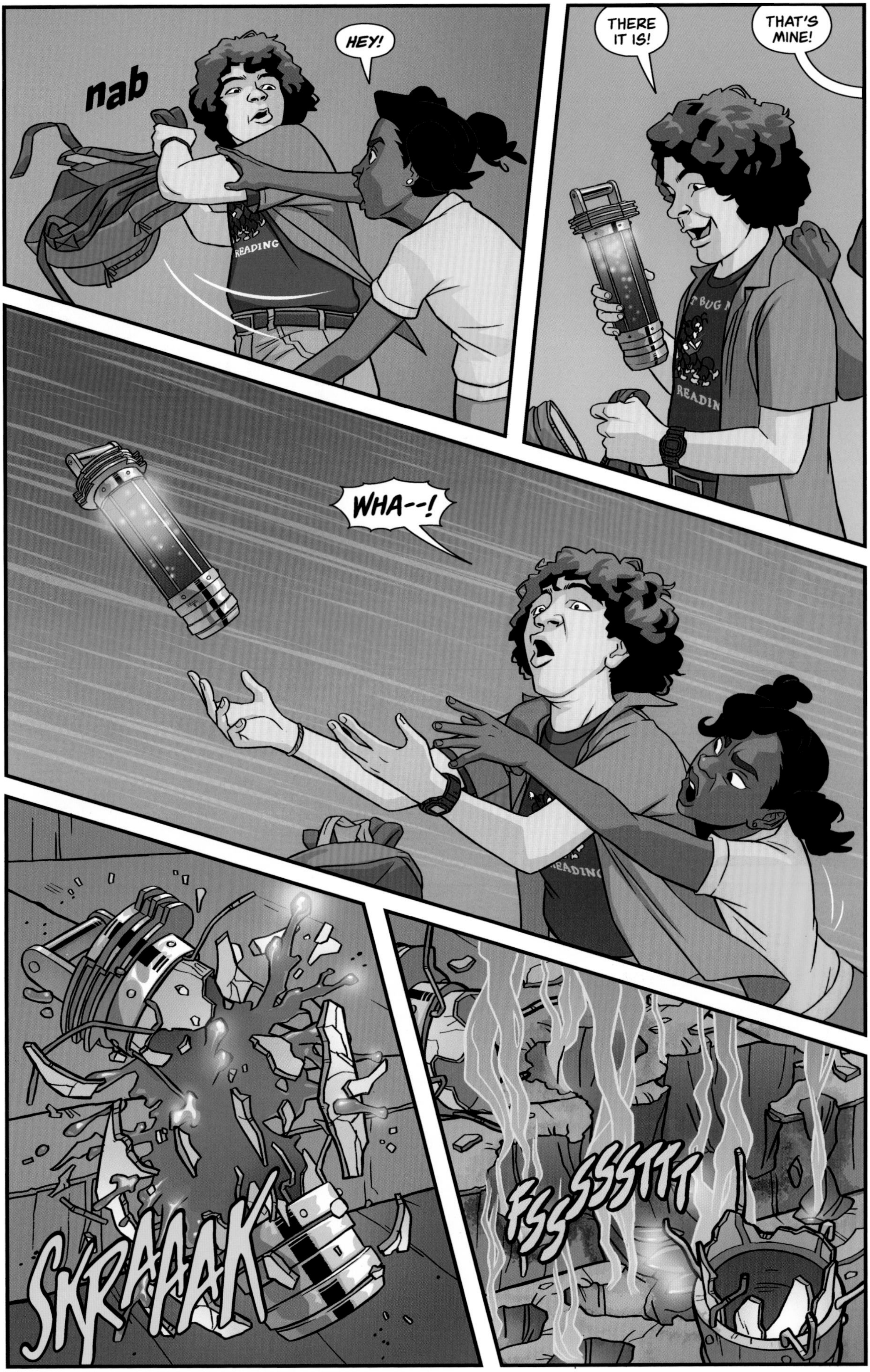
nab
HEY!
THERE IT IS!
THAT'S MINE!
WHA--!
SKRAAAK
FSSSSSSTTTT

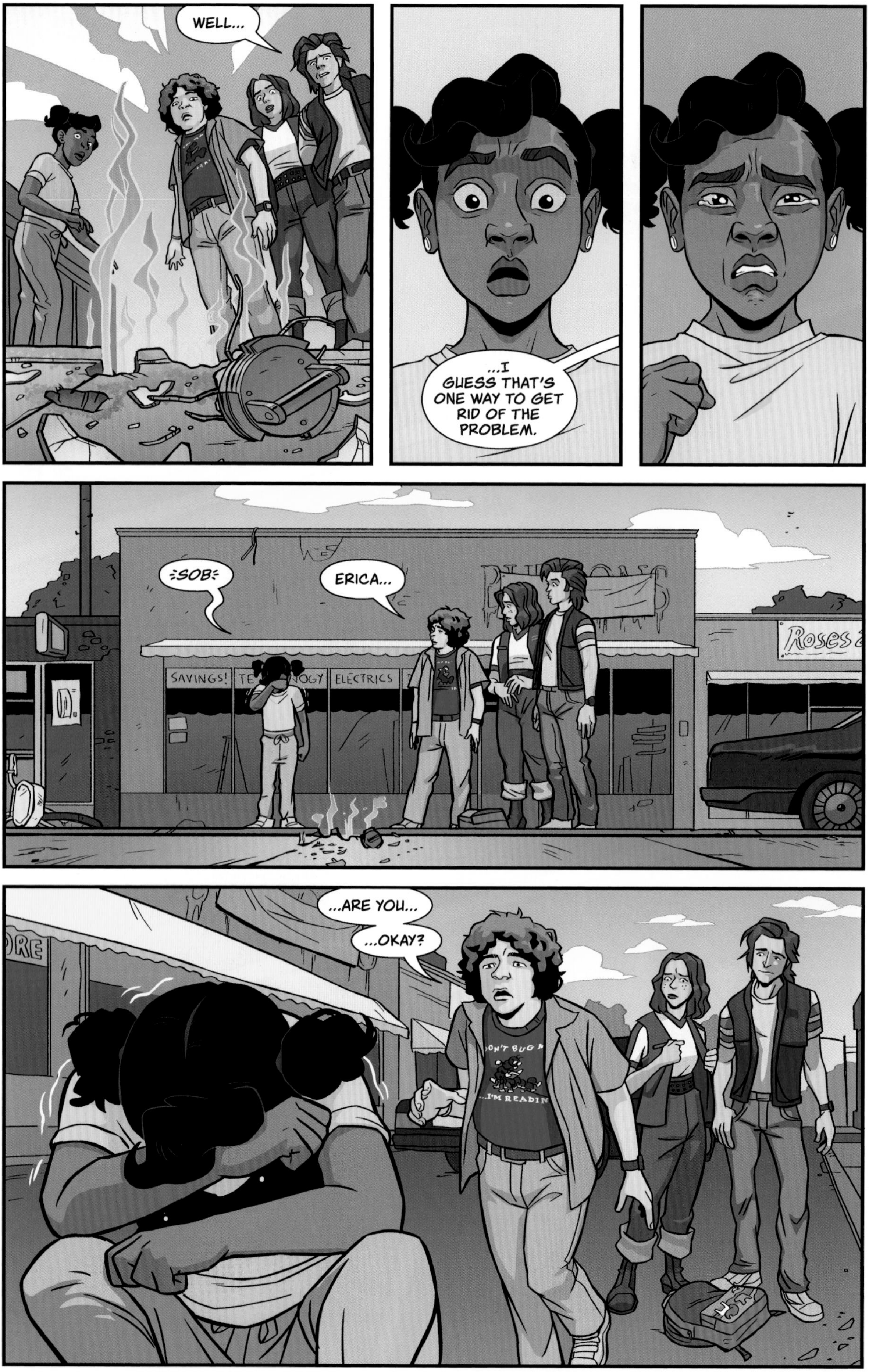
WELL...
...I GUESS THAT'S ONE WAY TO GET RID OF THE PROBLEM.
SOB
ERICA...
SAVINGS! TE NOGY ELECTRICS
Roses
...ARE YOU...
...OKAY?
DON'T BUG M
...I'M READIN

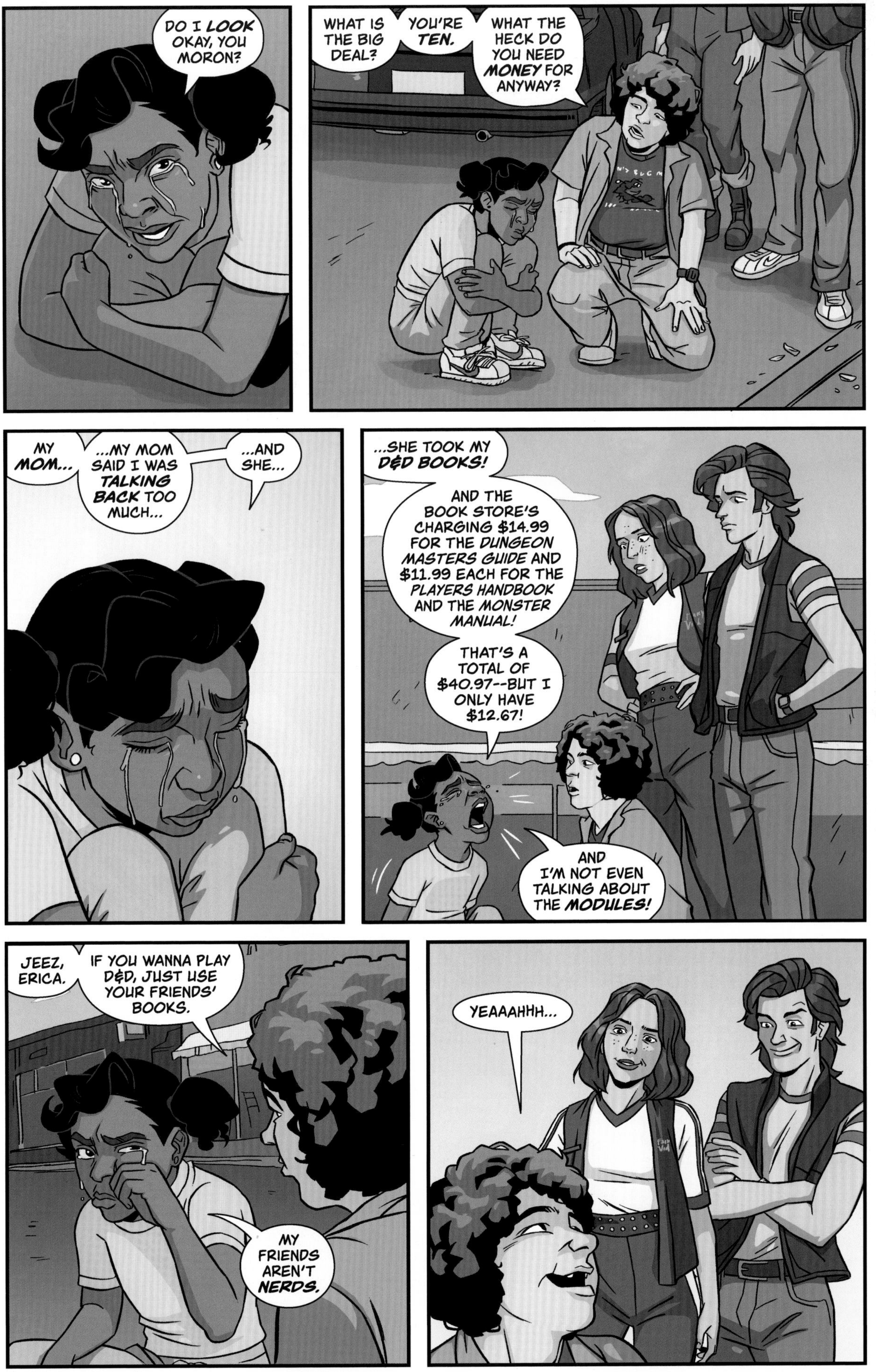
DO I LOOK OKAY, YOU MORON?
WHAT IS THE BIG DEAL?
YOU'RE TEN.
WHAT THE HECK DO YOU NEED MONEY FOR ANYWAY?
MY MOM...
...MY MOM SAID I WAS TALKING BACK TOO MUCH...
...AND SHE...
...SHE TOOK MY D&D BOOKS!
AND THE BOOK STORE'S CHARGING $14.99 FOR THE DUNGEON MASTERS GUIDE AND $11.99 EACH FOR THE PLAYERS HANDBOOK AND THE MONSTER MANUAL!
THAT'S A TOTAL OF $40.97--BUT I ONLY HAVE $12.67!
AND I'M NOT EVEN TALKING ABOUT THE MODULES!
JEEZ, ERICA.
IF YOU WANNA PLAY D&D, JUST USE YOUR FRIENDS' BOOKS.
MY FRIENDS AREN'T NERDS.
YEAAAHHH...

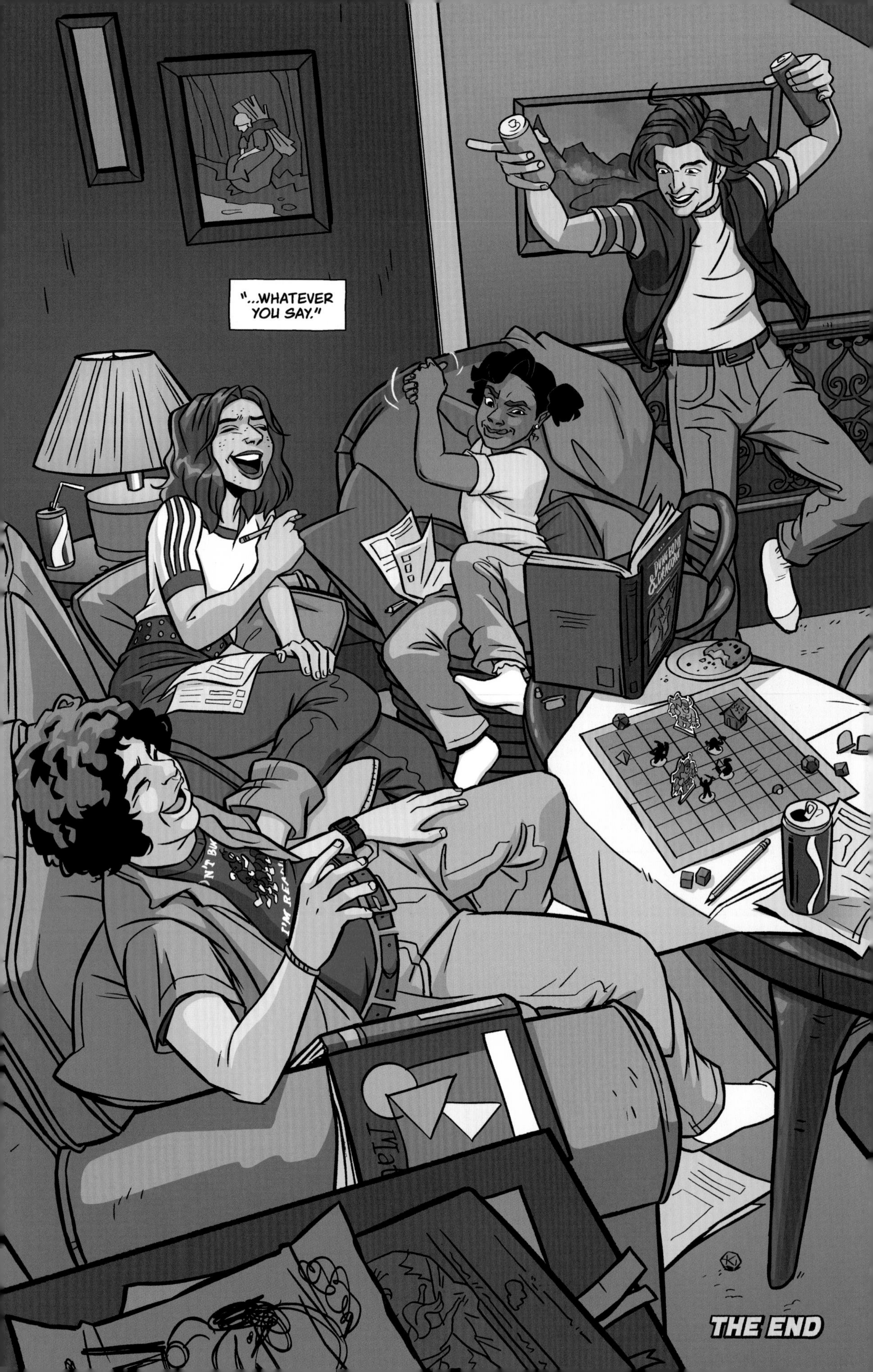
"...WHATEVER YOU SAY."
THE END

Art by FRANCISCO RUIZ

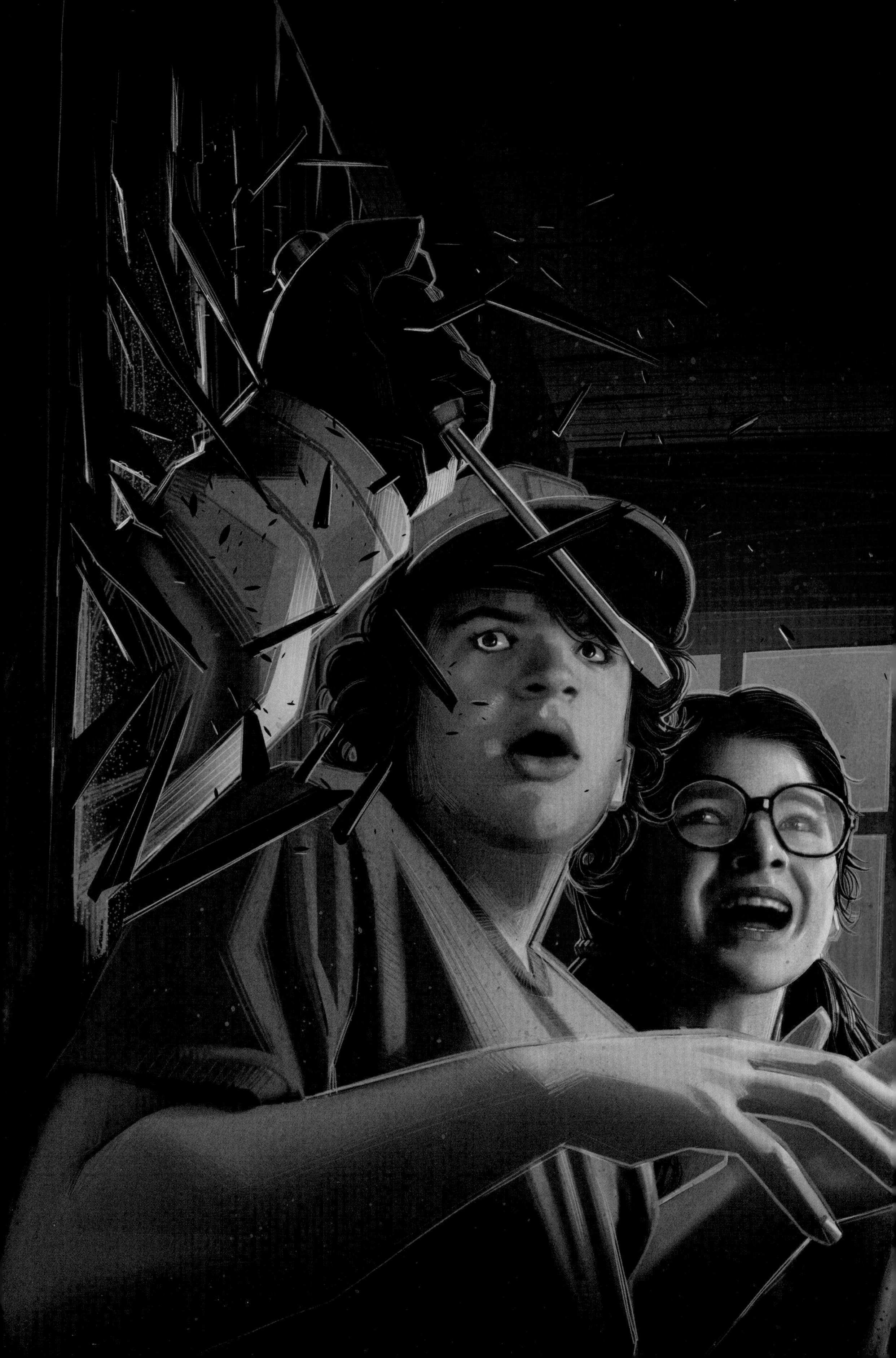

Art by TULA LOTAY

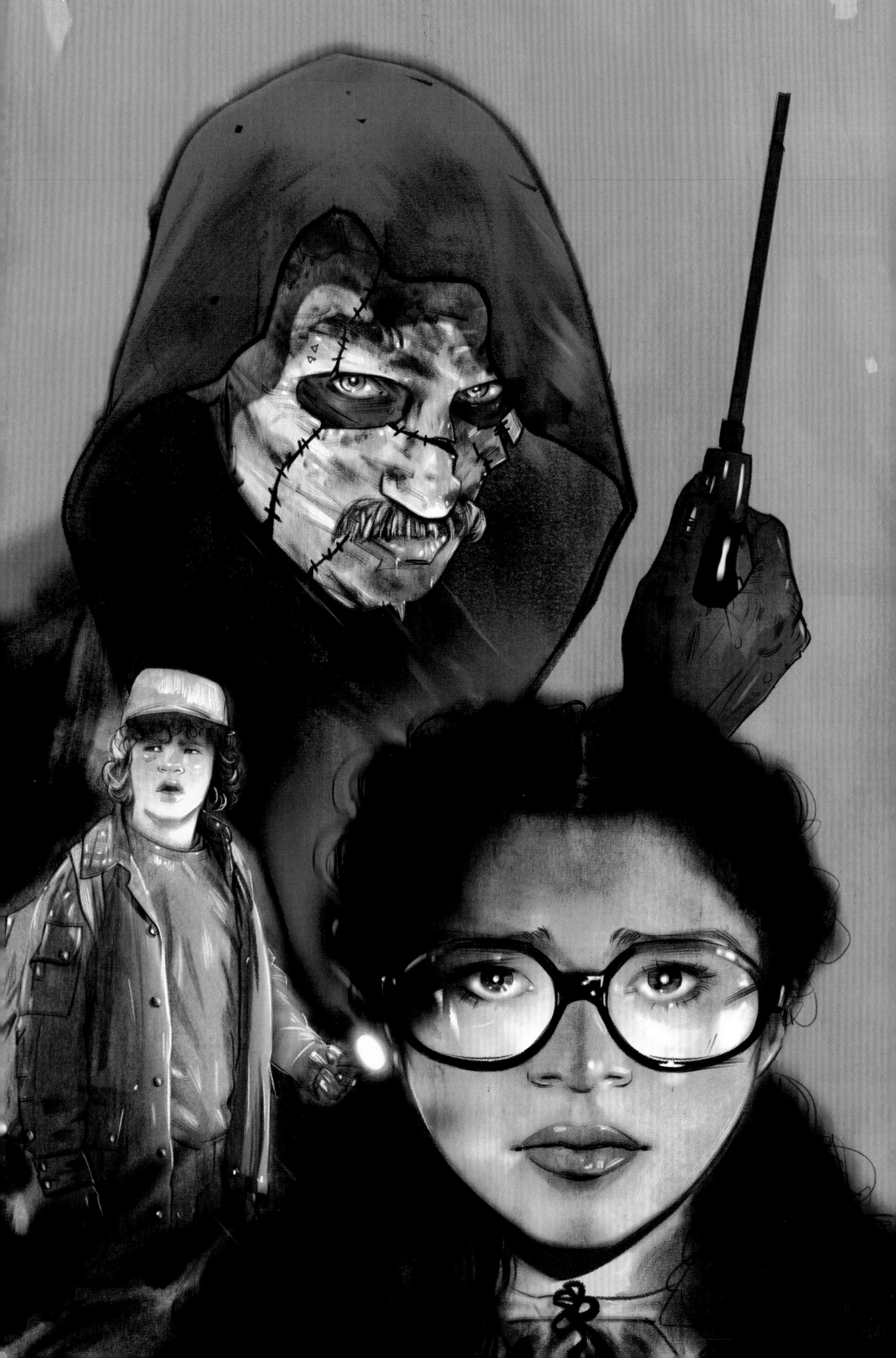

Art by ERIC NGUYEN

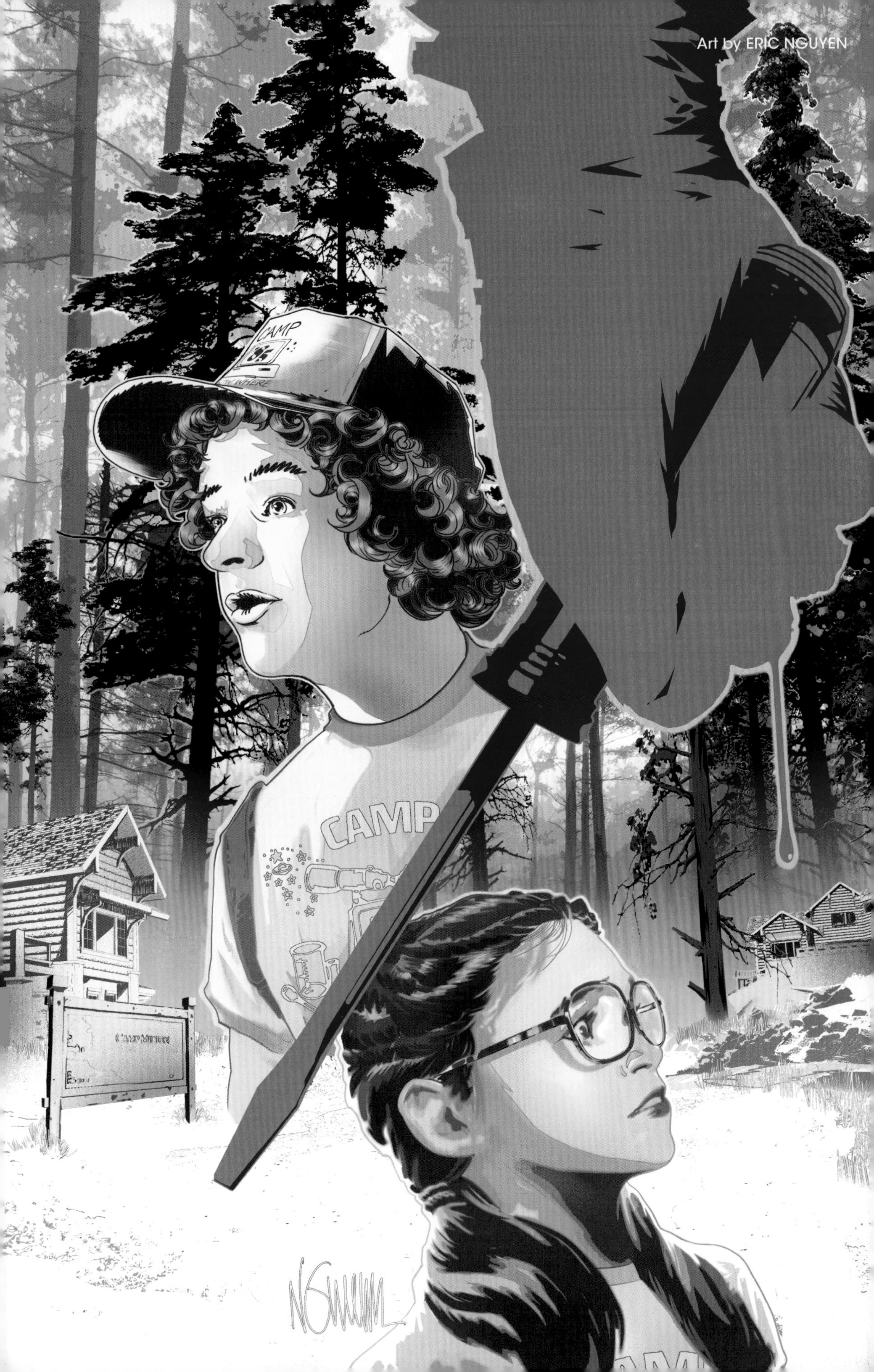
CAMP
CAMP

Art by RAUL ALLEN

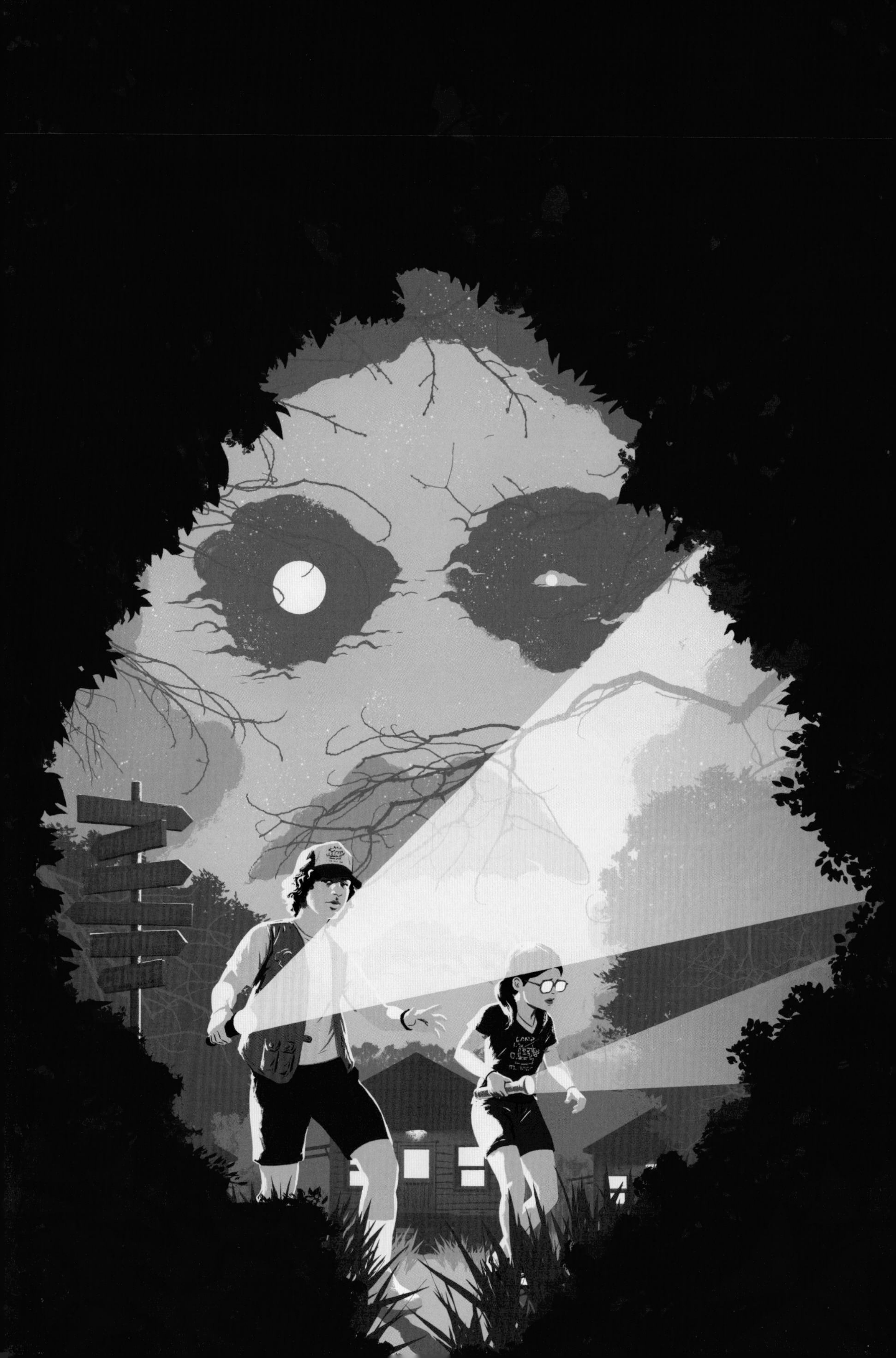

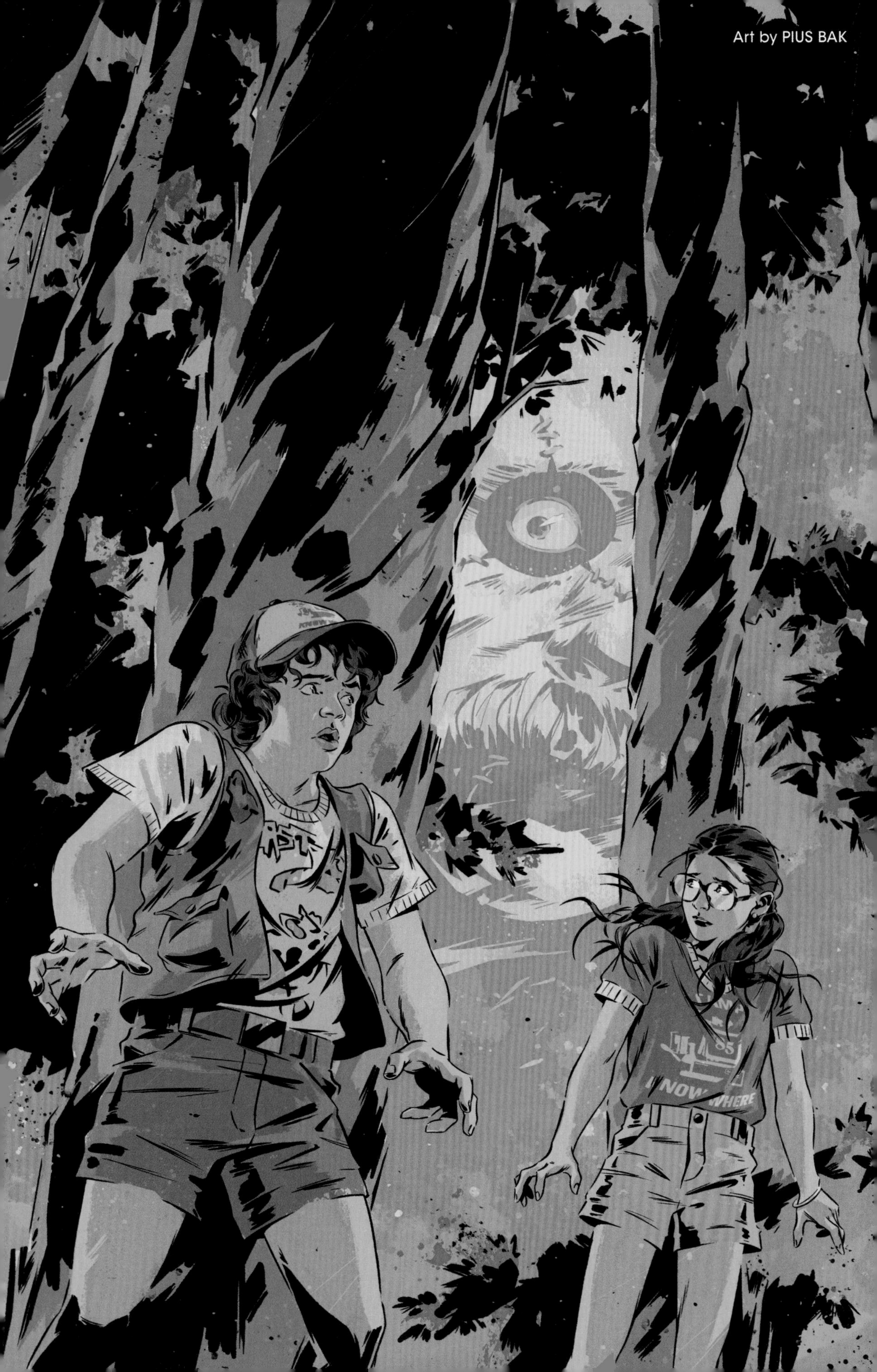

Art by PIUS BAK

Art by SEBASTIAN PIRIZ

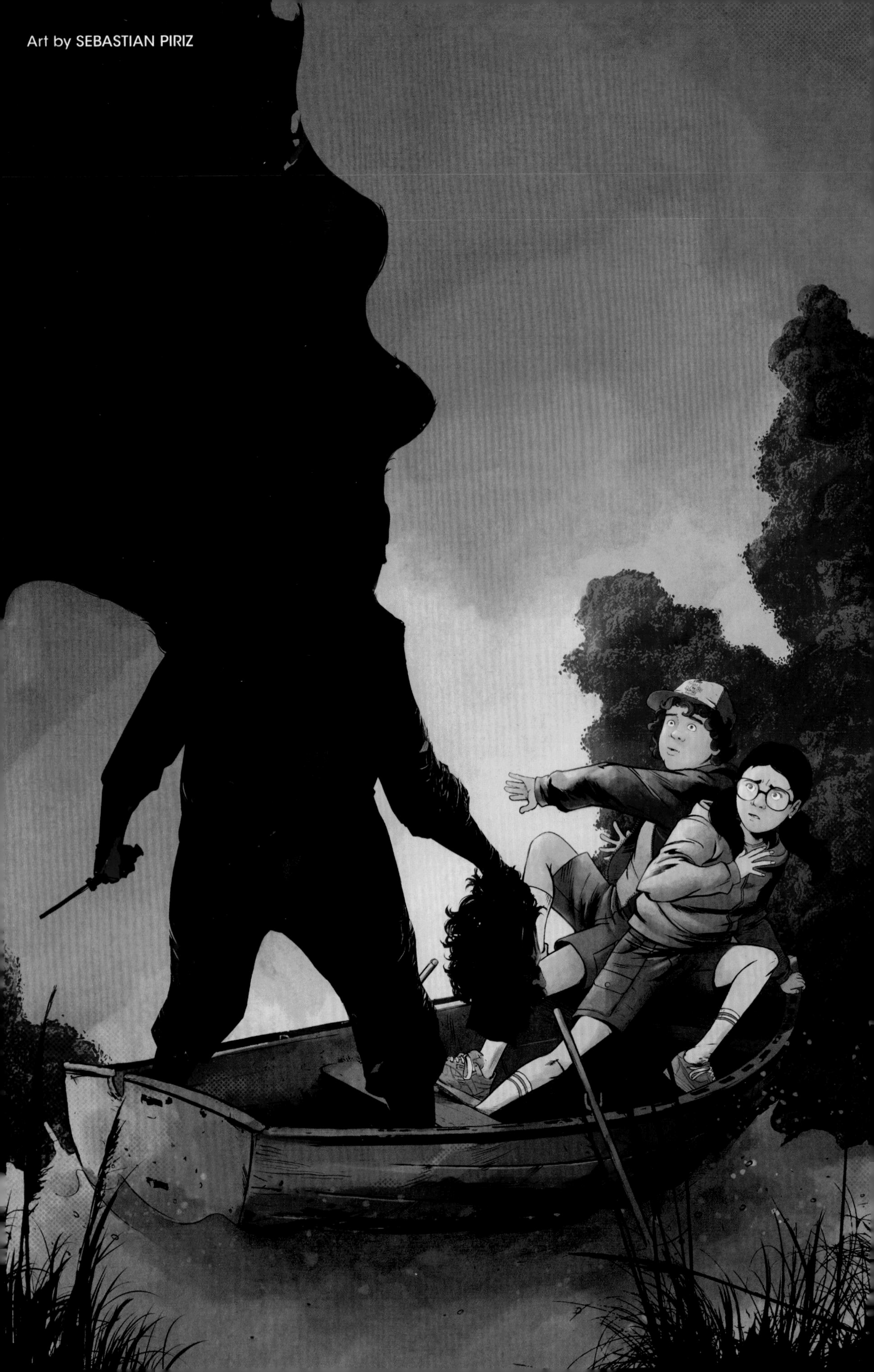

Art by PIUS BAK

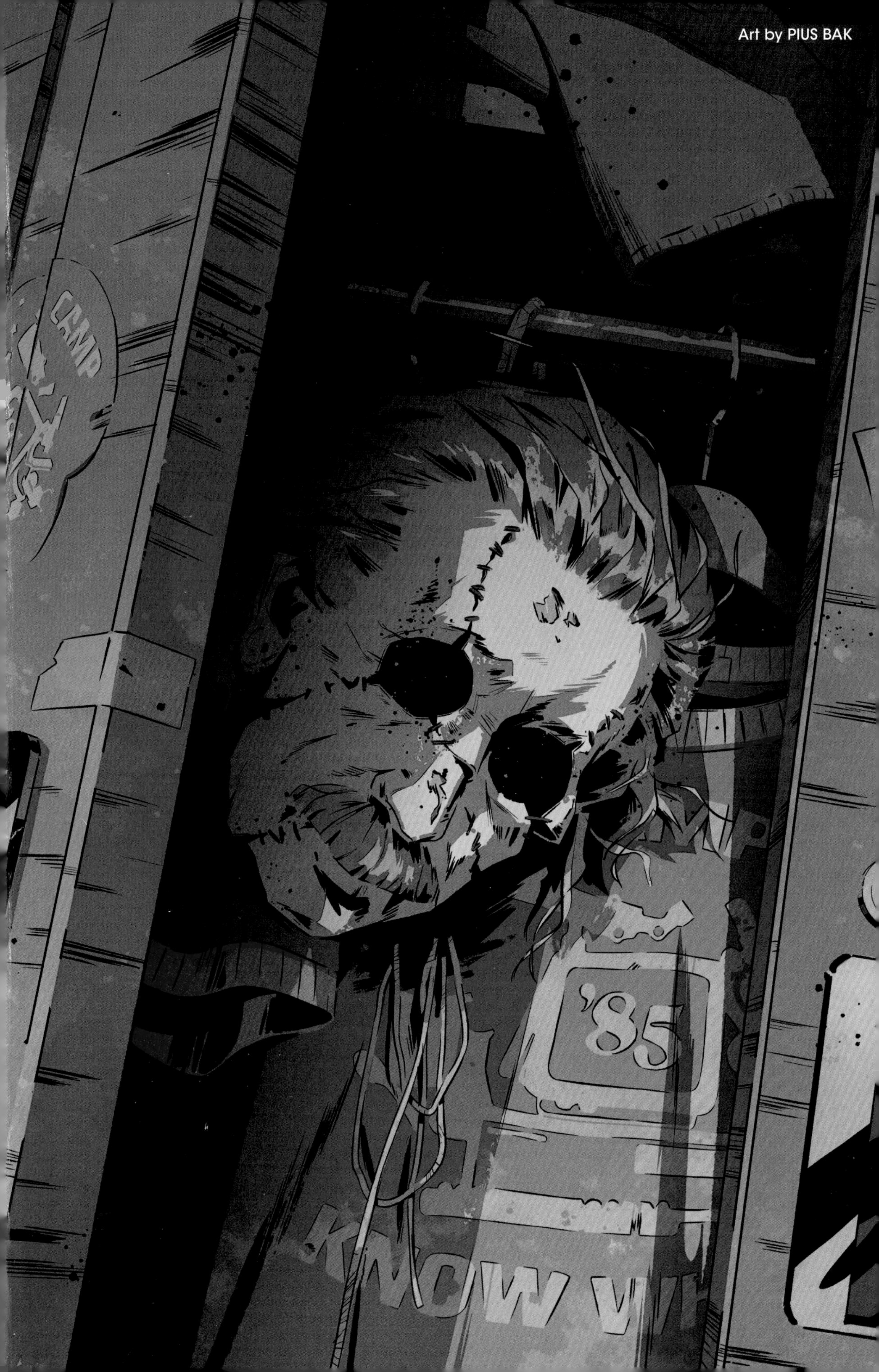
CAMP
'85
KNOW WI

STRANGER THINGS

THE NOSTALGIA-IGNITING HIT NETFLIX ORIGINAL SERIES COMES TO COMICS!

STRANGER THINGS VOLUME 1: THE OTHER SIDE
Jody Houser, Stefano Martino, Keith Champagne, Lauren Affe
ISBN 978-1-50670-976-5 • $19.99

STRANGER THINGS VOLUME 2: SIX
Jody Houser, Edgar Salazar, Keith Champagne, Marissa Louise
ISBN 978-1-50671-232-1 • $17.99

STRANGER THINGS VOLUME 3: INTO THE FIRE
Jody Houser, Ryan Kelly, Le Beau Underwood, Triona Farrell
ISBN 978-1-50671-308-3 • $19.99

STRANGER THINGS VOLUME 4: SCIENCE CAMP
Jody Houser, Edgar Salazar, Keith Champagne, Marissa Louise
ISBN 978-1-50671-576-6 • $19.99

STRANGER THINGS VOLUME 5: THE TOMB OF YBWEN
Greg Pak, Diego Galindo, Francesco Segala
ISBN 978-1-50672-554-3 • $19.99

STRANGER THINGS AND DUNGEONS & DRAGONS
Jody Houser, Jim Zub, Diego Gallindo, MsassyK
ISBN 978-1-50672-107-1 • $19.99

STRANGER THINGS: ZOMBIE BOYS
Greg Pak, Valeria Favoccia, Dan Jackson
ISBN 978-1-50671-309-0 • $10.99

STRANGER THINGS: THE BULLY
Greg Pak, Valeria Favoccia, Dan Jackson, Nate Piekos
ISBN 978-1-50671-453-0 • $12.99

STRANGER THINGS: ERICA THE GREAT
Greg Pak, Danny Lore, Valeria Favoccia, Dan Jackson
ISBN 978-1-50671-454-7 • $12.99

LOOK FOR OUR NEWEST COMICS SERIES NOW!

STRANGER THINGS LIBRARY EDITIONS

VOLUME 1
An oversized hardcover collecting
Stranger Things: The Other Side and
Stranger Things: Science Camp.
ISBN 978-1-50672-762-2 • $39.99

VOLUME 2
An oversized hardcover collecting
Stranger Things: Six and *Stranger
Things: Into the Fire.*
ISBN 978-1-50672-763-9 • $39.99

STRANGER THINGS: KAMCHATKA #1
Michael Moreci, Todor Hristov, Dan Jackson
$3.99